Cats
&Art

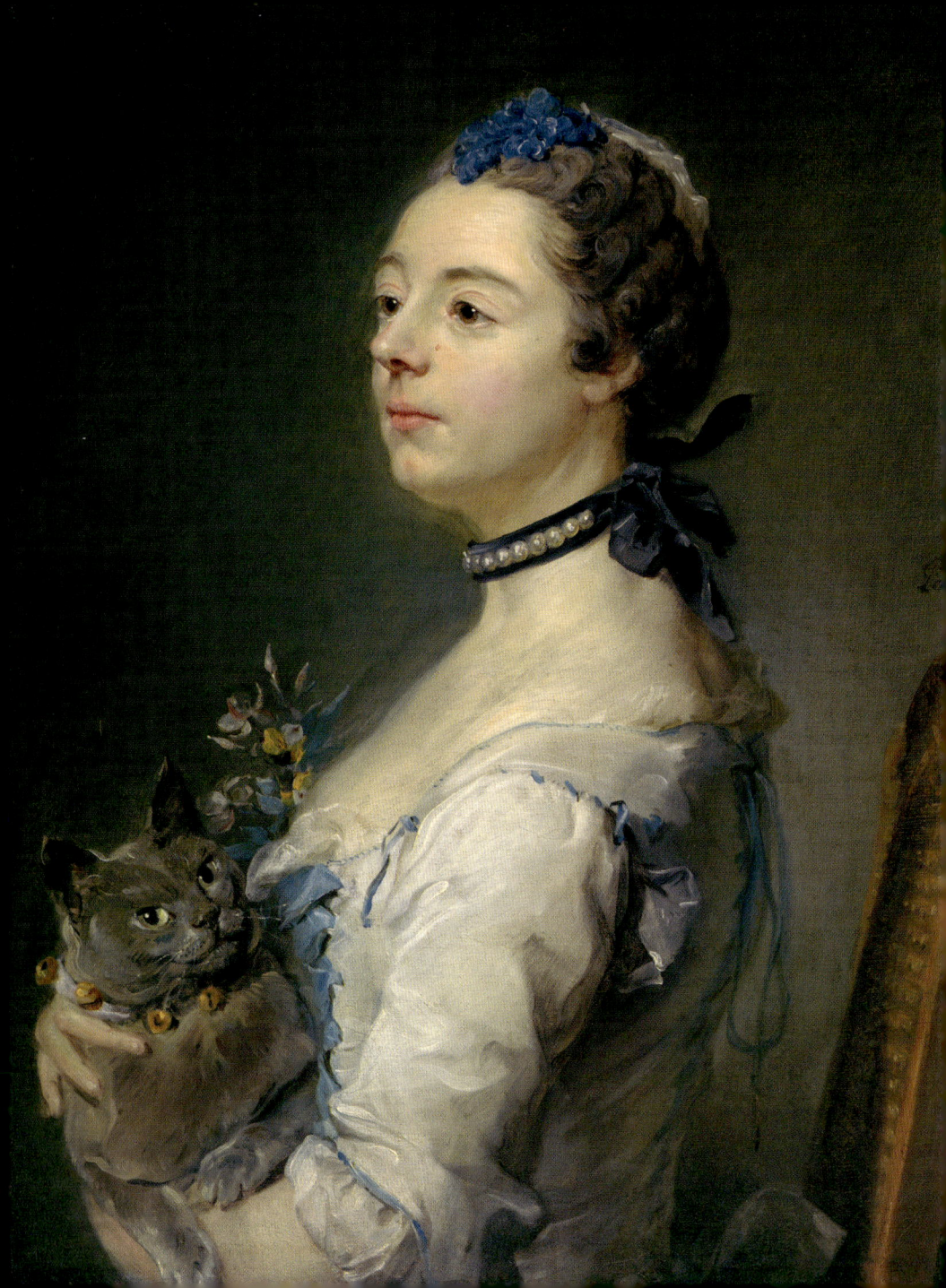

Cats & Art

50 MASTERPIECES & THEIR CAT BREEDS

Susie Hodge

G:

Contents

Introduction

"The smallest feline is a masterpiece."

Leonardo da Vinci

Often elusive and fascinating, frequently affectionate and amusing, soft and gentle, sharp and ruthless, cats have been human companions, artistic muses and icons in many cultures for thousands of years. They are frequently featured for symbolic reasons, sometimes in portraits to relax the sitter, sometimes simply for their amusing actions, beauty or grace, or even as a contrast to the surroundings. Whether they are sleeping or playing, the centre of attention or hiding in a composition, they are always in artworks as a way of drawing the viewer's attention. Across history, cats have been the chosen companions of celebrities, royalty, nobility, writers, artists and more, valued for their company and for the solace and inspiration they bestow.

A brief history

It has often been said that cats choose to mix with humans rather than vice versa. Wild cats, particularly the African wildcat, *Felis silvestris lybica* (meaning "the cat of the woods"), are believed to be the ancestors of domestic cats, and this domestication probably began around 9,000 or 10,000 years ago in the so-called Fertile Crescent of the Near East, specifically in the regions that constitute present-day Turkey, Israel, Egypt and Cyprus. Humans and wildcats formed a symbiotic relationship whereby the cats protected fields and granaries from rodents, and people provided them with shelter.

Ancient Egyptian affection and respect for cats as skilful predators led to the development of religious cults and temple worship around them, making them revered in many

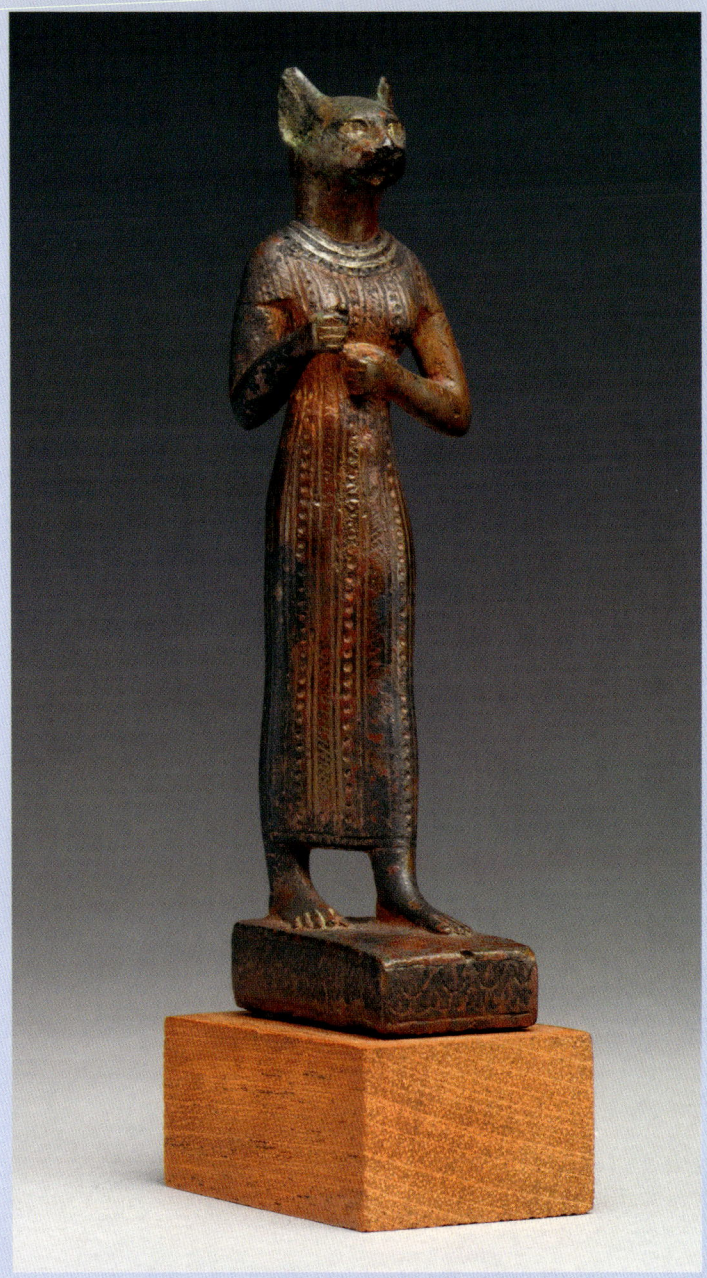

UNKNOWN ARTIST

Goddess Bastet

664–30 BCE

Leaded bronze, precious metal and black bronze inlays

4⅛ × 1¼ × 1⅞ in (10.5 × 3.2 × 3.9 cm)

The Metropolitan Museum of Art, New York, USA

households. In ancient Egypt, when a pet cat died, the owner often shaved off their eyebrows in mourning.

To the ancient Romans, cats symbolized freedom, and they were described as *libertus sine labore* (liberty without labour). Valued for their ability to control rodent populations on ships and in settlements, they accompanied traders and explorers to different parts of the world. However, by the Middle Ages in Europe, superstitions had arisen that associated cats with witchcraft, so they faced persecution. In 1232 Pope Gregory IX instructed the Inquisition to watch black cats closely because he believed they were suspicious. Nevertheless, cats (if perhaps not black ones) remained integral to many households for their control of pests. This dual perception of value and threat was widespread. In Norse mythology, for example, the goddess Freya – whose chariot was drawn by two cats – was worshipped as the goddess of love and fertility, but also of war, prophecy and magic.

From 1620 European settlers introduced cats to North America, where they played a crucial role in controlling rodent populations in cities and on farms. By the nineteenth century they had also become treasured household pets in many parts of the world, appreciated for their endearing, amusing characteristics as well as their affection, company, beauty and calming qualities. The first organized cat show took place in London in 1871, marking the beginning of the establishment of cat breeds and an appreciation of cats for their appearance.

Present-day tabbies probably look much like the sacred cats of ancient Egypt. The black cat was the first known domestic variation of this wild tabby colouring. It is likely that a darker tabby coat with thicker stripes and swirls appeared first in the Middle Ages, the pattern an adaptation that helped the animal to hide better in the shadows. The tortoiseshell coat probably developed in nineteenth-century Britain, where the Victorians made cats their beloved pets and bred them for colour varieties and other aesthetic characteristics. Various colours, shapes and features have developed across the world at different times, and many are discussed in this book. Over time, the selective breeding of cats focused primarily on appearance and temperament rather than performance. This is by way of contrast with dogs, which were bred for various tasks, such as hunting, herding and guarding. As a result, there are fewer cat breeds than dog breeds.

Cats in art

In ancient Egyptian art, cats were depicted in various forms, and symbolized protection, fertility and grace. The goddess Bastet (see page 7), who is often shown with the head of a lioness

UNKNOWN ARTIST
Nekomata (detail)
c. 1700
Scroll
17⅓ × 600⅓ in (44 × 1,525 cm) (entire scroll)
Brigham Young University, Provo, Utah, USA

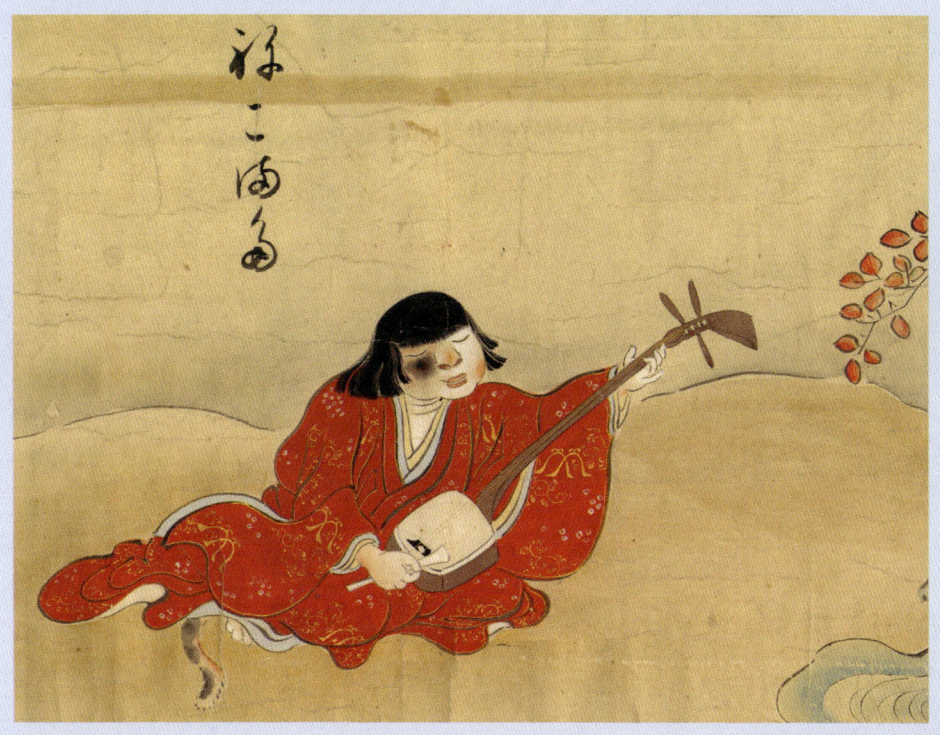

or a domestic cat, appeared in many tombs, in paintings and in sculptures. Depictions of cats are also found in the art of Sumer, where they were admired for protecting grain stores from rodents.

The *maneki-neko* (beckoning cat) represents good luck and prosperity in Japan. Often portrayed with a raised paw, these cats invite fortune and wealth. Cats also appear in traditional Japanese *ukiyo-e* woodblock prints and paintings, conveying charm and elegance. Additionally, cats in Japan are associated with such mythical creatures as Bakeneko and Nekomata, which have supernatural powers. Cats feature prominently in Chinese art and folklore, symbolizing prosperity, luck and protection. In Indian art, they are sometimes depicted in religious and myth-ological contexts, signifying different qualities based on the cultural beliefs of each region, or associated with goddesses, such as Shashthi and Durga.

Cats are occasionally depicted in Islamic art, such as in manuscript illustrations or architectural ornamentation, although direct representations of living beings in Islamic art are uncommon. The Quran does not prohibit such visual representa-tion, but a recognized collection of Muhammad's sayings forbids the making of images of living beings, so, to avoid confusion, these are generally avoided.

In parts of Africa, cats are depicted in symbolic and mys-tical contexts, representing themes of guardianship, spirituality and connections with the supernatural, and sometimes they feature in masks, sculptures and textiles to embody such qual-ities as agility, cunning and protection.

The portrayal of cats in European art has varied over time. For instance, during the Middle Ages, as we have seen, they were often negatively portrayed, but during the Renaissance they reappeared as companions and symbols of domestic life in Christian imagery. In this context they have frequently been seen as symbols of independence, self-sufficiency, vanity or purity. They were also associated with the so-called feminine virtues, including patience, cleanliness and fertility. They sometimes appeared in paintings alongside saints or religious figures, often curled at their feet or sitting nearby. This was meant to highlight the saint's gentleness, compassion or connection to the natural world. Conversely, cats were sometimes used in Christian art to represent negative qualities, such as lust, gluttony or sloth. Where the artist intended the viewer to focus on these characteristics or vices, paintings featuring cats served as moral lessons or warnings.

In Europe at the end of the eighteenth century and in the first half of the nineteenth, Romantic art often included cats as subjects, emphasizing their independence and beauty. Such artists as Théophile-Alexandre Steinlen (page 129) and Gwen John (1876–1939) depicted them in urban settings, celebrating their mysterious allure. They continued to feature in art movements worldwide from the late nineteenth and twentieth centuries into the twenty-first.

Artists' muses

Many artists have been famed for cherishing their cats. Leonardo da Vinci (page 31) famously regarded all animals as equal. Numerous beloved cats kept Gustav Klimt (1862–1918) company in his studio in Vienna, and helped to relax the people – especially wealthy women – who came to have their portraits painted. Klimt's cats sometimes caused chaos, but he encouraged it. And Suzanne Valadon (page 138), it is said, gave her pet cats beluga caviar as a treat every Friday.

Wassily Kandinsky (1866–1944) loved colour, music, horses – and cats. When he worked at the Bauhaus design school, he and his good friend Paul Klee (1879–1940) lived in adjacent staff houses, and their cats would laze in their directly opposite windows, perhaps watching each other. Kandinsky's second wife, Nina Andreievskaya, wrote: "Paul Klee loved cats. Dessau, his cat, always looked out of the study window. He saw me perfectly from my room. Klee told me that the cat was watching me. [He said]: 'You can't have secrets; my cat will explain everything to me.'" Over the years, Klee had various cats: tabbies named Fritzi and Skunk; Bimbo and Bimbo II; and the long-haired Mysis and Nuggi. His cats inspired him, and he featured them in at least thirty of his artworks, encouraging them to pad across his wet paintings for unexpected results.

Henri Matisse (1869–1954) had three cat companions: Minouche and her daughters Coussi and La Puce. Minouche was a petite grey cat, Coussi was striped and La Puce was black. Through ill health during the last decade of his life, Matisse was restricted to a wheelchair or bed, and his cats stayed with

PAUL KLEE
Cat and Bird
1928
Oil and ink on plaster-primed gauze mounted on plywood
15 × 21 in (38.1 × 53.2 cm)
Museum of Modern Art, New York, USA

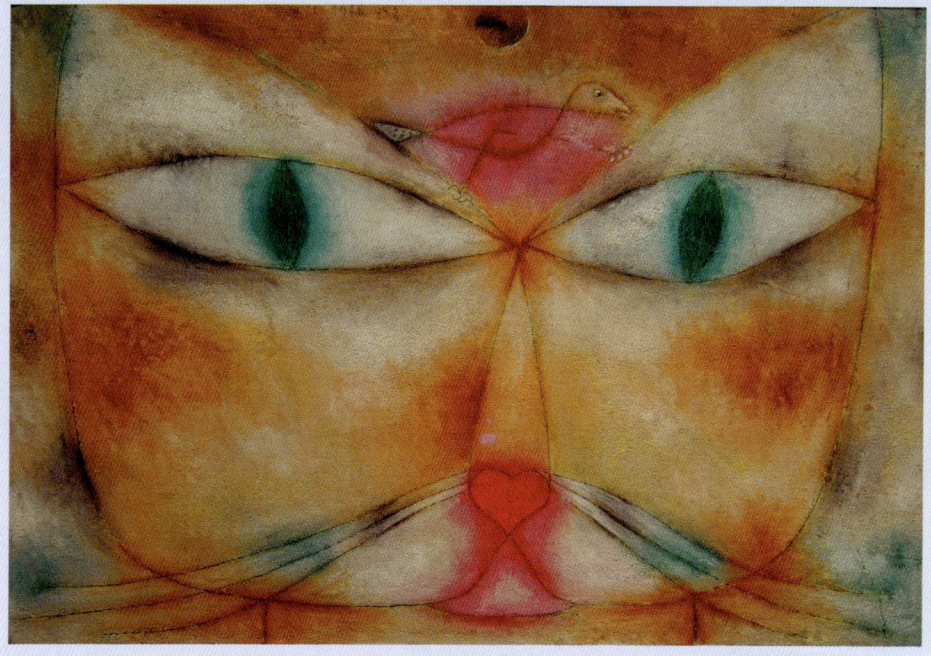

him. Salvador Dalí (1904–89) had two pet ocelots that he took everywhere, even to restaurants and hotels, while Andy Warhol (1928–87) kept 25 cats in the New York apartment he shared with his mother. He even published a book, *25 Cats Name Sam and One Blue Pussy* (1954), featuring his own hand-coloured lithographs.

For these artists and others, cats have been a comfort and a source of inspiration. Thanks to their elegance, grace and mystery, they feature frequently in art for many purposes, whether spiritual or secretive, symbolizing freedom, solitude, love, independence, comfort, or even laziness or indifference. They have been constant, reliable muses, and their calm, relaxing presence has nurtured many artists' creativity.

Free spirits

overleaf
JEAN-JACQUES BACHELIER
Angora Cat Chasing a Butterfly
c. 1760
Oil on canvas
26 × 31⅞ in
(66 × 81 cm)
Musée Lambinet, Versailles, France

This book investigates the rich diversity of cats in art, examining how they have been portrayed and honoured across continents and eras, and exploring their versatility as a subject. However they have been conveyed – whether as precious family pets, controllers of rodents, deities, free spirits, symbols of human nature or the spiritual world, revered idols, talismans, or icons of protection, grace or mysticism – cats have contributed unequivocally to the vibrant tapestry of artistic expression. Whether you are a devoted cat-lover, an art enthusiast or both, or simply curious about the countless ways in which felines have inspired creative expression over time and place, this book will enlighten and captivate you. Through 50 artworks from different periods and various locations, it explores the enduring legacy of the cat as the ultimate muse.

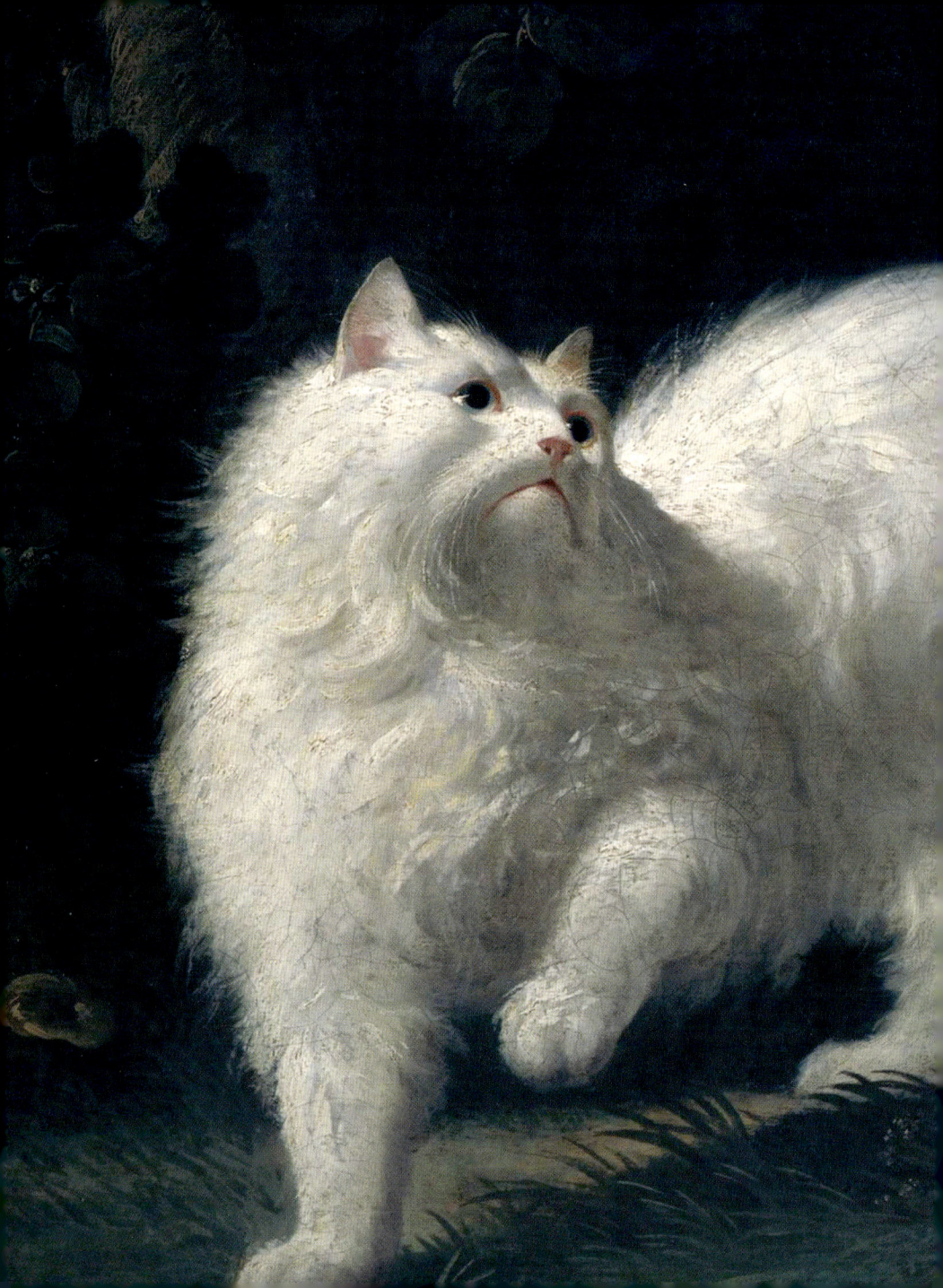

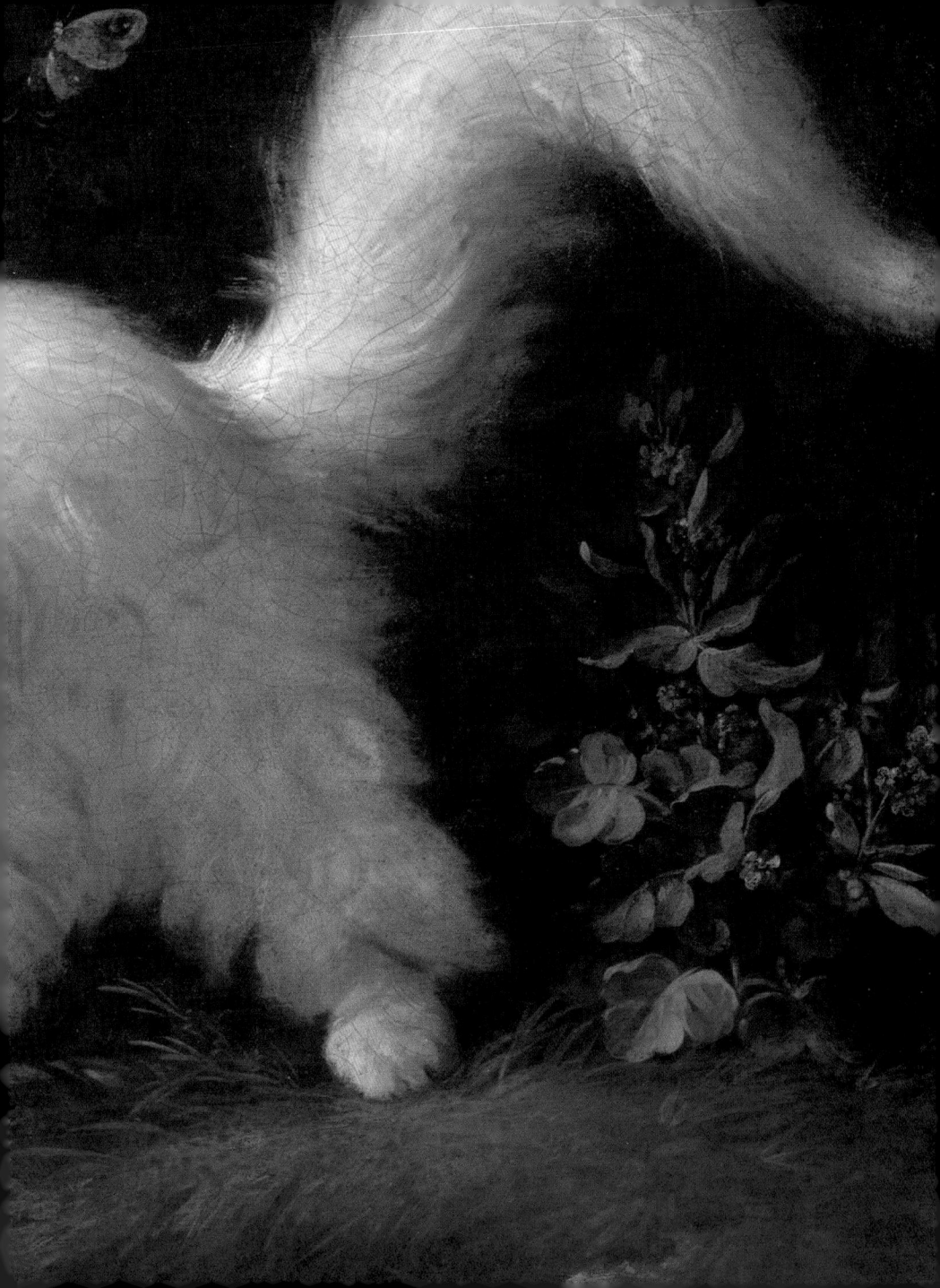

Individuality

The Tomb of Nebamun is an ancient Egyptian burial from the Eighteenth Dynasty (1550–1292 BCE), on the west bank of the Nile at Thebes (present-day Luxor). This fragment of a scene painted on the wall of the tomb shows the nobleman Nebamun and his family hunting in the marshes of the Nile. He is the largest figure, appearing to stride forward on his skiff, holding three herons to lure and attract birds, and a throwing-stick to kill them. His wife, Hatshepsut, stands to his left, their daughter sits beneath him, and his cat hunts with him on his right. Unlike most ancient Egyptian paintings, this image blends established rigid rules with individuality. For example, the energetic, carefully rendered cat displays a sense of naturalism. Poised in action, it balances on two flower stems, catching wild birds, which were perceived as enemies of light and order. Its coat is finely painted with tiny, individual stripes and dots, creating the appearance of fur and markings. Gold was an emblem of the sun, and the tiny fleck of gold leaf on the cat's eye – the only example of gilding yet found on a Theban wall painting – has led experts to believe that the cat might represent the sun god Ra. Cats were also sacred to the goddess Bastet, Ra's daughter.

EGYPTIAN MAU

The Egyptian Mau may have descended from the domestic cats of ancient times. The association of felines with the goddess Bastet remained strong during the Roman rule of Egypt, so it is likely that Romans took these cats back to Italy; that could be how the breed arrived in Europe. The breed has several unique characteristics: spots appearing in random patterns on the coat, a distinctive "M" or scarab shape on the top of the head, and dark lines running from the corners of the eyes to the cheeks. The tail is banded with a dark tip and striped along its full length. Maus are fast compared with other breeds.

1
UNKNOWN ARTIST
The Tomb of Nebamun
1400–1350 BCE
Earth pigment on plaster
Dimensions unknown
British Museum, London, UK

Overleaf: detail

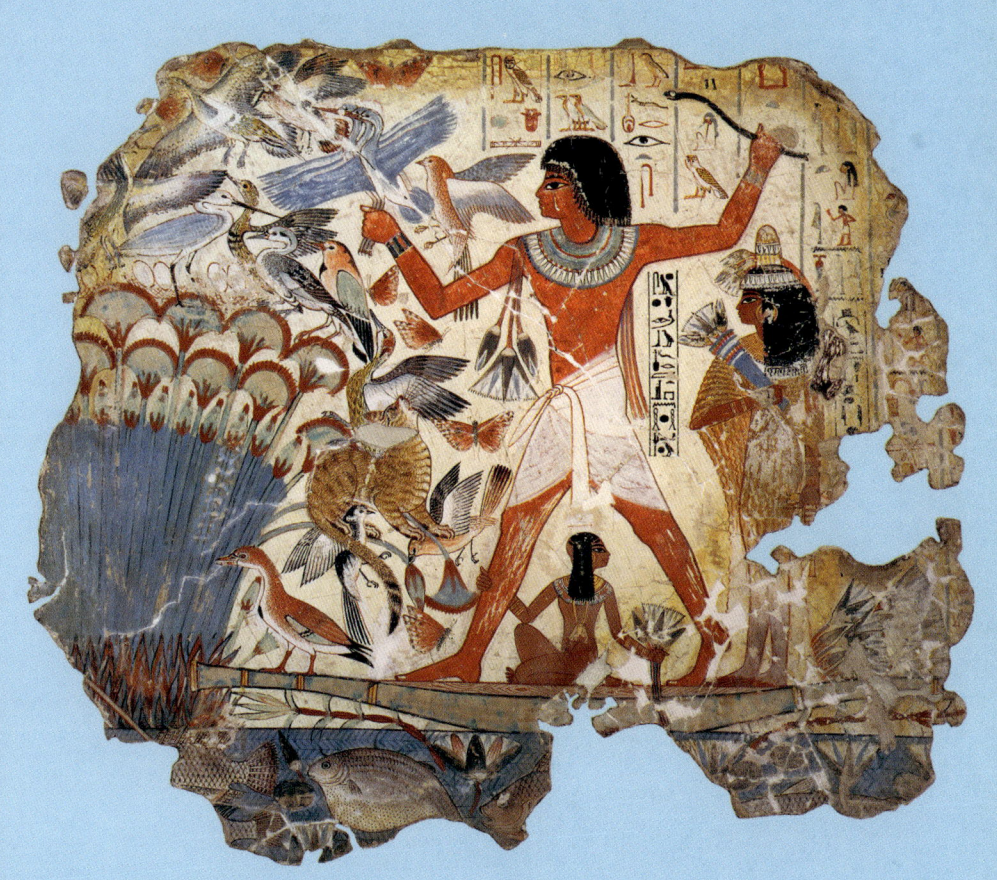

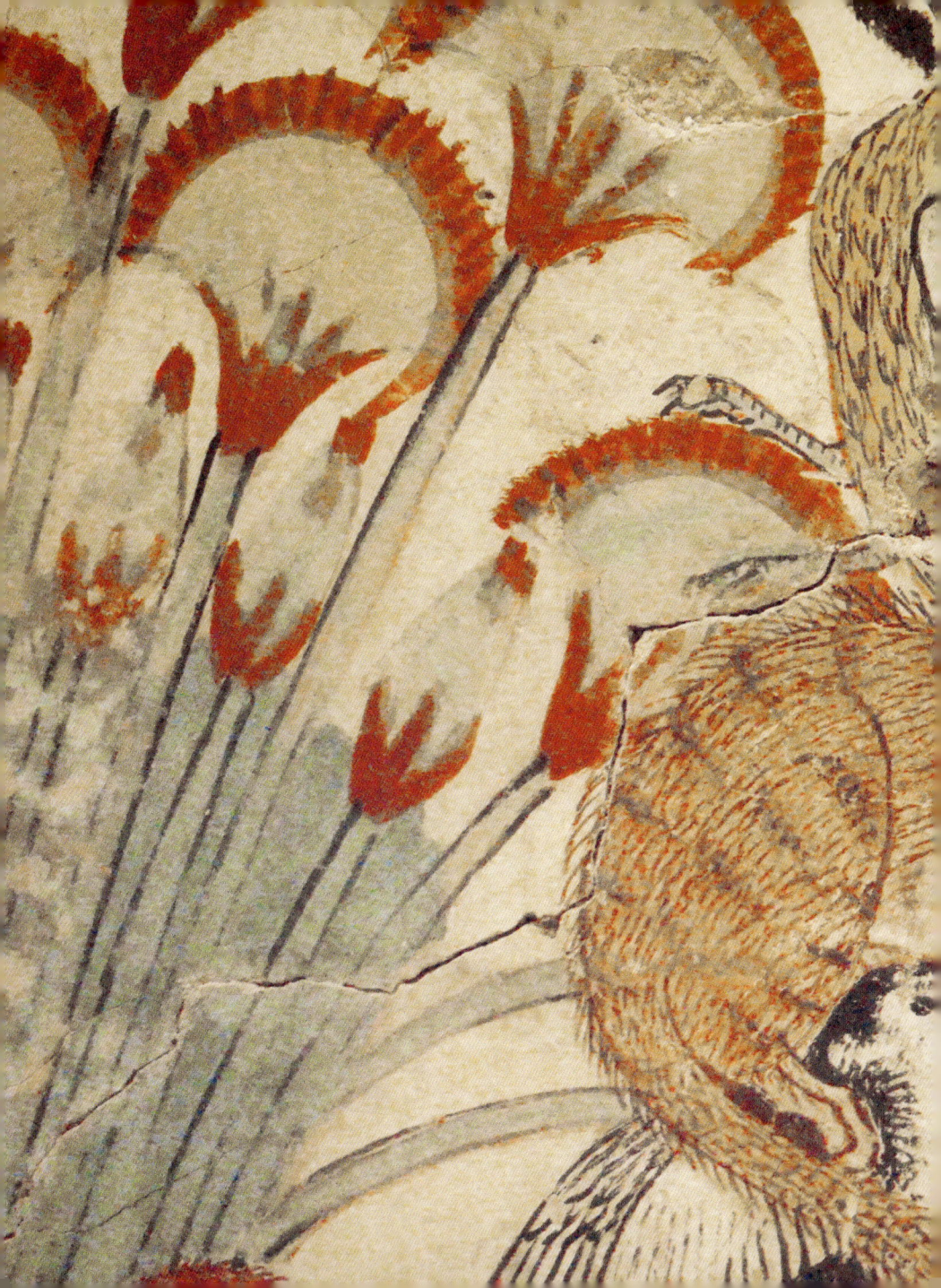

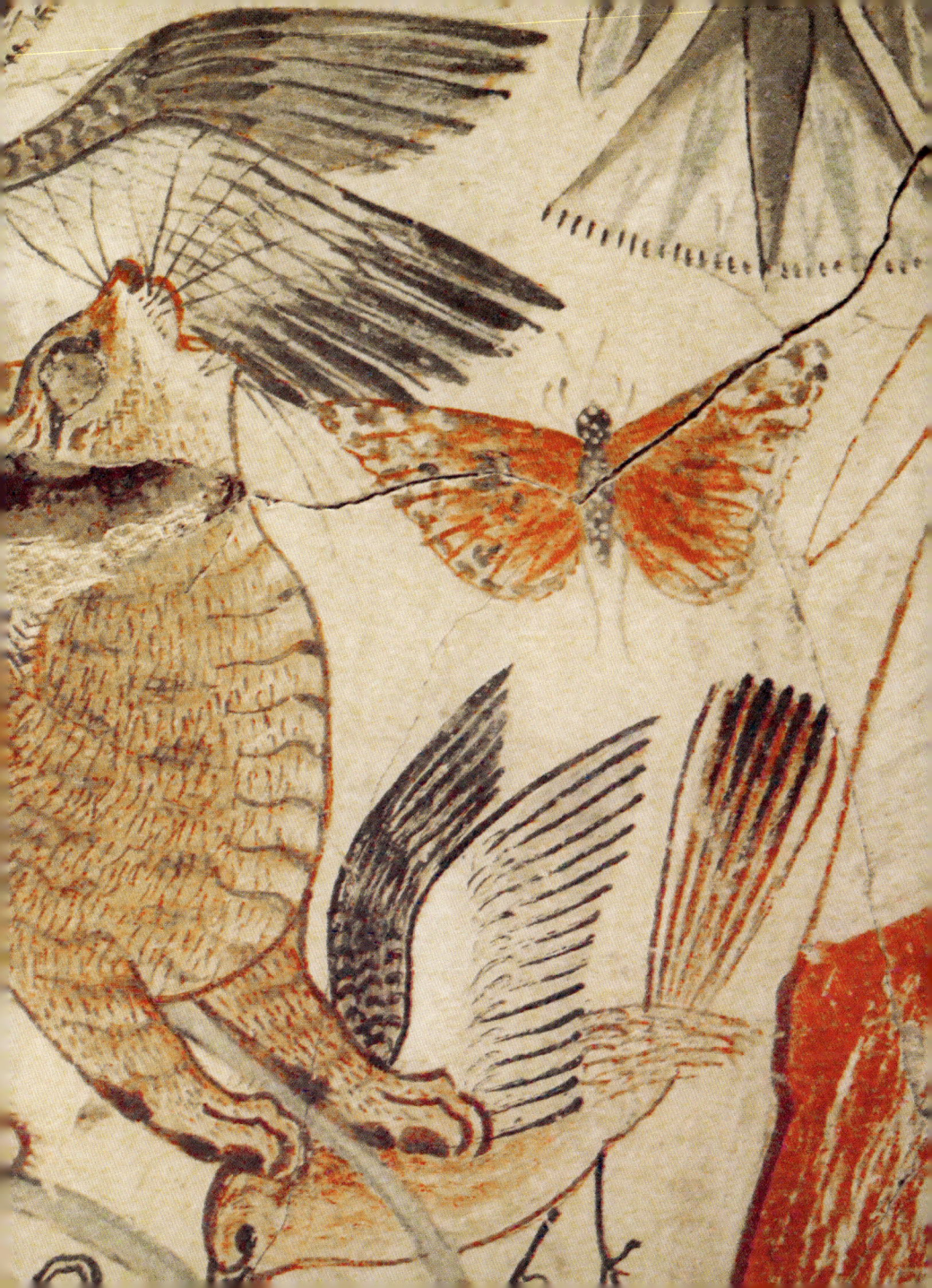

House of the Faun

Featuring a fairly lifelike cat clutching a quail or partridge, this mosaic was probably made for the centre of a floor in the Casa del Fauno (House of the Faun) in Pompeii. For this grand Hellenistic palace – preserved under ash after the eruption of Mount Vesuvius in 79 CE – the animals were carefully crafted with tesserae (small pieces of stone) to create a sense of realism, with darker and lighter tones and detailed markings. The mosaic is an example of the *opus vermiculatum* (wormlike work) method, whereby the images are outlined. The cat has shining eyes, and fine whiskers and claws, and there is a realistic impression of soft fur. It looks surprised to have caught a bird that almost matches it in size. Below the action are more animals, including fish, shellfish, ducks and other birds. The craft and materials displayed in this villa were of higher quality even than in most other noble houses in Pompeii. In ancient Roman culture, cats were often associated with protection and good fortune. Legions kept them in their forts to protect the food stores, armour and equipment. The Romans also saw cats as mascots and companions, and they were the only animals to be allowed inside religious temples. In Roman mythology, cats symbolized freedom and were depicted accompanying the goddess Libertas.

2
UNKNOWN ARTISTS
Cat and Ducks
c. second half of 2nd century BCE
Mosaic
20¾ × 21 in (53 × 53.5 cm)
National Archaeological Museum, Naples, Italy

TABBY CATS

Tabby patterning on a cat arises from the agouti gene, which comes in different variants, or alleles. For example, one allele may result in a tabby pattern with bold swirls, while another may produce spots. Other genes also contribute to the individual appearance of a cat, such as those that affect colour or pigmentation, and those that control the length and texture of the fur, or how well defined the pattern appears. The ancient Romans valued tabbies for their hunting skills and their ability to keep homes free from vermin, but owning a tabby cat was also seen as a sign of prosperity and good fortune.

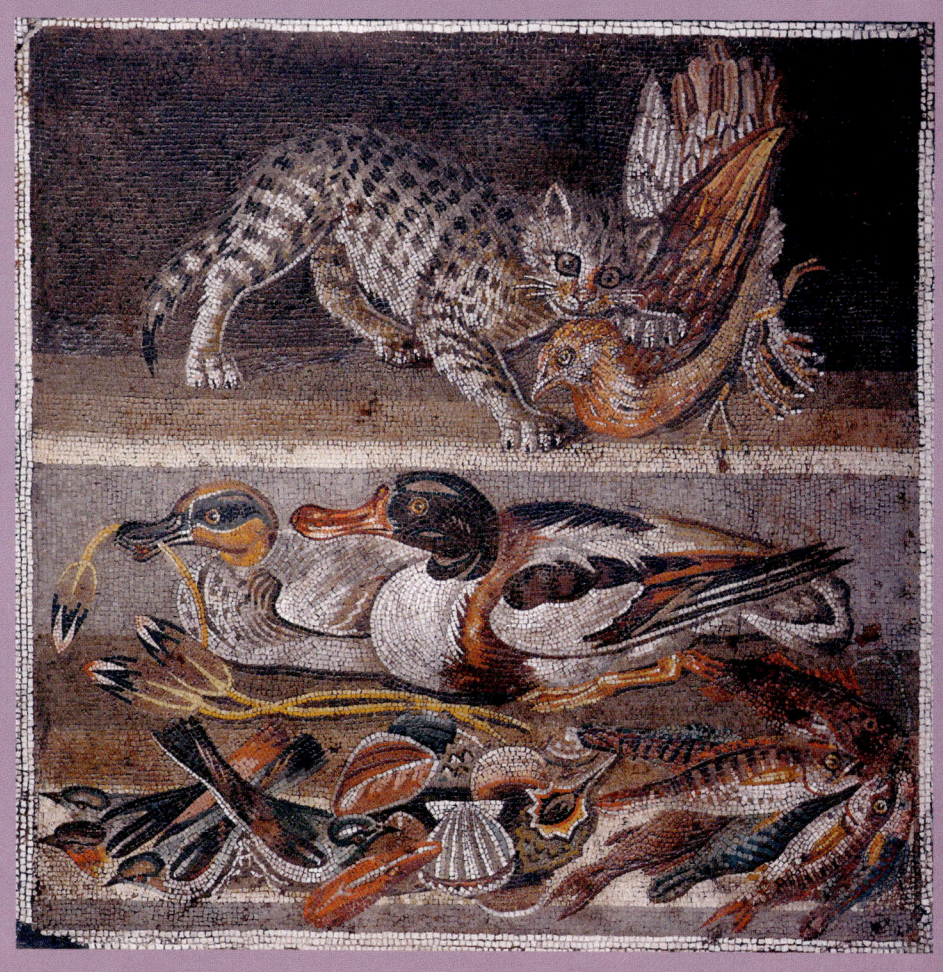

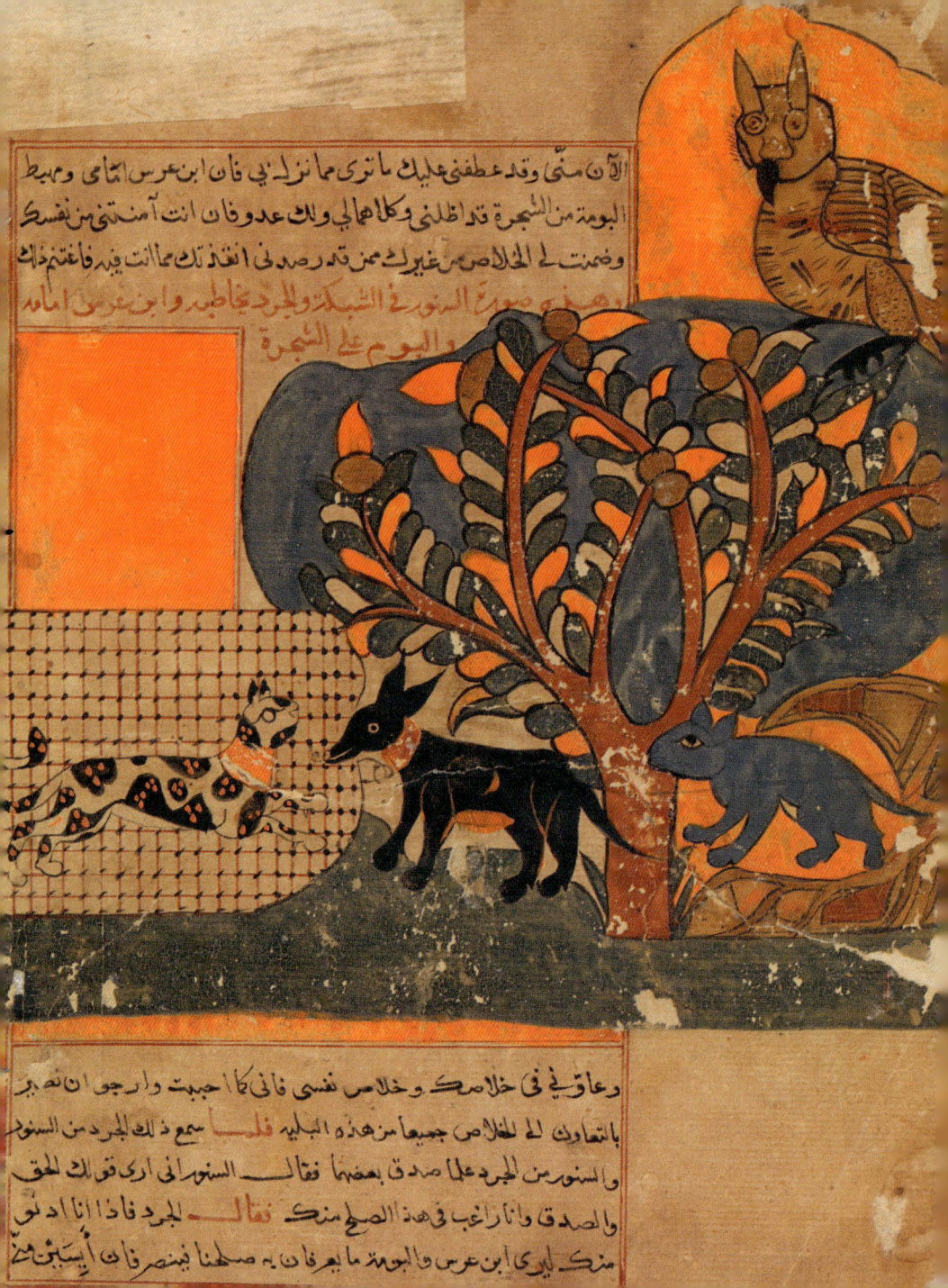

الآن إذ متى وقد عطفني عليك ما ترى ما نزل بي فإن ابن عرس اعدائي وهبط
البومة من الشجرة تدعاطلني وكلاهما لي ولك عدوان انت امنتني من نفسك
وضمنت لي الخلاص غيرك من قدر من نفذني في العذاب ما انت فيه فاغتنم ذلك

هذه صورة السنور في الشبكة والجرذ يخاطبه وابن عرس امامه
والبوم على الشجرة

دعاني في خلاصك وخلاص نفسي فاني كما احببت وارجو ان يجبر
بانتعاونك لي للخلاص جميعا من هذه البلية سمع ذلك جميع الجرذ من السنور
وسنور من الجرذ على بعضها فقال السنور اني ارى قولك الحق
والصدق وانا راغب في هذا الصلح منك فقال للجرذ فاذا دنا
منك ليرى ابن عرس والبومة ما بيننا من صلح فانه بعرف ان بيننا فانبسط

Moral tales

The *Kalila wa-Dimna* is the Arabic version of a book of fables featuring anthropomorphized animals that originated in the Sanskrit text *Panchatantra*, written by Vidyapati (also known as Bidpai) in about 200 BCE. The book features 15 stories, each of which gives a moral lesson. Throughout, a lion is the king, his servant is an ox, and two jackals, Kalila and Dimna, feature as both narrators and protagonists. This illustration, which depicts the story "The Trapped Cat and the Frightened Mouse", echoes the style of Mamluk Egypt, with its rich colour palette and dark outlines. A cat is trapped in a hunter's net, and a mouse (or rat) appears looking for food. At first, he rejoices to see the cat ensnared, but then he notices an owl and a weasel waiting to pounce on him. He offers to set the cat free in return for protection, but as he starts gnawing through the net, the owl and the weasel rush away. The mouse then wonders if the cat will eat him once it is freed, so after much deliberation he decides to postpone the final bite. The hunter returns and the mouse bites through the last cord. He bolts down his hole and the cat shoots up a tree.

3

UNKNOWN ARTIST

"The Trapped Cat and the Frightened Mouse", from the *Kalila wa-Dimna*, trans. Ibn al-Muqaffa'Abd Allâh

1220

Illuminated manuscript, paper, ink and paint

11 × 8⅓ in (28 × 21.5 cm)

The Metropolitan Museum of Art, New York, USA

TURKISH VAN

The grey-and-white cat illustrated here is possibly an ancestor of the Turkish Van, a semi-long-haired breed of domestic cat that was developed in Britain in the mid-twentieth century from various cats found in Turkish cities. It is a large animal, with broad patterns on the head and tail. The Turkish Van may have blue or amber eyes, or be odd-eyed (having one eye of each colour, a condition known as heterochromia). Some Turkish Vans also have random patterns on their bodies, but these are not as large as those on their heads and tails. The breed has a moderately long body and tail, and large paws. It has been nicknamed the "swimming cat", owing to its unusual (for cats) fascination with water.

Waiting for scraps

Domenico Ghirlandaio (1448–94) painted the scene of the Last Supper three times in a short period. The scene shown overleaf was the last of the three. The Apostles sit at a long table in front of a wall. Christ is in the centre, with a distraught-looking John leaning against him. Peter is on his right, while Judas, the traitor, is separated from the others, sitting in front of the table. Everything is neatly depicted, including crockery, decanters, knives, bread and cherries. Outside, large pomegranate trees and birds can be seen against a bright sky, representing the glorious beauty of Paradise, and inside, on the right-hand wall, a peacock perches, representing resurrection and immortality. On the floor near Judas, a cat waits patiently for scraps, lending a sense of intimacy and domesticity to the scene, while also symbolizing deceit and treachery. The image is a fresco, whereby pigment is dissolved in water before being painted on to a thin layer of wet plaster known as *intonaco*. The colour range of frescoes was limited because only specific colours – including black and white, as well as reds, yellows and greens – would react with the alkaline of the lime in the plaster. Most blues had to be applied to the plaster after it had dried, which brought with it the risk that the colour would flake off the wall.

4
DOMENICO GHIRLANDAIO
Last Supper
1480–86
Fresco
13 × 26 ft
(4 × 8 m)
San Marco, Florence, Italy

Opposite and overleaf: details

POPE GREGORY AND CATS

Cats were for centuries regarded as useful creatures that guarded food supplies from rodents. However, many people also believed that they were associated with the devil. In this painting, the cat sitting next to Judas verifies the prevailing Catholic belief that the animals were the embodiment of Satan. Pope Gregory IX, anxious to counteract any leanings away from Catholicism, started the idea. He had people tortured so that they would tell stories of devil worship being connected to cats. In 1233 he issued a papal bull, *Vox in Rama*, which condemned the heresy of Luciferianism said to be widespread in Germany, and proclaimed that all cats were symbols of the devil.

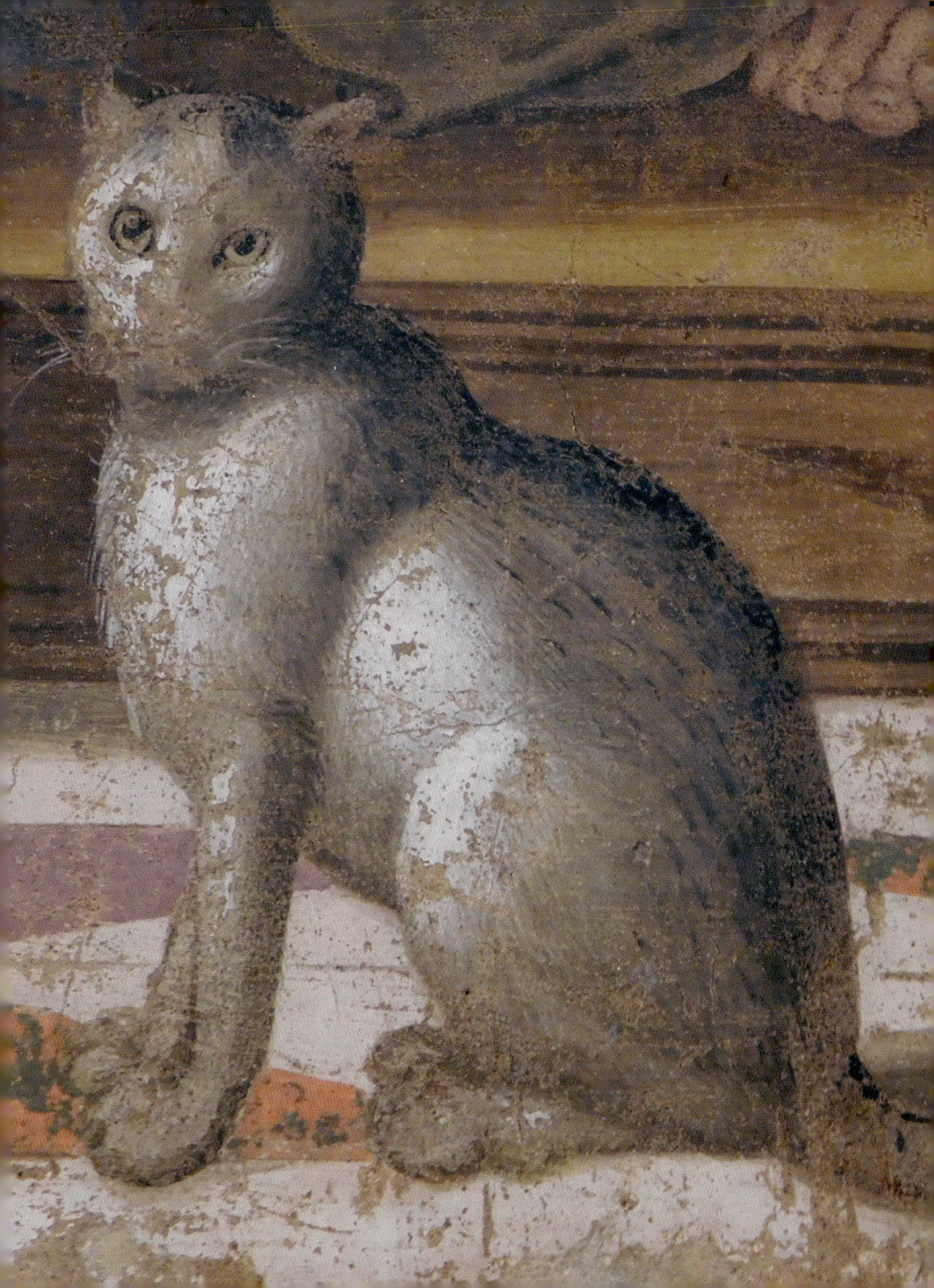

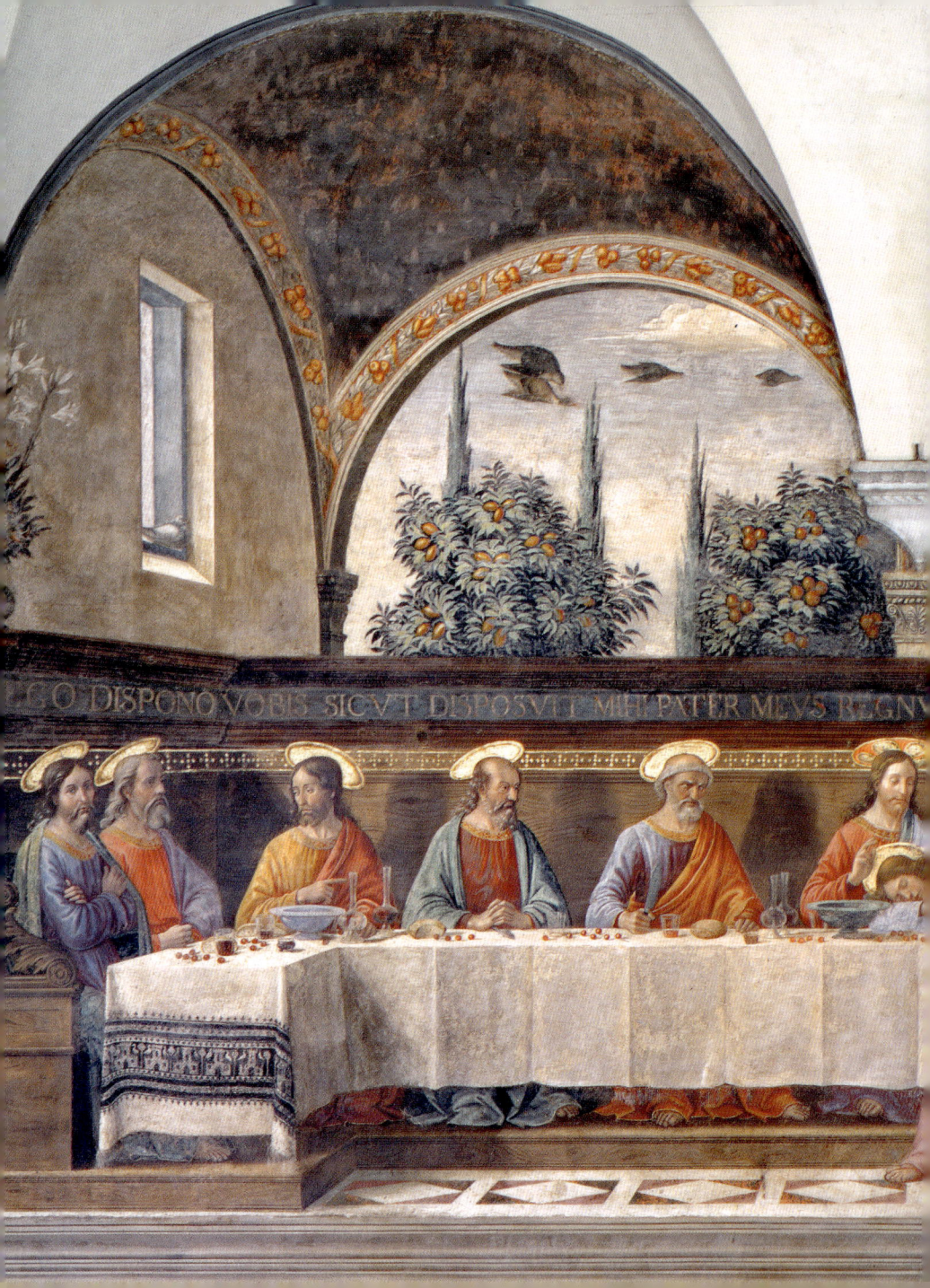

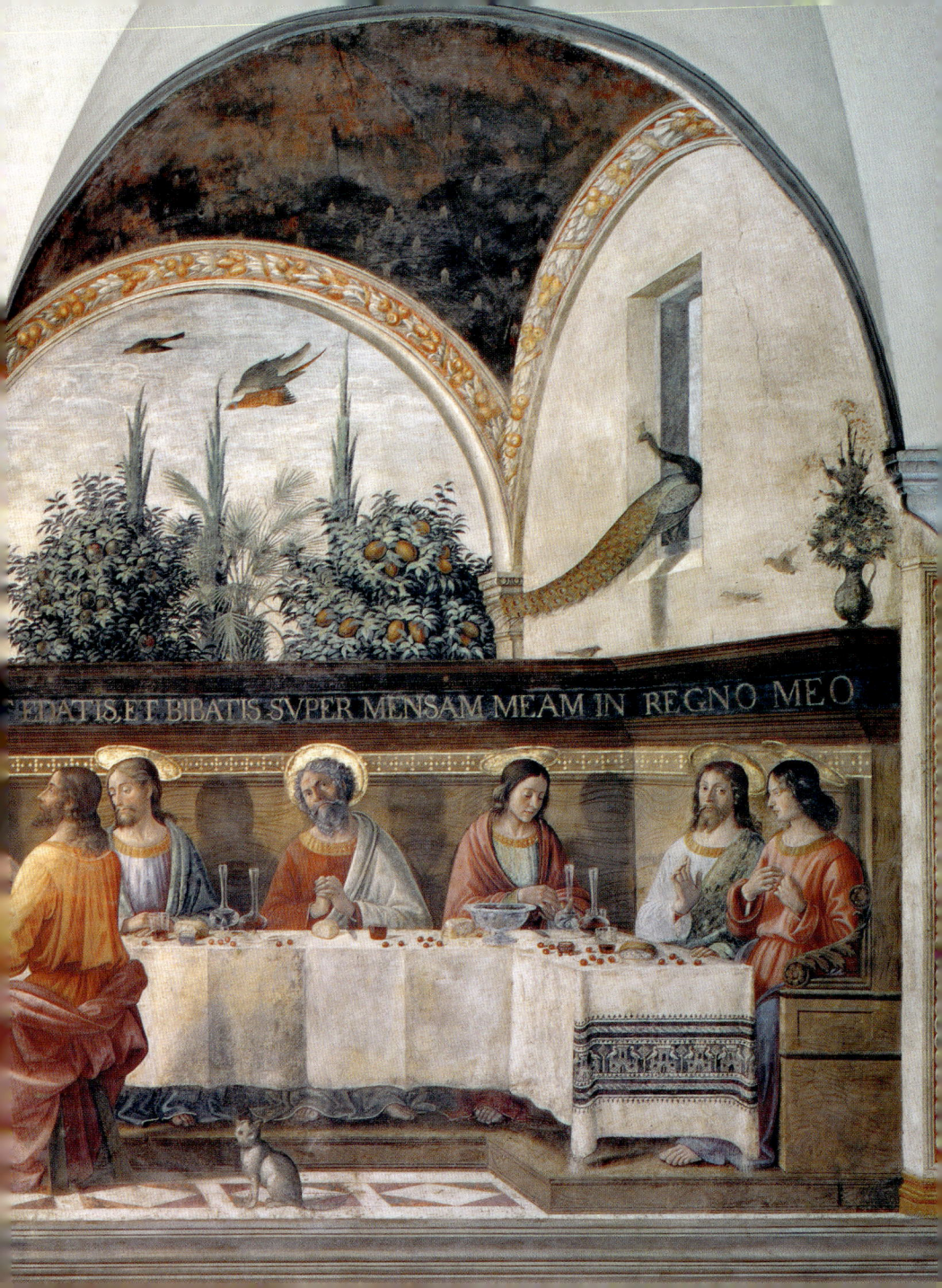

Symbol of volatility

One of the most famous and important printmakers in history, the Northern Renaissance artist Albrecht Dürer (1471–1528) was also a draughtsman and painter who successfully integrated a detailed Northern style with Italian ideals of balance and harmony. This engraving is one of two works on the same subject that he executed in different media. Adam and Eve stand in the Garden of Eden, surrounded by symbolic animals. It is the moment in the Old Testament when Adam and Eve defy God and eat from the Tree of Knowledge. Dürer, who created the work soon after returning from Italy, follows ancient Greek and Roman ideals of body proportions and poses. The couple stand in front of a German forest. A parrot sits on a branch, and the snake signifies the devil, while the rabbit, ox, cat and elk represent the four "humours". According to ancient Greek and Roman doctors and philosophers, everyone has varying amounts of four bodily fluids or humours, and an excess or deficiency in any affects personality and health. Here, the elk represents black bile and a melancholic personality; the ox symbolizes a phlegmatic or unemotional disposition; the rabbit signifies blood and sanguinity or hopefulness; and the cat denotes choleric humour or yellow bile, which results in a hot-headed personality.

5

ALBRECHT DÜRER
Adam and Eve
1504
Engraving with burin on copper
9⅞ × 7⅞ in (25.1 × 19.8 cm)
The Metropolitan Museum of Art, New York, USA

TICKED TABBY

The cat in this scene is a ticked tabby, one of the four tabby patterns, the others being mackerel, classic and spotted. Ticked tabbies have several colours on each strand of hair, known as agouti hairs. In common with other tabbies, they also have an "M" marking on the forehead, and often stripes on the face. Some ticked tabbies have faint stripes on the tail, legs or stomach, known as "ghost striping" because these can be seen only in certain lighting or by looking closely. Although the stripes closely match the primary fur colour, they are a shade darker. Some ticked tabbies also have a darker colour along the spine, and many have dark outlines around the eyes.

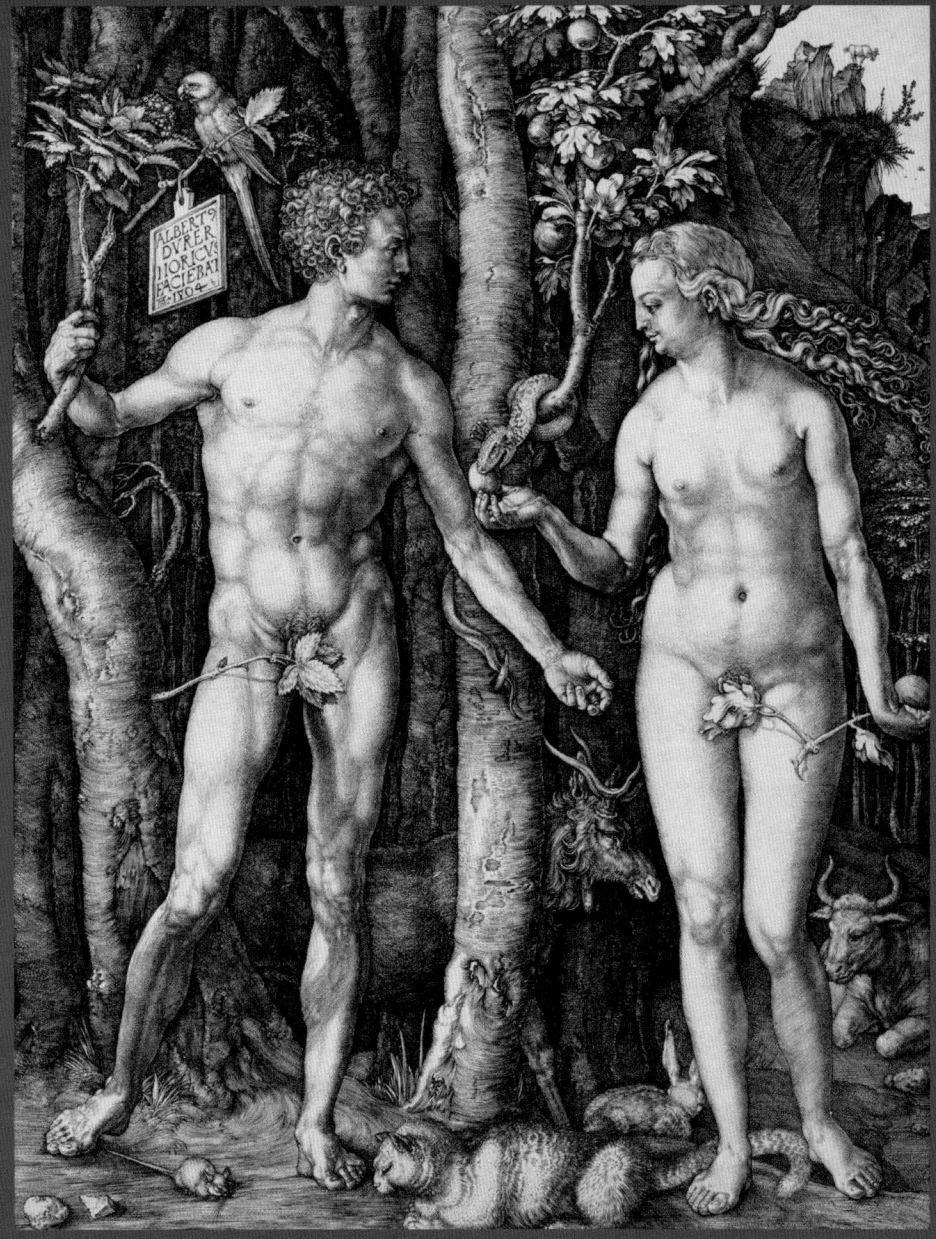

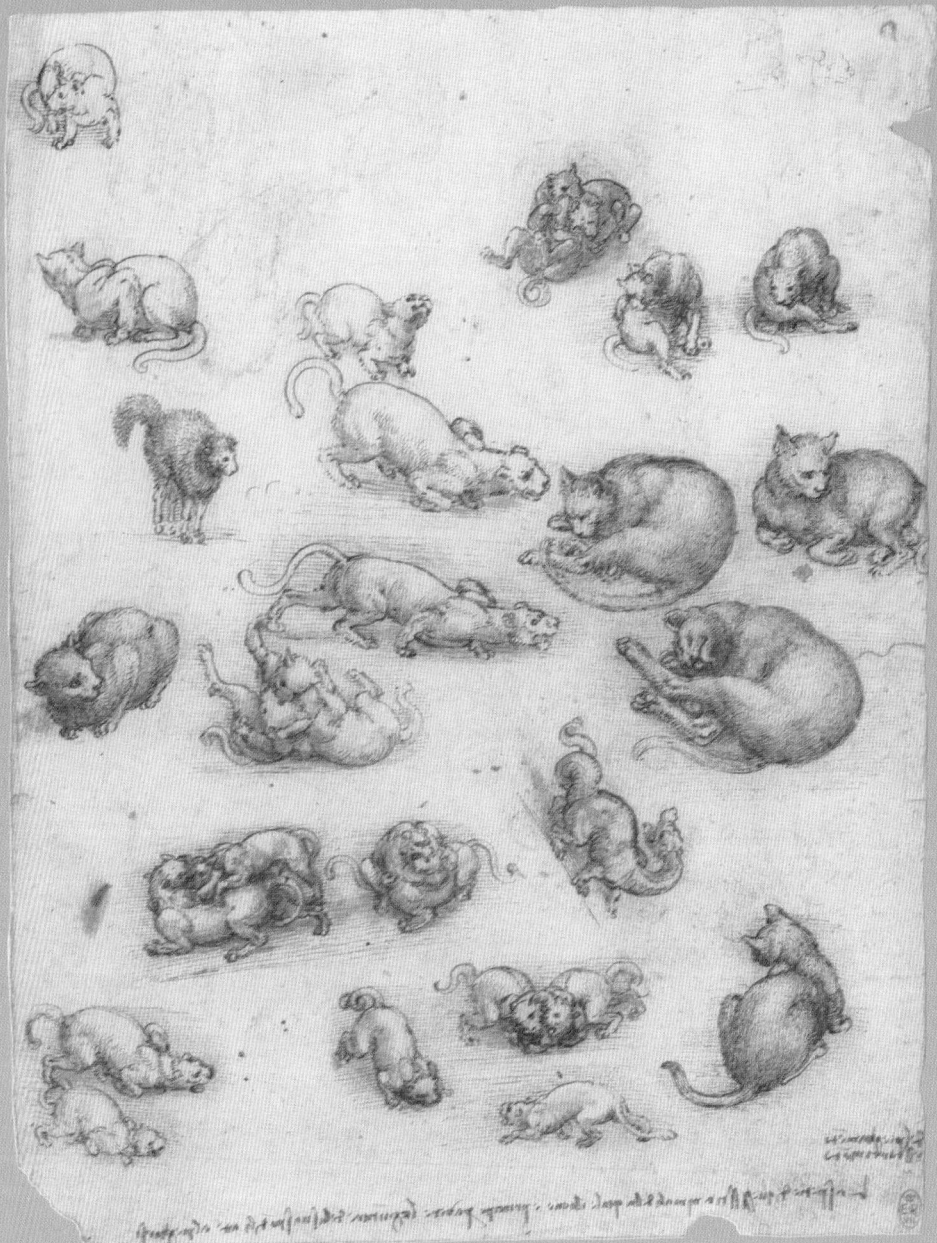

Dynamism and anatomy

Leonardo da Vinci (1452–1519) made numerous studies of the human body, complex engineering projects and plans for machines. Many of his drawings also included anatomical and physiological studies of animals, and his notes about his study of cat movements suggest that he intended to write a treatise on the subject. Here, he drew approximately 20 cats in various positions: sleeping, sitting, prowling, playing, fighting and hissing. One arches its back, its fur standing on end. In the fights, it is difficult to discern which limb belongs to which cat. A little dragon also appears in the lower part of the sheet, showing how the artist's study of real animals helped him to imagine the movements of fictitious ones. Surrounding the domestic cats are drawings of a lioness, mostly crouching or prowling. Lions were known in Italy at the time because they were a symbol of Florence, and some were kept in cages behind the Palazzo Vecchio, the city's town hall. Here, Leonardo shows his deep understanding of them, and these spontaneous sketches convey his empathy for cats and his proficiency with pen, ink and gouache (bodycolour). Both sketchy lines and firm contours convey their movements, and areas of brown ink and gouache suggest their three-dimensionality.

6

LEONARDO
DA VINCI

Cats and a Dragon

c. 1513–17

Pen and brown ink, brush with touches of gouache and charcoal on paper

10⅔ × 8 in
(27.1 × 20.5 cm)

Royal Library, Windsor, UK

Overleaf: detail

LEONARDO AND CATS

Animal lover Leonardo was particularly fond of cats, although no record exists of him keeping a specific breed, and pet-keeping was a novel idea in Europe at the time. These sketches appear to depict domestic shorthairs, which were then the most common European domestic cats. At a time when Christianity was against cats, Leonardo almost single-handedly changed people's minds, saying, "Evil could not enter a cat, because the animal itself was forged by the Supreme Artist and Architect." He planned to paint a Madonna with Jesus and a pet cat to show that if Jesus loved cats, they must be good. Over the next century, other artists increasingly portrayed cats as gentle.

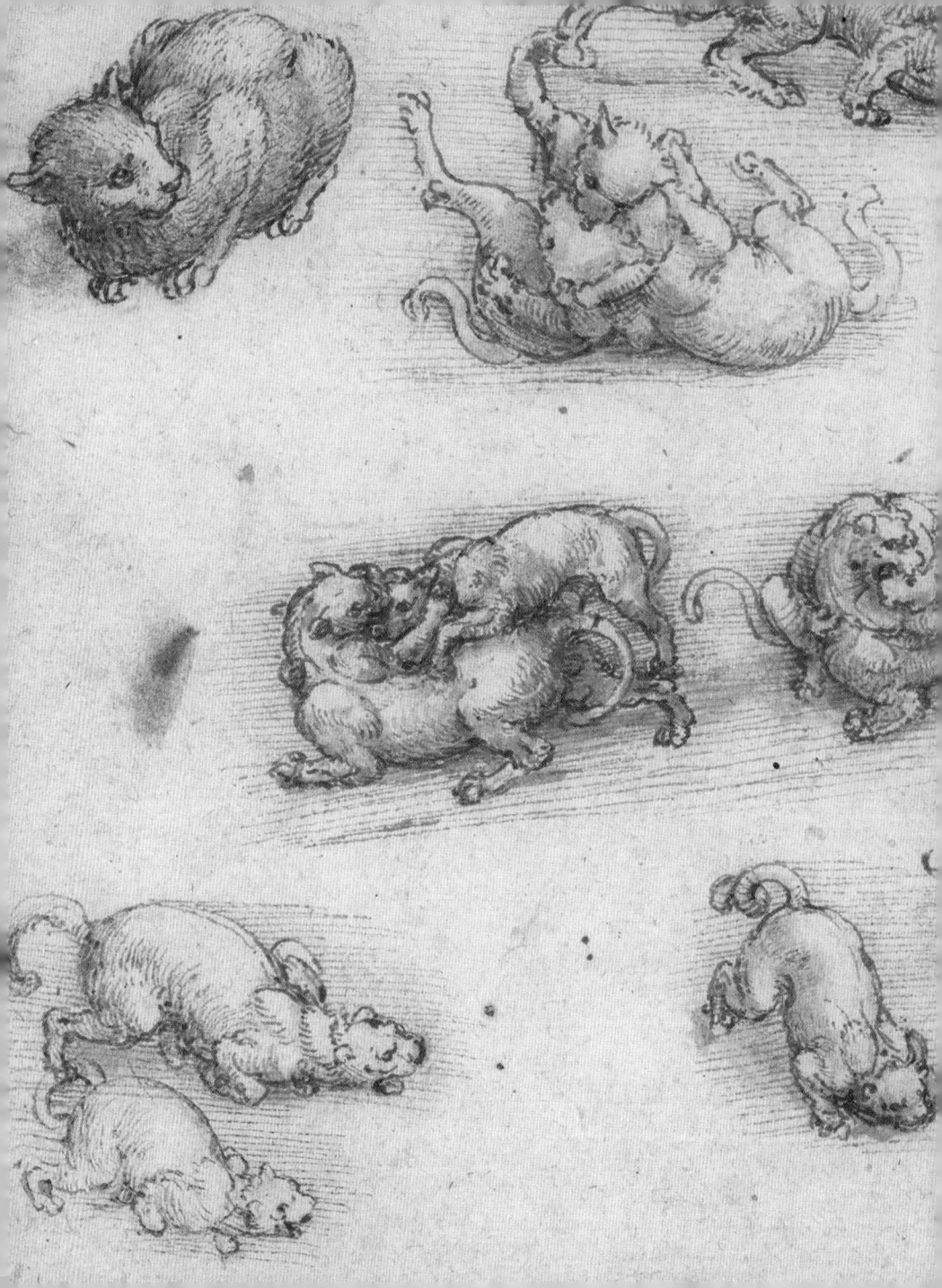

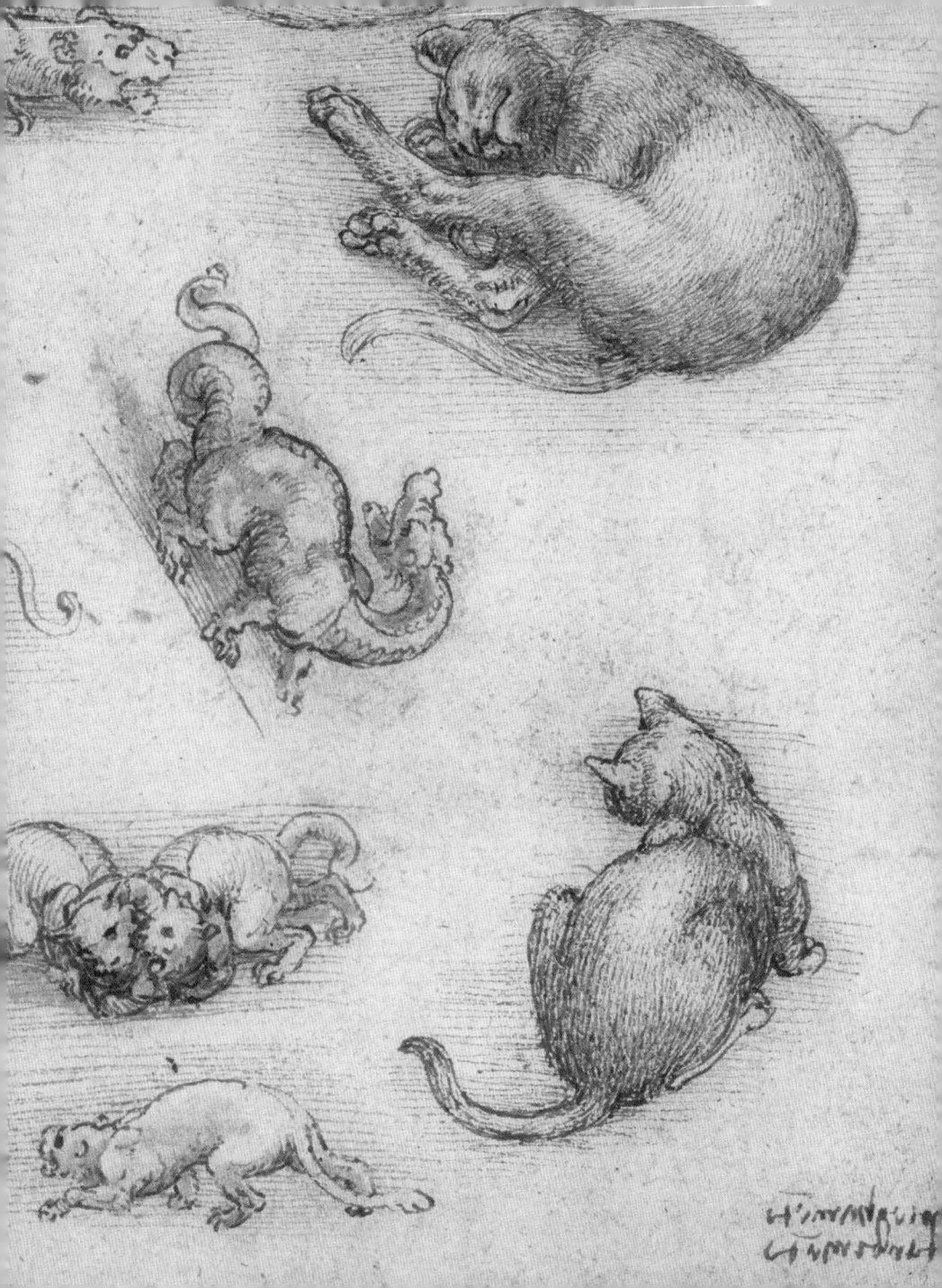

A sidelong glance

The real name of the artist known as Bachiacca or Bacchiacca (1495–1557) was Francesco d'Ubertino. Born into a family of painters, he spent most of his life in Florence, having been apprenticed to Pietro Perugino, who also famously taught Raphael. Bachiacca developed an individual, colourful style showing the influence of Perugino, Albrecht Dürer (page 28), Jacopo Pontormo and others, although this painting displays more of the influence of Leonardo da Vinci (page 31), especially his portrait *Lady with an Ermine* of about 1490. Unlike the Leonardo portrait, however, this young woman holds a cat rather than an ermine. Tilting her head and looking to one side, she appears to be flirting with the viewer, while the cat, its paws crossed, gives a similarly knowing sidelong glance. The woman's seductive expression, elaborate jewellery and bright yellow dress all suggest that she is a courtesan. In Renaissance Italy, most cities had laws demanding that prostitutes wore yellow. Pearls were also linked with such women, who were often given them as payment. The way in which this woman strokes her cat adds to the impression of eroticism and enticement, allowing us to interpret the portrait as an image of sexual temptation.

RENAISSANCE CAT SYMBOLISM

In different places as the Renaissance continued, animals carried various symbolic meanings. Cats could symbolize domesticity and femininity, reflecting the role of women in managing the household. In some cases, cats – being known for their free-spiritedness – also symbolized a woman's independence, a quality that was not always admired at the time. As we have seen, cats were still sometimes linked to witchcraft and the supernatural, which could add an element of mystery to a subject's character. Conversely, they were also seen as protectors, since they kept homes free of pests, so they could symbolize good luck and the safeguarding of the household. The cat shown in this portrait is a brown mackerel tabby.

7
BACHIACCA
Portrait of a Young Lady Holding a Cat
c. 1525–30
Oil on panel
21⅛ × 17¼ in
(53.6 × 43.8 cm)
Private collection

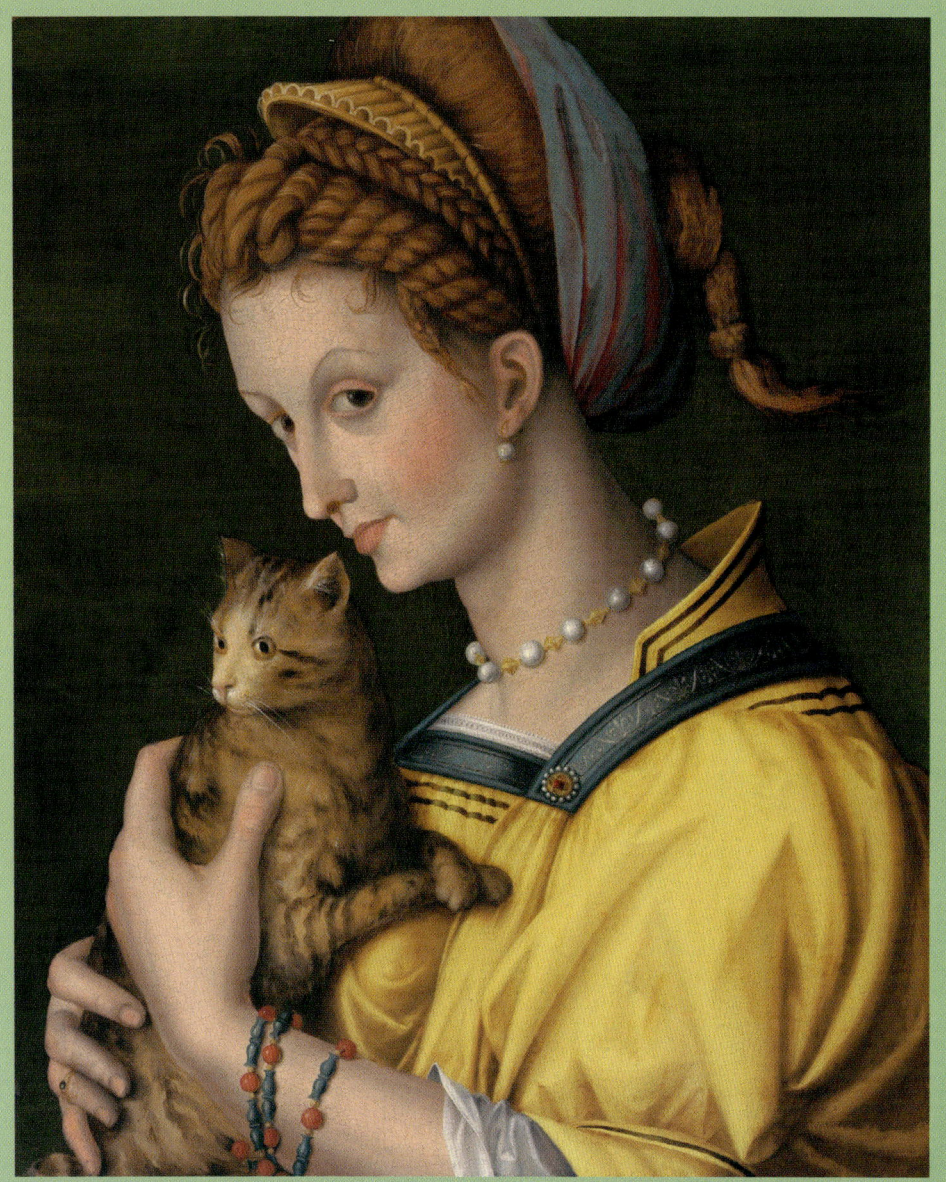

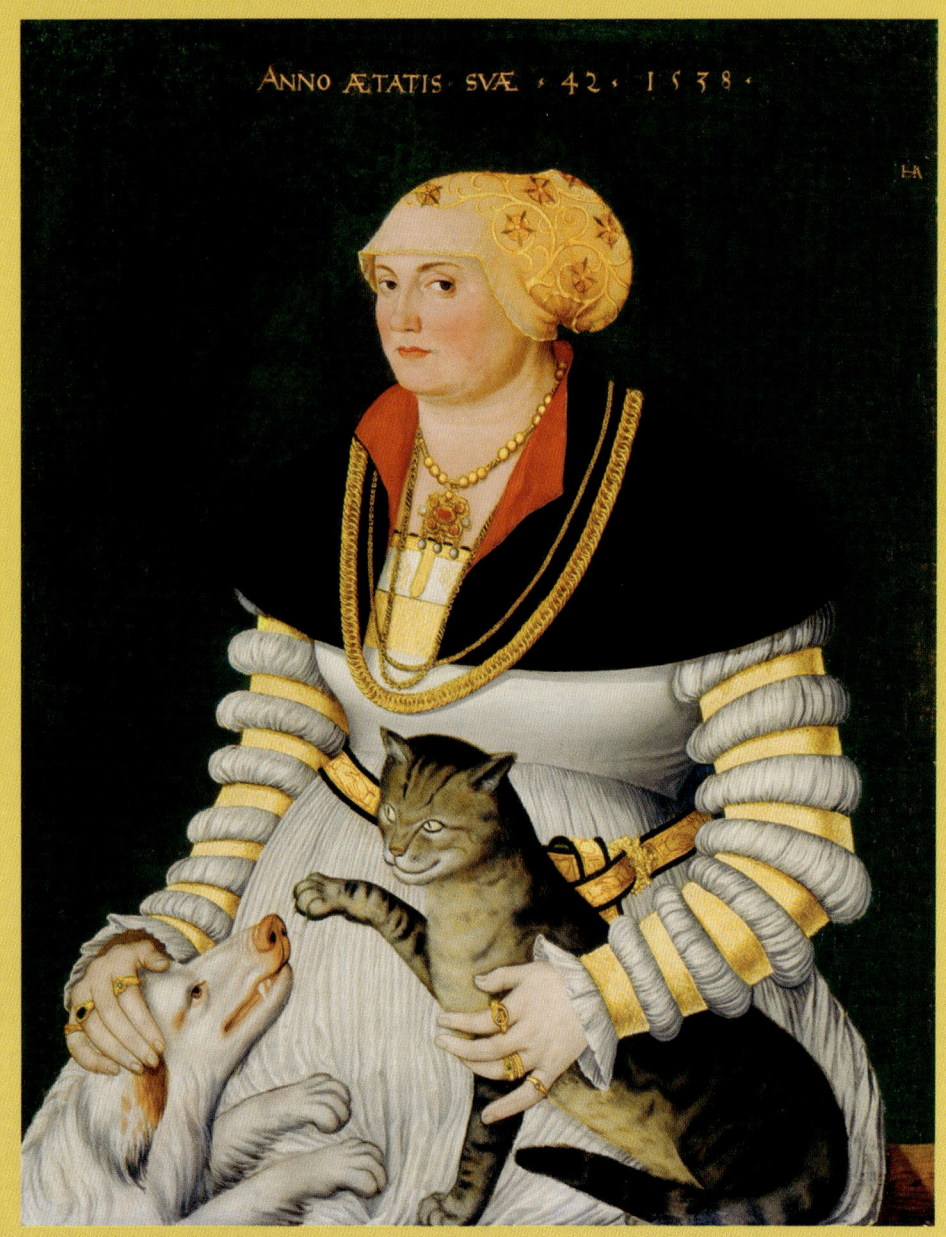

ANNO AETATIS SVAE · 42 · 1 5 3 8 ·

Pictorial allusion

Known for his portraits, the Swiss artist Hans Asper (c. 1499–1571) created this three-quarter view of a young woman in an elaborately pleated gown and shoulder cape, stroking a dog and holding a cat on her lap. The bonnet indicates that she is married, and the expensive jewellery around her neck and on her fingers conveys her wealth. She was Cleophea Holzhalb *née* Krieg von Bellikon. The painting closely follows the *Portrait of the Artist's Family* of 1528–9 by Hans Holbein the Younger, which Asper owned. Holbein, who had been Asper's teacher, focused especially on portraits because during the Protestant Reformation few religious works or landscapes were in demand, or even allowed, and portraits were popular. However, Asper's approach to painting was more decorative, simplified and flat-looking than Holbein's realistic style. In place of the two children of the earlier painting, Asper included a dog and a cat, a pictorial allusion to the sitter's family name: *Krieg* means "war" and *Bellen* "bark". The motif of crossed hands on her belt symbolizes marital fidelity, and Asper used a reduced colour palette to unify the painting. Particularly noticeable is the serious expression on the sitter's face, while her dog and cat seem to be smiling.

8

HANS ASPER

*Portrait of
Cleophea Krieg
von Bellikon*

1538

Tempera and oil
on panel

30⅓ × 24 in
(77 × 61 cm)

Kunsthaus Zürich,
Online Collection

BROWN TABBY

Brown tabby markings can be found in almost any breed, including Maine Coons, Bengals, Abyssinians, British and American shorthairs, and Scottish Folds. This is a brown mackerel tabby with black stripes on a predominantly brown background. It is generally believed that all tabby patterns came from the selective breeding and mutation of the mackerel pattern inherited from the African or Near Eastern wildcat. With their dark brown colouring and unique patterning, brown tabbies are well camouflaged in the wild. They are often described by their owners as being particularly affectionate, although this has not been scientifically proven.

Scrutiny and judgement

In about 1600 the Dutch-born German artist Hendrick Goltzius (1558–1617), who was already famous across Europe for his outstanding skill as a draughtsman and printmaker, started to paint. The large painting overleaf of Adam and Eve reclining in the Garden of Eden contrasts with earlier renderings of the biblical story. Dramatically close to the viewer, the two almost life-sized figures appear totally absorbed with each other. Unlike the usual emphasis on shame and punishment, their physical attraction and sensuousness are obvious. With her back to the viewer, Eve has taken the first bite of the apple and looks at Adam, who is clearly enthralled by her. Above Eve, the serpent, with a female face, represents both deception and redemption. The two goats symbolize the sins of humanity, and the elephant in the distance denotes the unshakeable power of God. The cat, which commonly symbolized lust and sensual pleasure, also reminds viewers not to enjoy what they should denounce in case it causes more harm than good. The cat's wise, scrutinizing look is there to remind the viewer not to condemn others for vices of which they may also be guilty. Overall, Goltzius is showing the viewer that an inability to restrain physical appetites will result in dire consequences.

9
HENDRICK GOLTZIUS
The Fall of Man
1616
Oil on canvas
41⅛ × 54½ in
(104.5 × 138.4 cm)
National Gallery of Art, Washington, DC, USA

Opposite: detail

CYPRUS CAT

Also known as the St Helen cat, St Nicholas cat, Aphrodite Giant or Aphrodite cat, this breed originated on the Mediterranean island after which it is named. It is probably one of the oldest cat breeds in the world, and is also one of the largest, with fairly short fur, an athletic build and almond-shaped eyes. A Byzantine legend explains that in the fourth century CE St Helen saved her monastery, which was infested with venomous serpents, by importing hundreds of Cyprus cats from Egypt or Palestine. The monastery had two bells; one called the cats for their meals, and the other reminded them to go to the fields and hunt snakes and rodents.

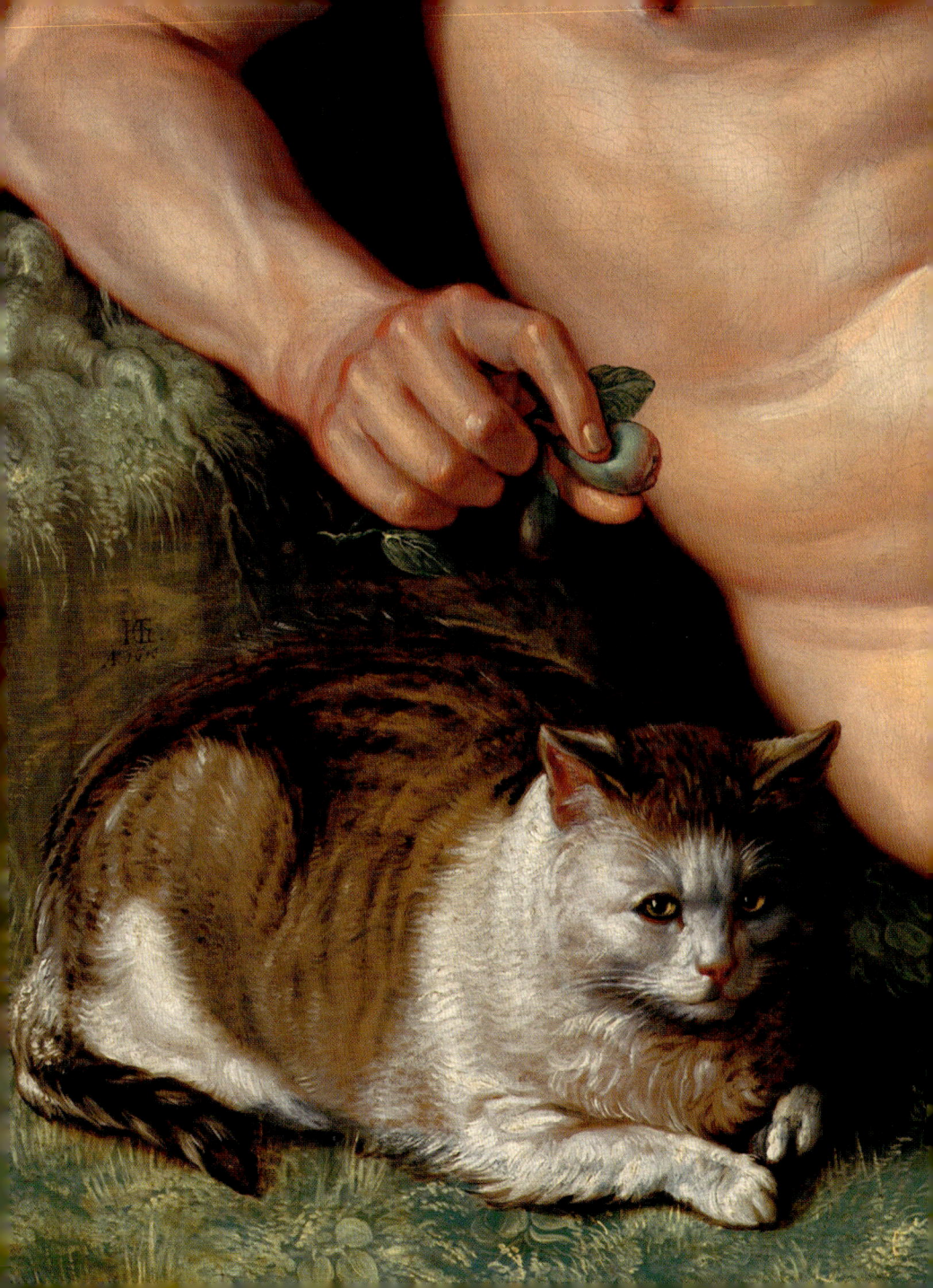

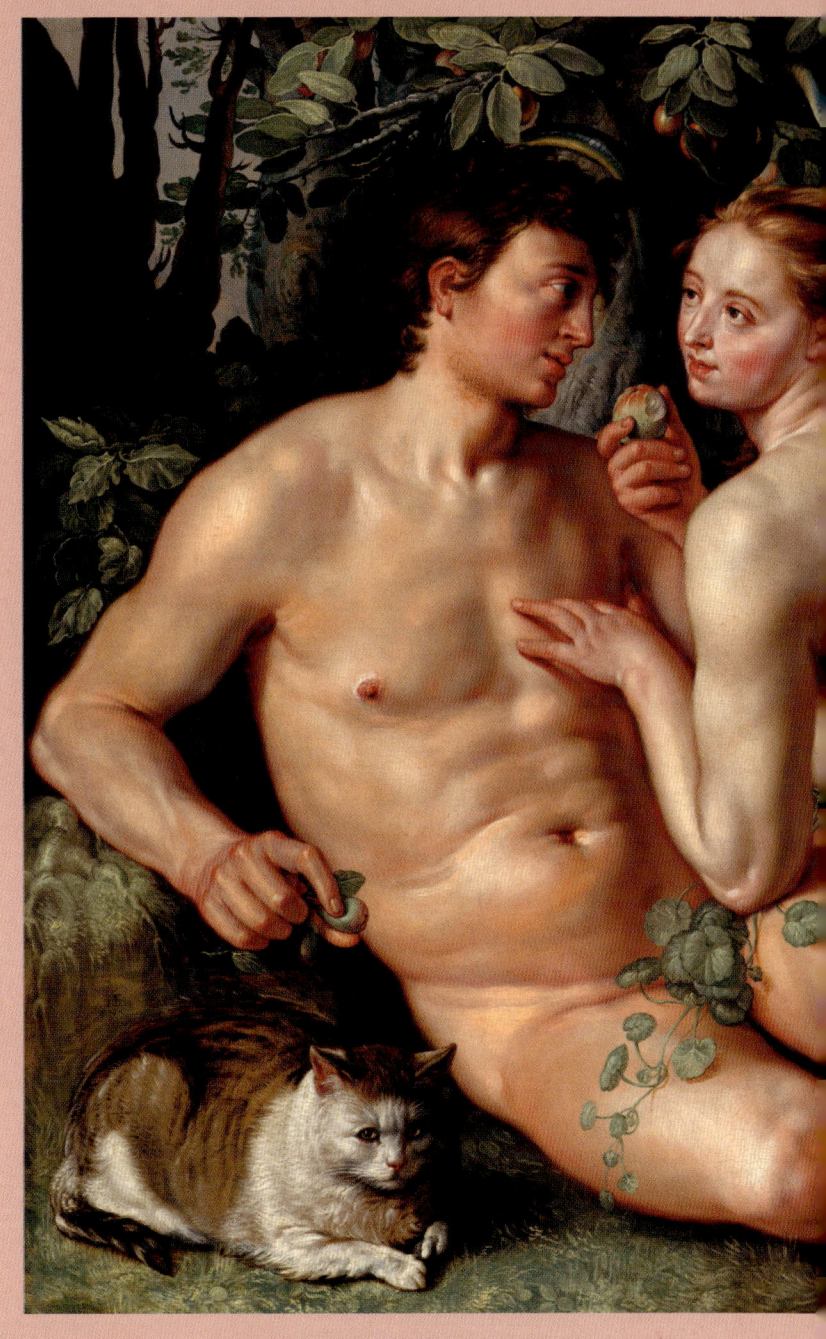

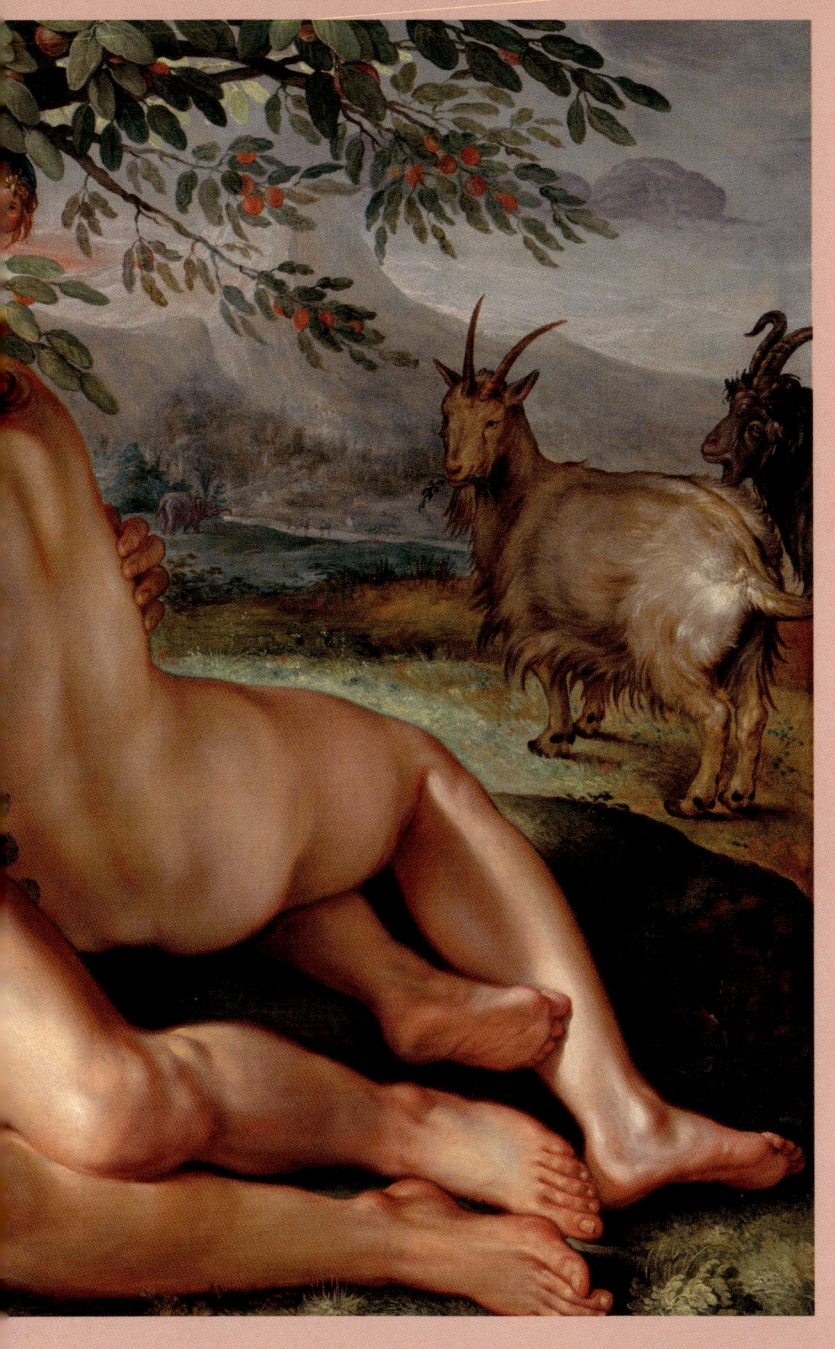

Mary and cats

This painting depicts the Annunciation, the moment when the Angel Gabriel announces to the Virgin Mary that she will be the mother of Christ. Peter Paul Rubens (1577–1640) merged the lifelike style that was popular in his native Flanders with traditions of the Italian Renaissance, developing a powerful and exuberant Baroque style that emphasized movement, colour, drama and sensuality. This is his second Annunciation painting. He made it relevant to contemporary viewers by adding domestic elements that would be recognized instantly, such as a wicker basket containing sewing equipment and, next to it, a sleeping pet cat. Blending the everyday with the extraordinary, a golden-haired angel descends from a divine beam of light, while winged cherubs cast petals down on Mary. Silky cloaks and robes billow gracefully, and Mary looks as though she is about to kneel and pray in this middle-class Flemish room. Darkness surrounds the figures, who glow with holy radiance. Even the white dove – representing the Holy Spirit – turns gold in the bright shaft of light. Every figure is moving except the cat, which is in a deep sleep and unaware of the dramatic events. Rubens's method of making the spiritual more accessible shows how the divine can be present in all aspects of life.

10
PETER PAUL RUBENS
Annunciation
c. 1628
Oil on canvas
120 × 70⅓ in
(310 × 178.6 cm)
Collection Rubenshuis, Antwerp, Belgium

Overleaf: detail

"M" ON THE FOREHEAD

This is a grey mackerel tabby, and the "M" shape on the forehead of this breed is linked to several stories. One Islamic legend says that the Prophet Muhammad had a tabby cat named Muezza. While Muhammad was resting, Muezza went to sleep on his robe. Rather than disturb the cat, Muhammad cut off his sleeve and gently stroked the cat's forehead, marking it with the "M". The ancient Egyptians revered cats, and some people believe the "M" stands for *mau*, the Egyptian word for "cat". A Christian story suggests that when baby Jesus was crying in the manger, a tabby cat curled up beside him and Mary stroked the cat's forehead, leaving the "M" mark for her name.

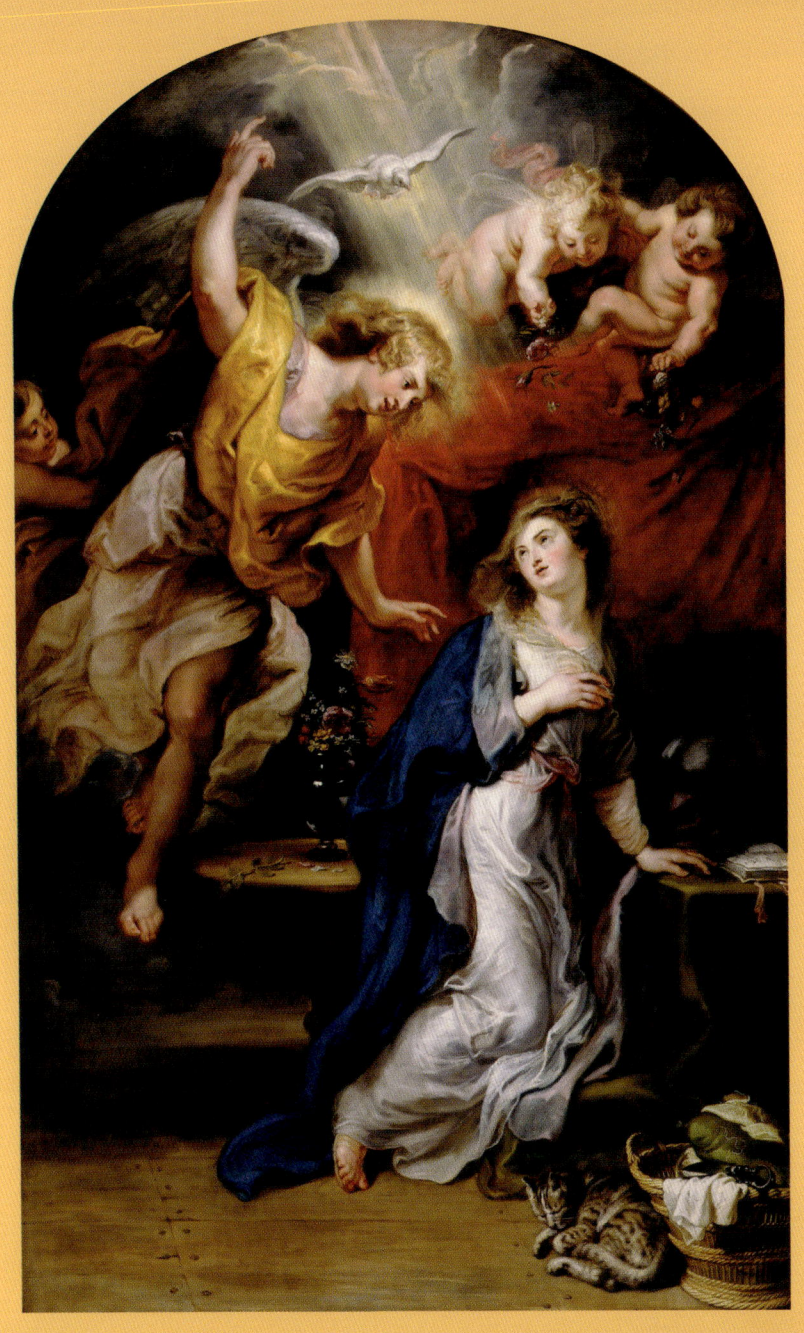

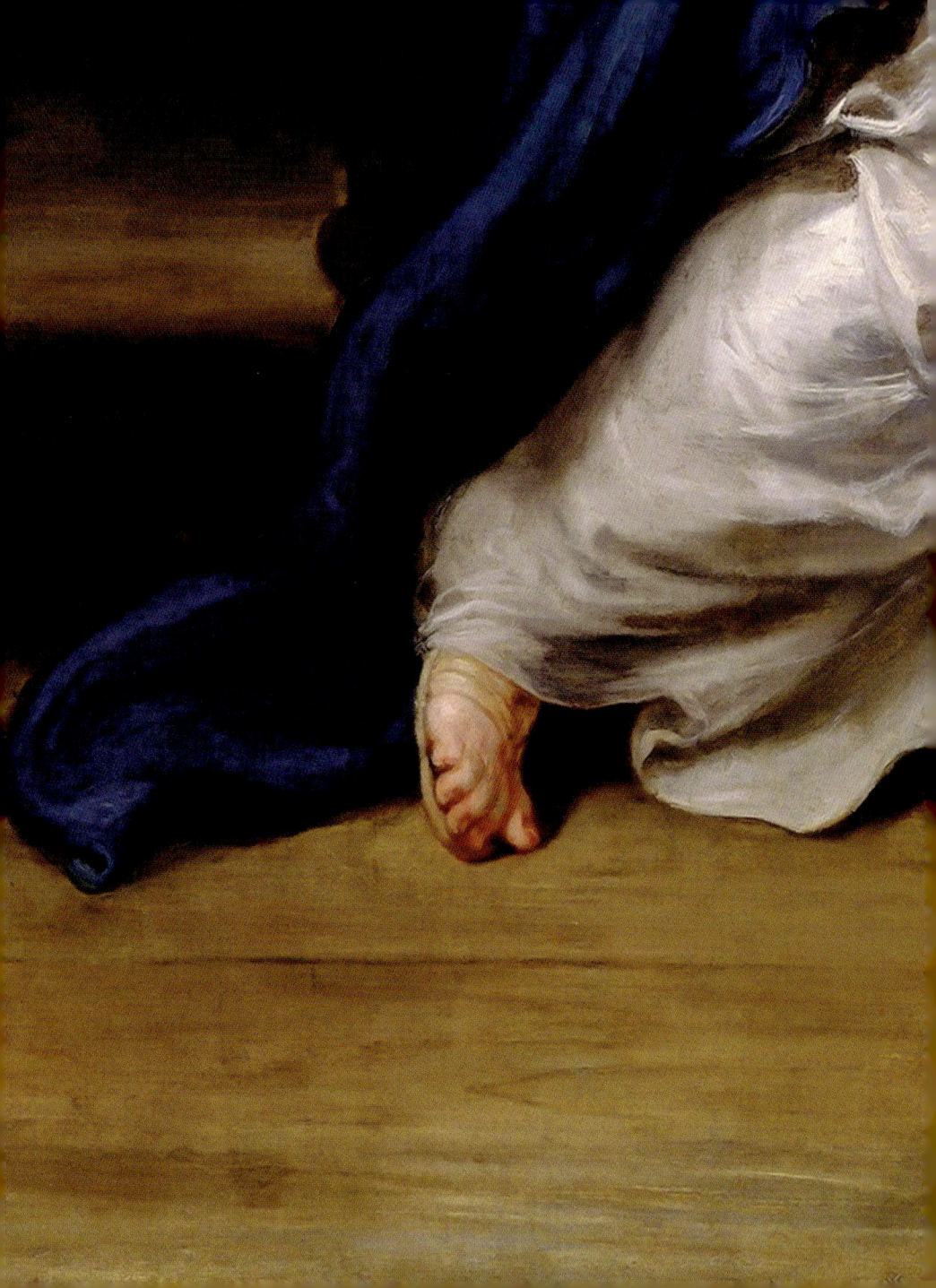

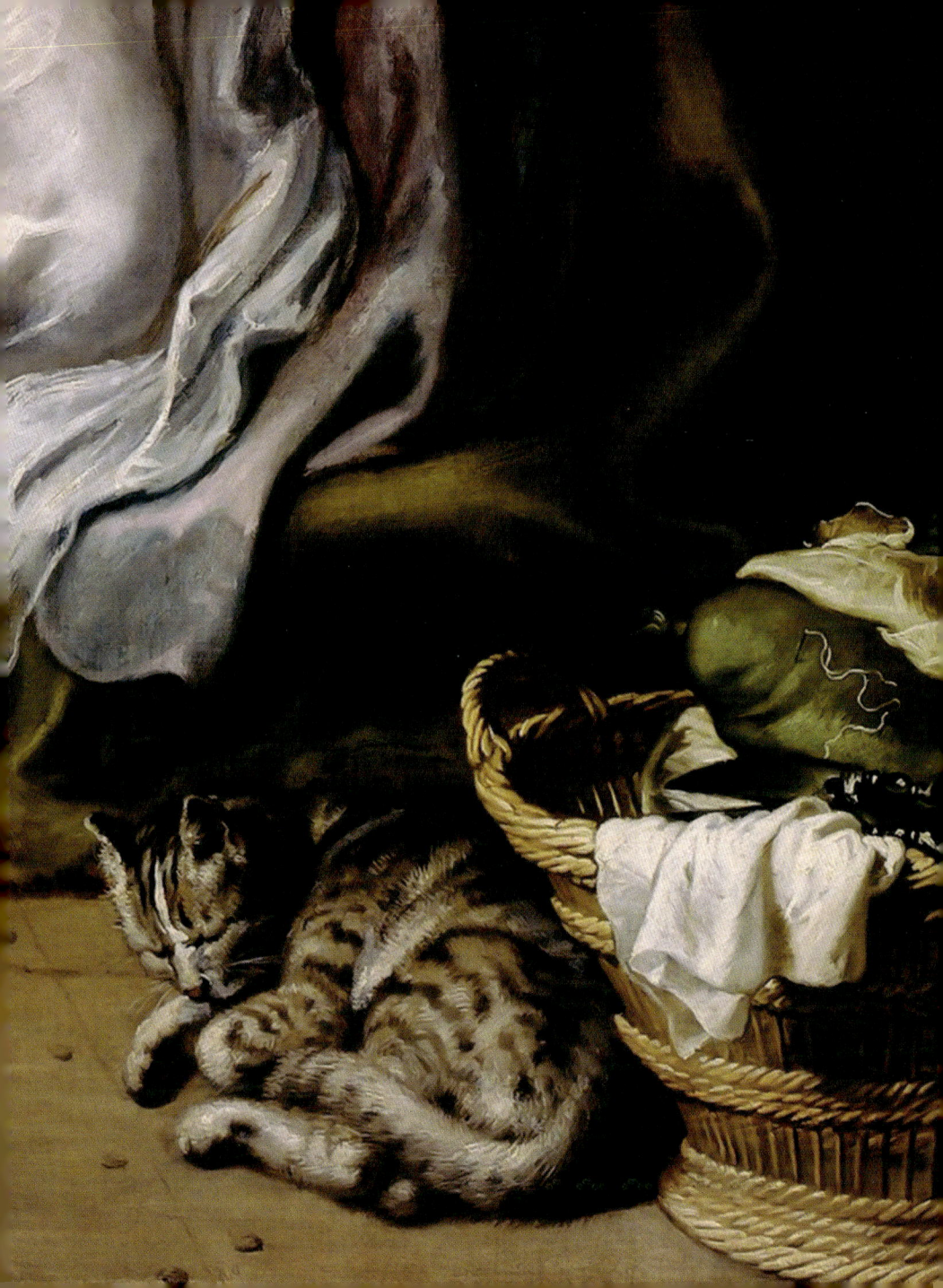

Take care

One of the leading painters of what is often called the Dutch Golden Age or the Dutch Baroque, Judith Leyster (1609–60) was famous during her life, financially successful and respected by her peers. Nonetheless, she was largely forgotten after her death, mainly because she was a woman. Only about 20 of her paintings are known now, yet she worked prolifically. Her canvases were in huge demand, and she was frequently commissioned to produce genre scenes, domestic interiors and portraits. This work captures a lively, spontaneous moment through quick brushstrokes and touches of paint. Two young children laugh as they tease a kitten. One wears a jaunty red hat with a black feather and a mustard-yellow coat with blue trimmings. He holds the kitten in his left hand while playfully snatching away its treat in his right and keeping the kitten from being grabbed by the other child. The cat seems afraid of the little boy and might lash out unexpectedly. Leyster was known for her energetic, informal, yet technically precise style, and here she has created a natural-looking scene, conveying colour and texture as well as the emotions of the three living creatures she depicts.

PROTESTANTISM AND CATS

Because of the new Protestant religion, Dutch artists had to find alternatives to traditional religious subjects while still conveying moralistic thoughts, warnings and instructions. Protestants generally did not hold to the same superstitions as Catholics; they did not encourage the fear of witchcraft, which some associated with felines, but rather valued cats for their practical role in keeping homes free of mice and rats. They also valued hard work, and the self-sufficiency and practicality of cats fitted well into this ethic. The Dutch were an important seafaring nation, and sailors took cats on their voyages to control rats on board ship, thus contributing to the spread of cat breeds around the world.

11
JUDITH LEYSTER
Two Children with a Cat
c. 1630
Oil on canvas
24 × 20 in
(61 × 52 cm)
Rijksmuseum, Amsterdam, The Netherlands

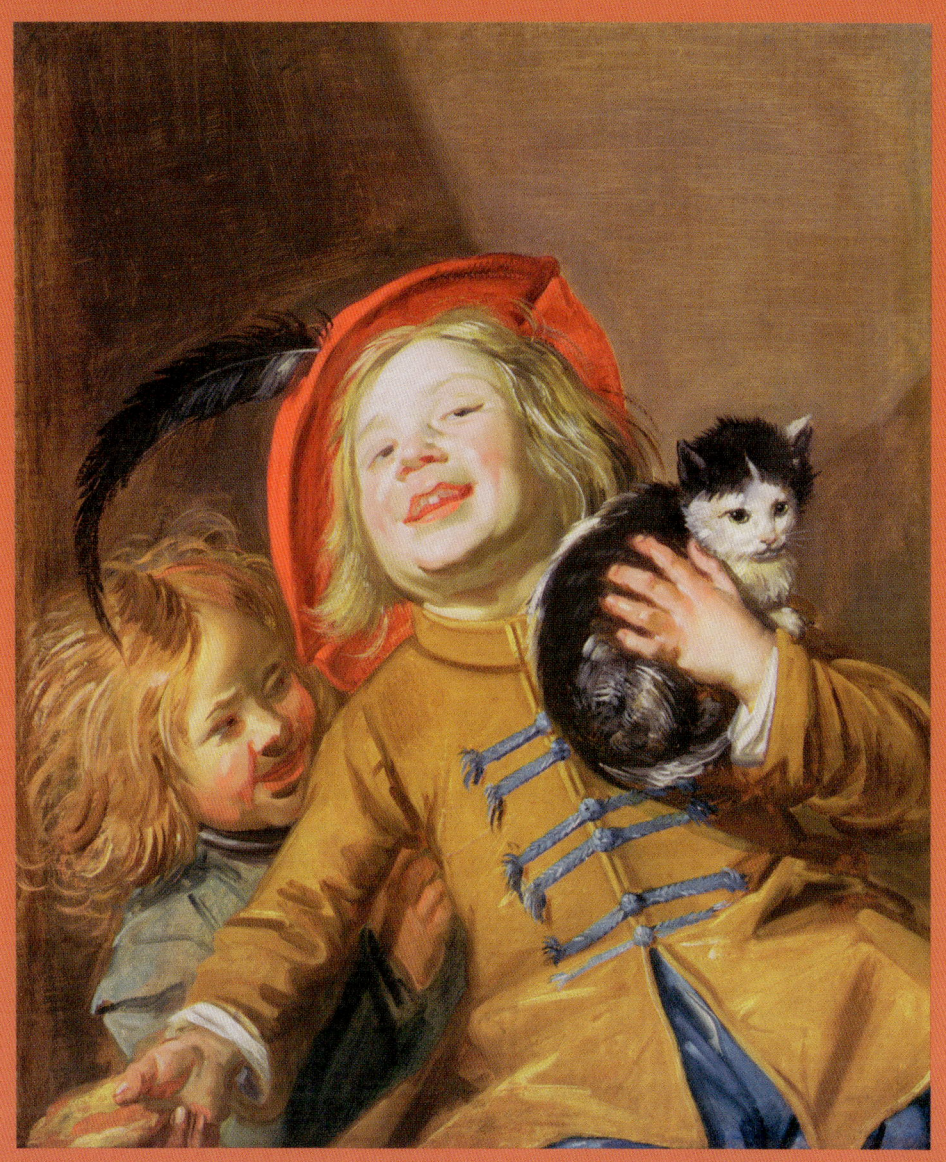

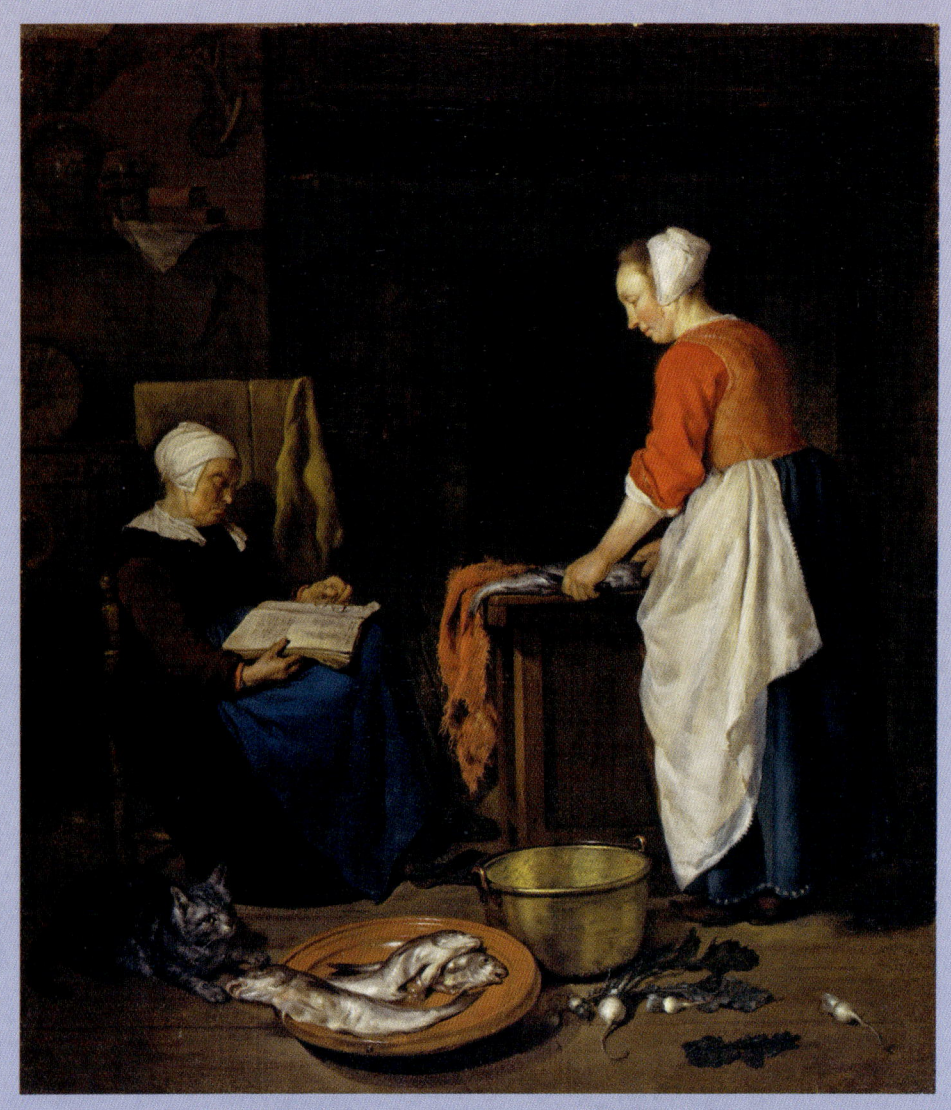

Potential thief

A successful Dutch painter of still lifes, portraits, and history and genre paintings, Gabriël Metsu (1629–67) did not adhere consistently to any style, technique or subject, but produced many "storytelling" images. Only 14 of his 133 known paintings are dated, of which this is one. In the midst of a fairly well-appointed contemporary room, the artist conveys the sin of sloth. An elderly woman has fallen asleep in a comfortable chair while reading the Bible. Her head lolls and the heavy book stays open on her lap. A maid is filleting fish, and a large plate on the floor holds several other fish that will be cooked along with the vegetables lying nearby. However, because the old woman is asleep, she has not noticed her cat hungrily eyeing the fish and sidling up to them. The scene therefore symbolizes the dire consequences of neglect and sloth. Metsu's use of light and shadow emphasizes the woman's peaceful yet defenceless state. Her pale, wrinkled face and hands stand out against the darker background, drawing attention to her figure and the book on her lap. The maid, who also contrasts with the dark background in her brightly coloured top and white apron, watches the grey cat, which looks back at her warily.

12

GABRIËL METSU

An Old Woman Asleep

1657–*c.* 1662

Oil on canvas

14¾ × 13 in (37.5 × 33 cm)

The Wallace Collection, London, UK

Overleaf: detail

GREY TABBY

The tabby is not a specific breed, but a common striped coat pattern found in pure-bred and mixed (randomly bred) cats. The pattern is thought to have come from the African wildcat (*Felis silvestris lybica*), and the silver or grey coat is caused by a melanin inhibitor gene that suppresses the development of the yellow pigment in the fur. Of the four tabby patterns, the cat in this painting seems to be a mackerel tabby. Also known as a "tiger cat", the mackerel is the original wild-type pattern; it consists of a dark stripe along the back and a fishbone pattern down the cat's side.

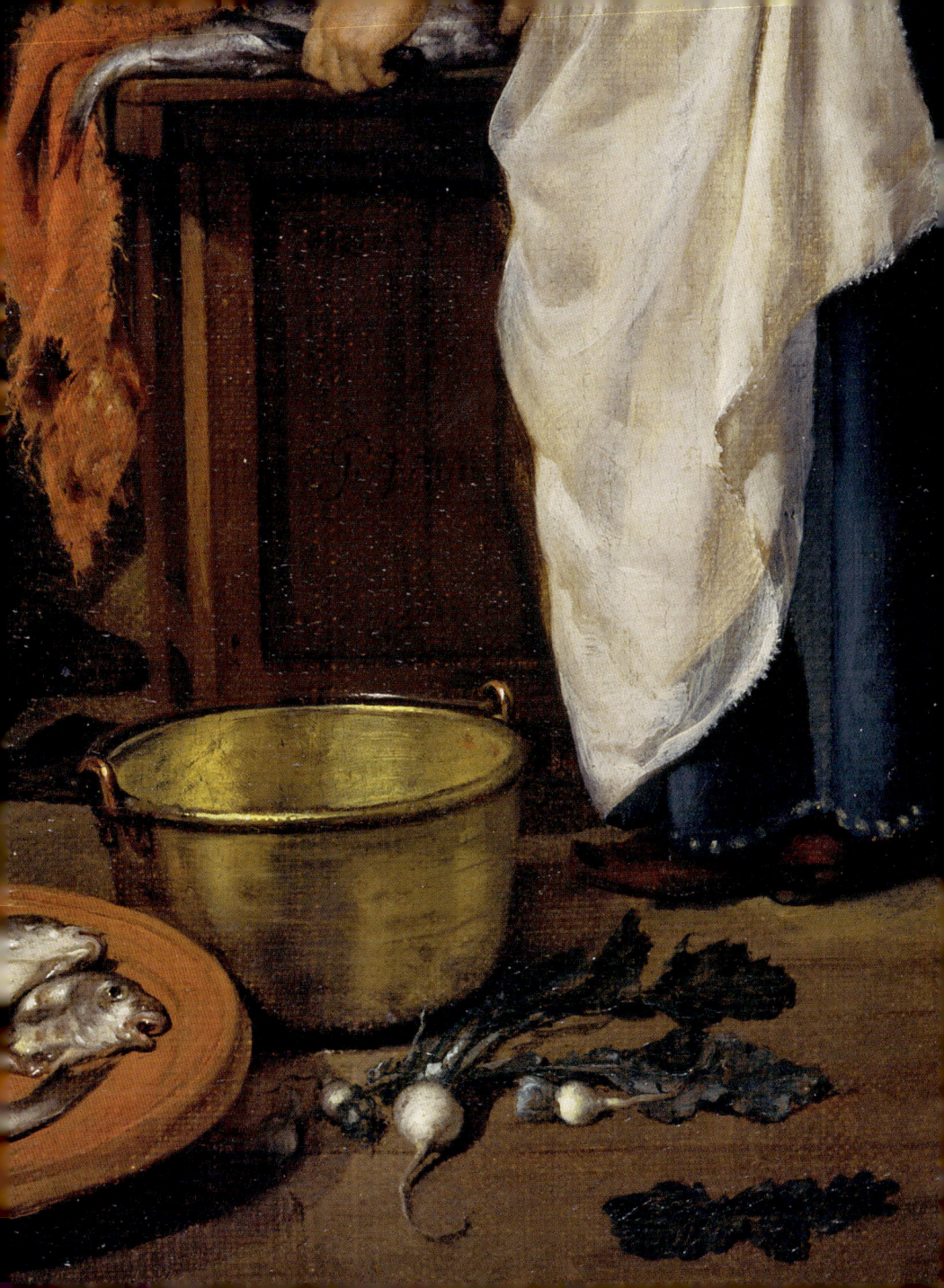

Calm companionship

Although he is often described as a master of still life, Jean-Baptiste-Siméon Chardin (1699–1779) is also celebrated for his genre paintings portraying children, kitchen maids and domestic activities. He was particularly skilled at conveying a sense of soft light, and of giving as much attention to the objects in his paintings as to the figures. The work opposite depicts a young washerwoman or laundress looking away from her work, distracted, as if she has heard something. Her pale, flushed face catches the light, while her hands stay submerged in the large wooden washtub. On a low stool close by, a young boy sits and blows a bubble, a symbol of the transience and fragility of life. The soft light and restricted colour palette produce a calm atmosphere; the laundress is still, the boy is quiet, the calico cat is relaxing. Only the figure through the door is busy, working hard in a steam-filled room. This technique of showing a figure through a doorway was an influence of Dutch genre painting. It makes the space appear larger, and brings a sense of companionship. Chardin's skill in capturing varied textures can be seen clearly in such elements as the steam, the iridescent bubble and the cat's thick fur.

CALICO CAT

Any breed of domestic cat with a tricolour coat can be described as calico. Most calico cats have white, orange and black patches, although they may have other colours as well. Calico cats are almost exclusively female. The name derives from a colourful printed fabric that originated in the city of Kozhikode (formerly Calicut) in southwestern India. Printed, finely patterned calico was made in Lancashire, northwestern England, in the 1780s, and the name soon became used to describe the mottled coats of these cats. Genetically, calico cats resemble tortoiseshells, except that the tortoiseshell has a black undercoat and the calico a white one.

13

JEAN-BAPTISTE-SIMÉON CHARDIN

The Washerwoman

1732–40

Oil on wood panel

15¼ × 17¼ in (38.7 × 43.8 cm)

Barnes Foundation, Philadelphia, USA

Overleaf: detail

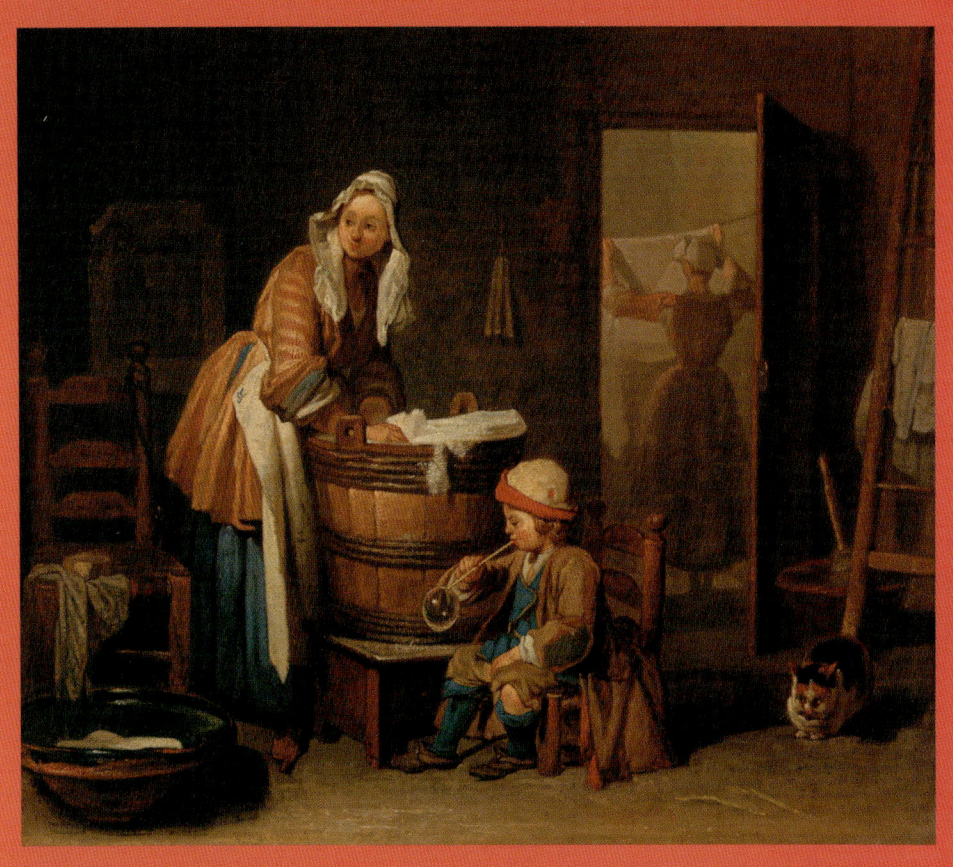

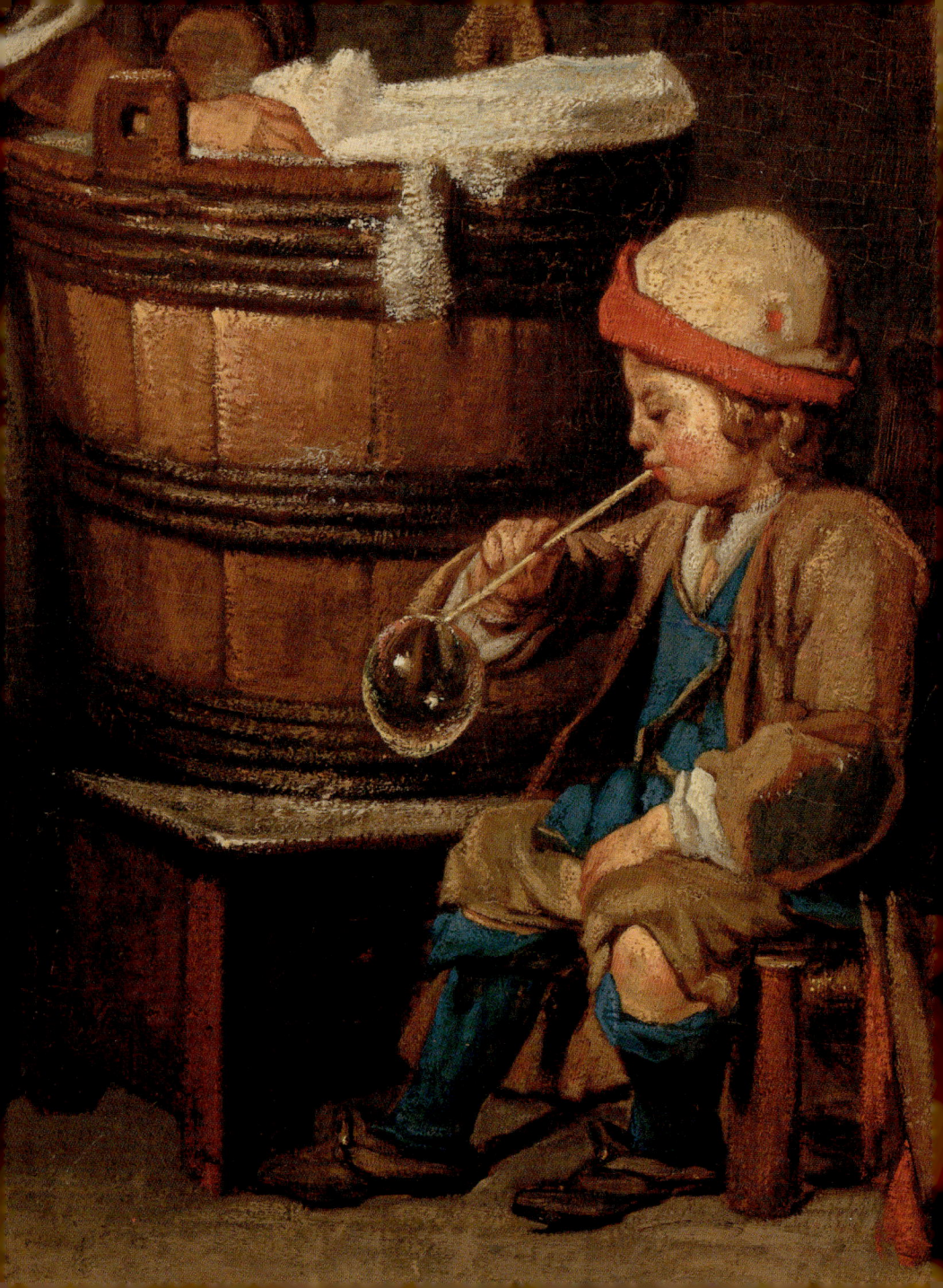

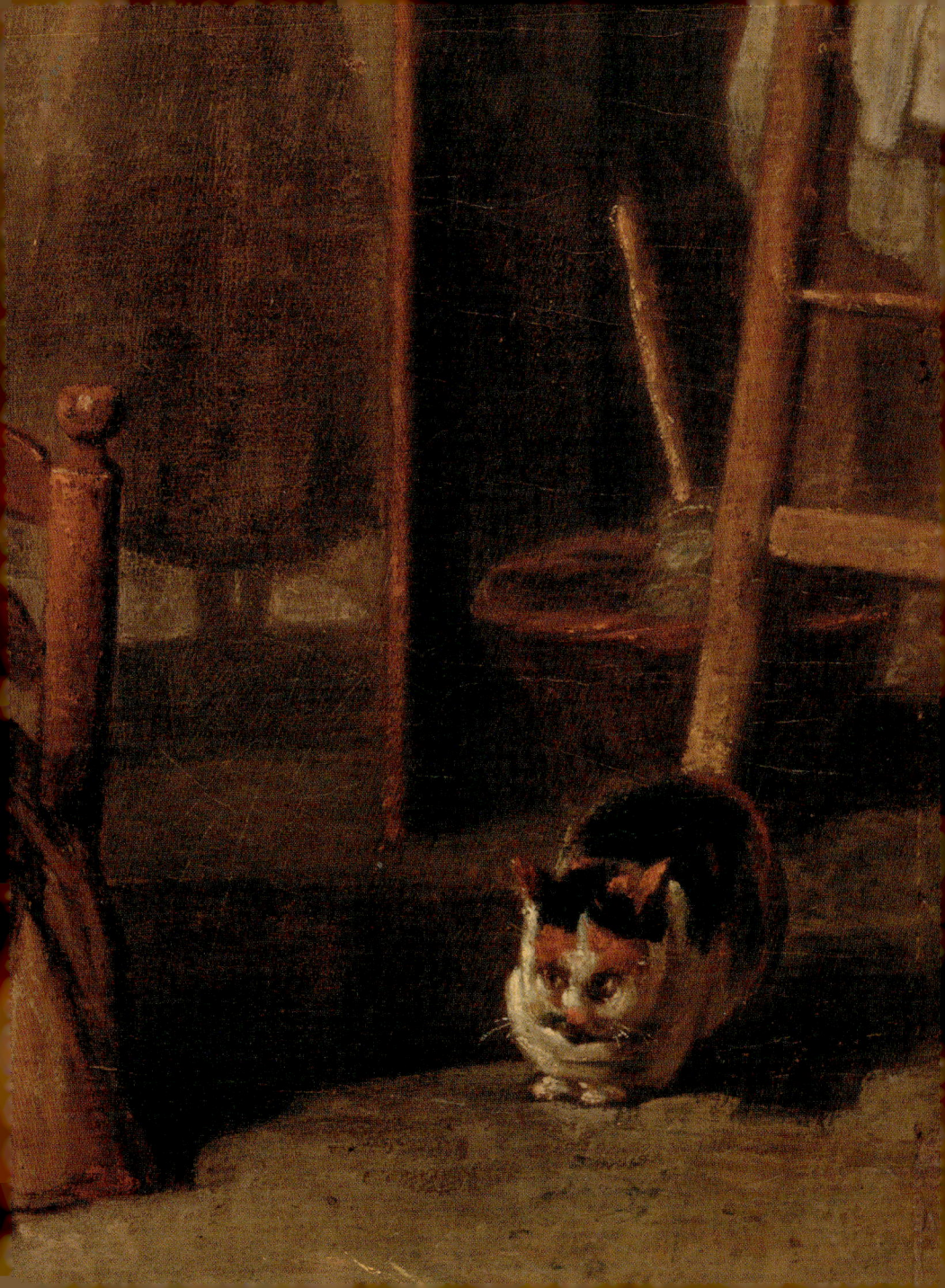

Lively and animated

Four well-dressed children, a cat and a bird are seen in a room. The children are those of Daniel Graham, apothecary to King George II, and the artist was the English painter and printmaker William Hogarth (1697–1764). Dressed in skirts and a bonnet – as was typical for all babies then until boys were "breeched" between the ages of two and five – Thomas is the youngest. The other children are Henrietta, Anna Maria and Richard. Surrounding them are luxurious furnishings reflecting the family's wealth. The bird is inside a gilded cage, and Thomas sits in an elaborate baby carriage with a gilded bird handle. He holds a piece of rusk but reaches for the red cherries in Henrietta's hand, while Richard plays a tune on a musical box. Yet underneath all this light-heartedness are reminders of death and the passing of time. Infant mortality was high in Britain during this period, and before Hogarth completed this painting, Thomas had died. It may have been made as a memorial for him. Cherries traditionally symbolize the fruit of Paradise, and the fruit and carnations on the floor could be a memento mori. A clock adorned with a winged cherub holding an hourglass and scythe are more reminders of time and death, and the goldfinch is a traditional symbol of Christ's Passion.

14
WILLIAM HOGARTH
The Graham Children
1742
Oil on canvas
63¼ × 71 in
(160.5 × 181 cm)
The National Gallery, London, UK

Overleaf: detail

TABBY CAT GENES

The tabby coat is linked to specific genes. The Taqpep gene, which was discovered in recent studies, plays a crucial role in determining whether a cat has a mackerel or classic tabby pattern. Mutations in this gene result in the classic pattern, whereas the gene's more active version produces the mackerel stripes. This genetic trait has been carried through millennia, ensuring the prevalence of tabbies in cat populations today. The agouti gene, meanwhile, controls the distribution of black pigment on individual hairs, which creates the "ticked" appearance of some tabby coats. When the agouti gene is active, tabby markings are the result. If it is inactive, the coat will appear solid.

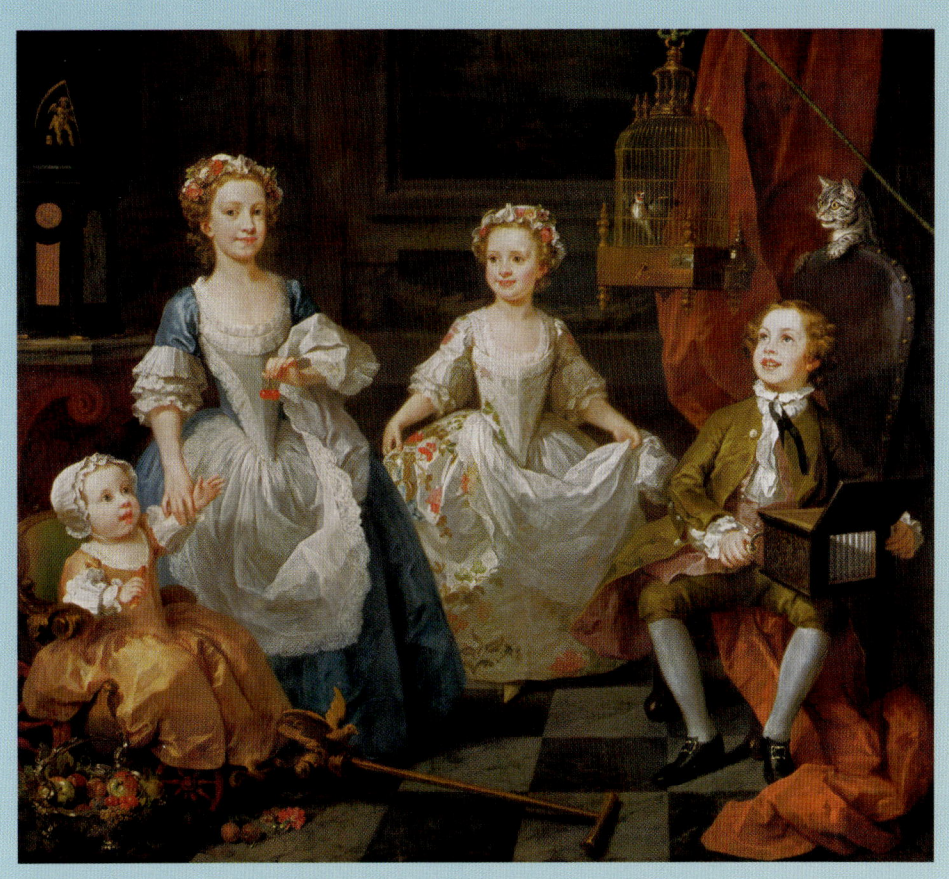

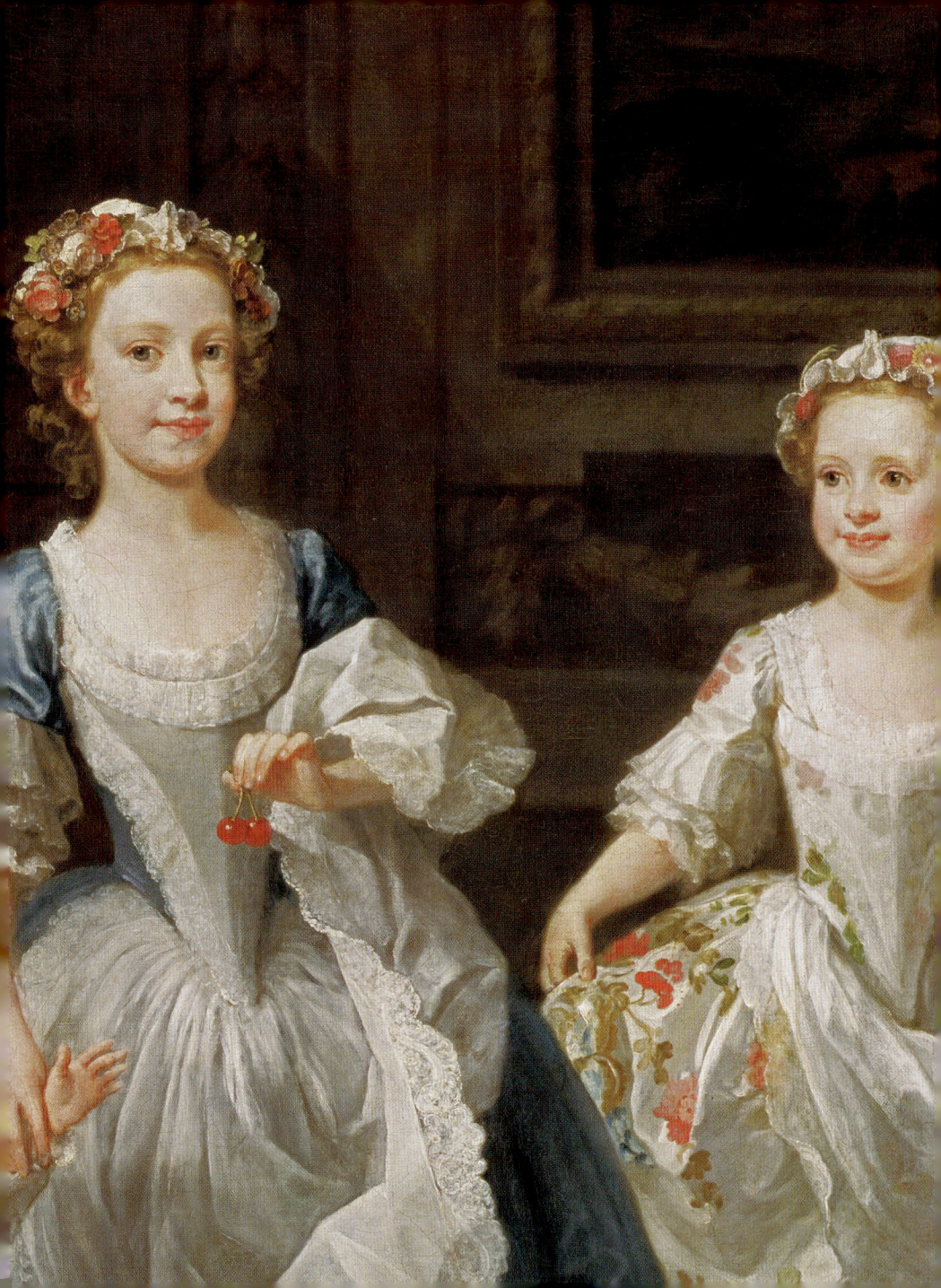

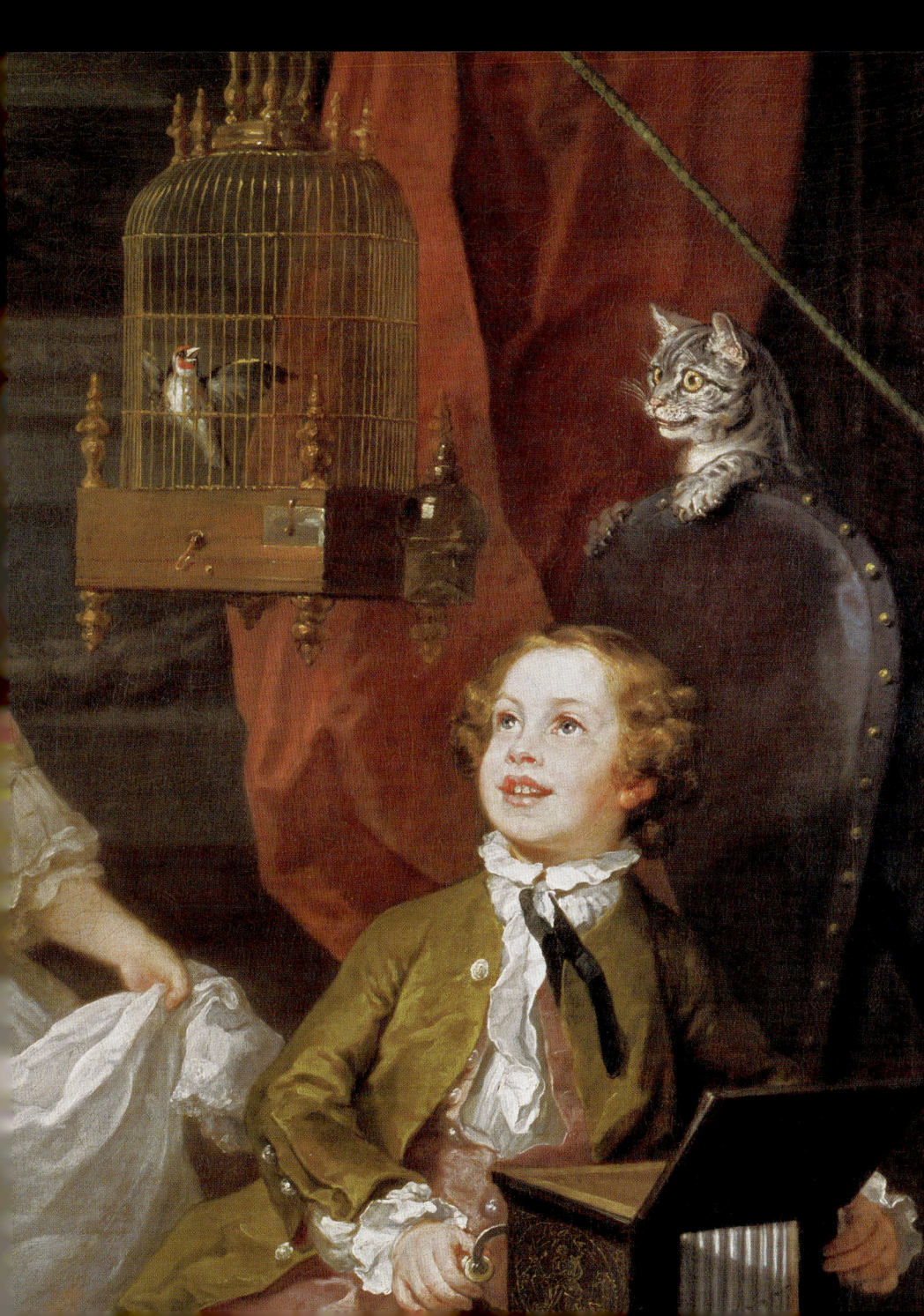

Harmless mischief

The Rococo style flourished during the eighteenth century, and the French painter, draughtsman and etcher François Boucher (1703–70) became one of its leading exponents, admired for his classical, decorative and pastoral scenes, but especially for his images of beautiful women. King Louis XV and his mistress Madame de Pompadour were among Boucher's greatest patrons, ensuring that his work became the height of fashion. In this ornate, messy boudoir, two fashionably dressed young women are daintily undertaking their morning tasks. Notions of delicacy, frivolity, light-heartedness and intimacy with a touch of sexuality are among the features of Rococo art, and Boucher conveys all this here. The painting evokes rustling taffeta and whispering cotton lawn, gentle chatter and a crackling fire. The elegant (and costly) yellow-papered walls and decorative screen set off the two figures. With her back to the viewer, the stylishly dressed maid holds out a delicately trimmed cap, while her mistress ties a pink ribbon around her silky stocking, revealing a glimpse of naked thigh. On the floor at the seated lady's feet, a cat plays with a small ball of wool. The animal's presence augments the sense of grace, elegance, femininity and mischief, while suggesting intimacy and domesticity.

ABYSSINIAN

The golden-brown cat seen here, with its white-tipped tail, is probably an Abyssinian, a breed known for its slender, elegant appearance. With its lean, graceful profile, the Abyssinian cat bears a close resemblance to ancient Egyptian cat statues and is one of the oldest cat breeds in existence. The name derives from the country to the southeast of Egypt, once called Abyssinia but now known as Ethiopia, although other research suggests that the breed originated in Southeast Asia, somewhere on the coast of the Indian Ocean. These cats have large eyes and unique ticked coats (meaning they are made up of striped hairs) in numerous colours.

15
FRANÇOIS BOUCHER
La Toilette
1742
Oil on canvas
20⅔ × 26 in
(52.5 × 66.5 cm)
Museo Nacional Thyssen-Bornemisza, Madrid, Spain

Overleaf: detail

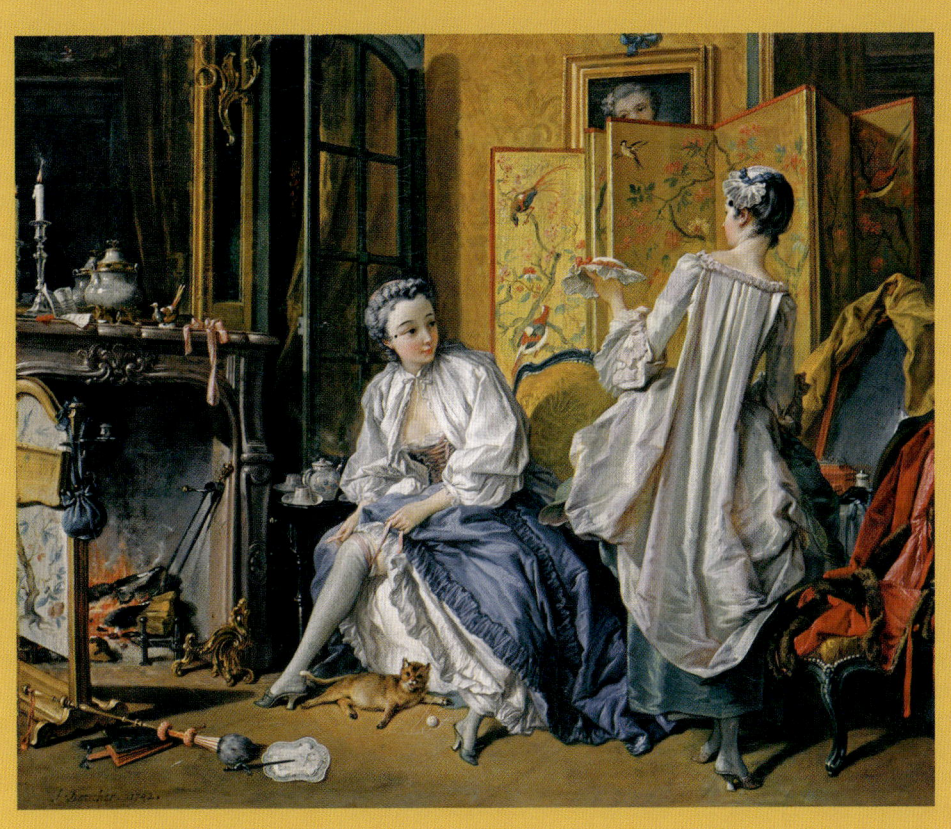

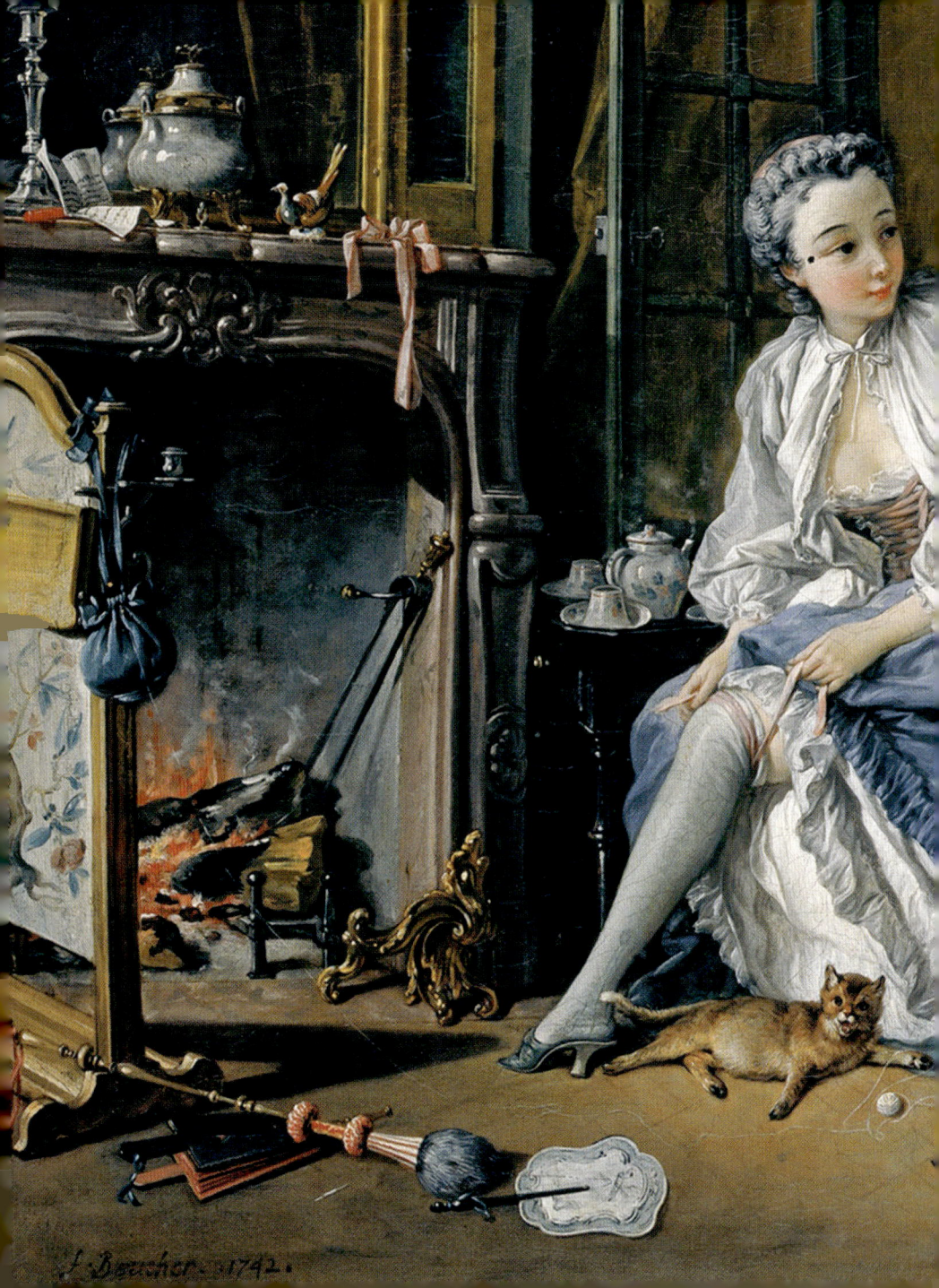

J. Boucher 1742.

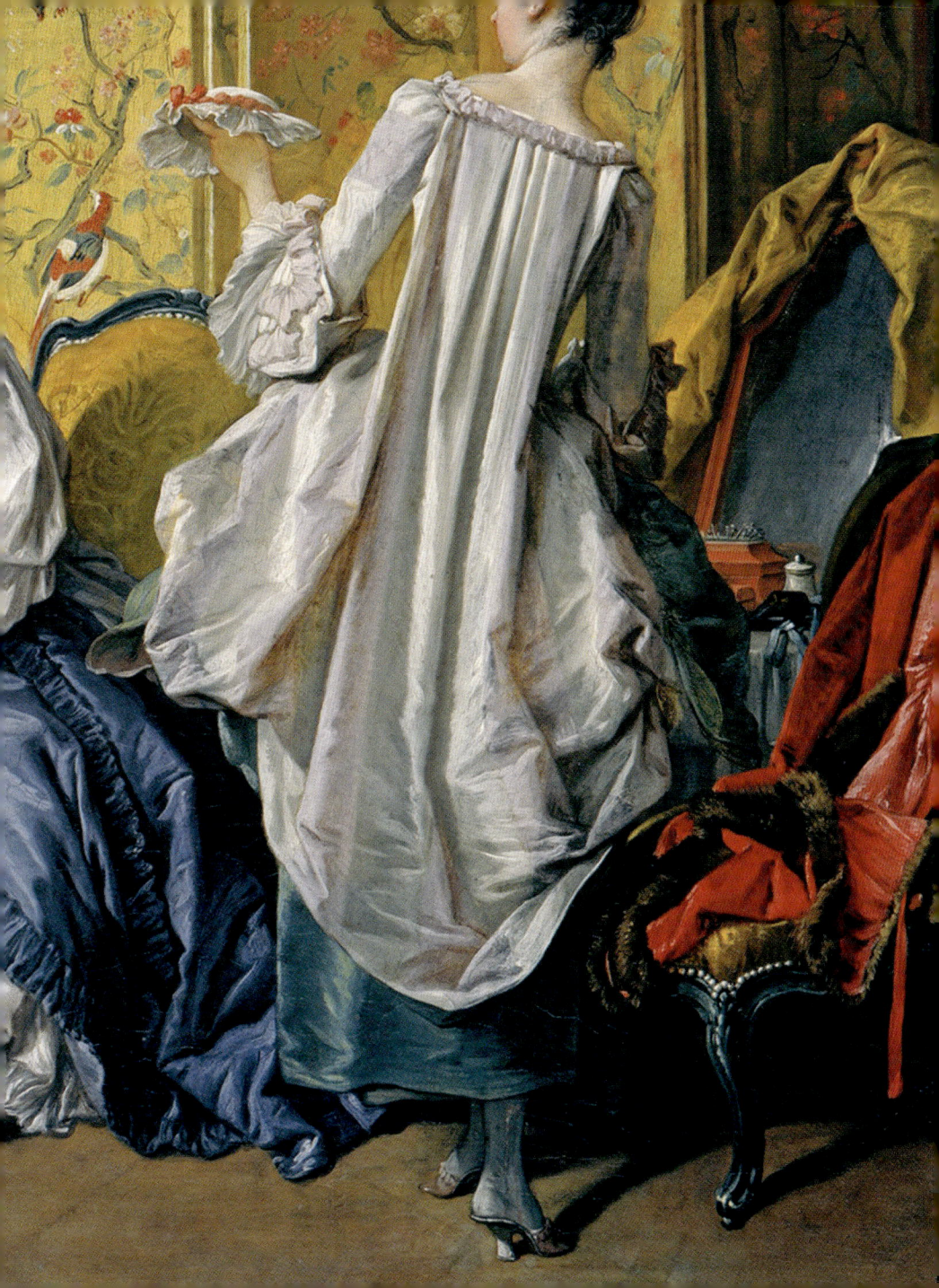

Pearls and bells

An artist who became especially well known for his inclusion of cats in portraits was the Parisian Jean-Baptiste Perronneau (c. 1716–83). He began his career as an engraver, but by the 1740s he was producing portraits in oils and, especially, pastels. His portraits of young women with pale, powdered faces often feature cats as well, and, along with his evident understanding of colour and of eighteenth-century fashion, he clearly empathized with his furry sitters. In this intimate portrait, Magdaleine Pinceloup de la Grange looks into the distance. The image was created as one of a pair with her husband, Charles-François, who seems more relaxed in his portrait; Magdaleine looks a little tense. Wearing a costly dress, headdress and choker embellished with pearls and flowers, she sits stiffly, leaning slightly forwards in the chair, holding her grey-blue Chartreux cat closely with both hands – perhaps to help her relax. Wearing a collar adorned with bells that echo the pearls around Magdaleine's neck, the cat seems rather uncomfortable and reluctant to be held so tightly. Perronneau included feline companions in several of his portraits of female subjects, probably to relax them, but also to emphasize each sitter's gentleness, elegance and sophistication.

16

JEAN-BAPTISTE PERRONNEAU

Magdaleine Pinceloup de la Grange, née de Parseval

1747

Oil on canvas

25⅝ × 20⅝ in (65.1 × 52.4 cm)

J. Paul Getty Museum, Los Angeles, USA

CHARTREUX CAT

The origin of this rare French cat breed is difficult to trace. The first mention of it was in a poem of 1558, and it had become particularly popular among the aristocracy by the late seventeenth century. It is commonly believed that the Chartreux cat was initially brought to France by Crusaders returning from Syria in the thirteenth century. With thick, short, almost woolly fur in a soft grey-blue colour, these nearly silent cats have strikingly contrasting orange or copper-coloured eyes. The head structure and tapered muzzle makes Chartreux cats appear to smile. In build and speed, they are muscular, athletic and quick hunters.

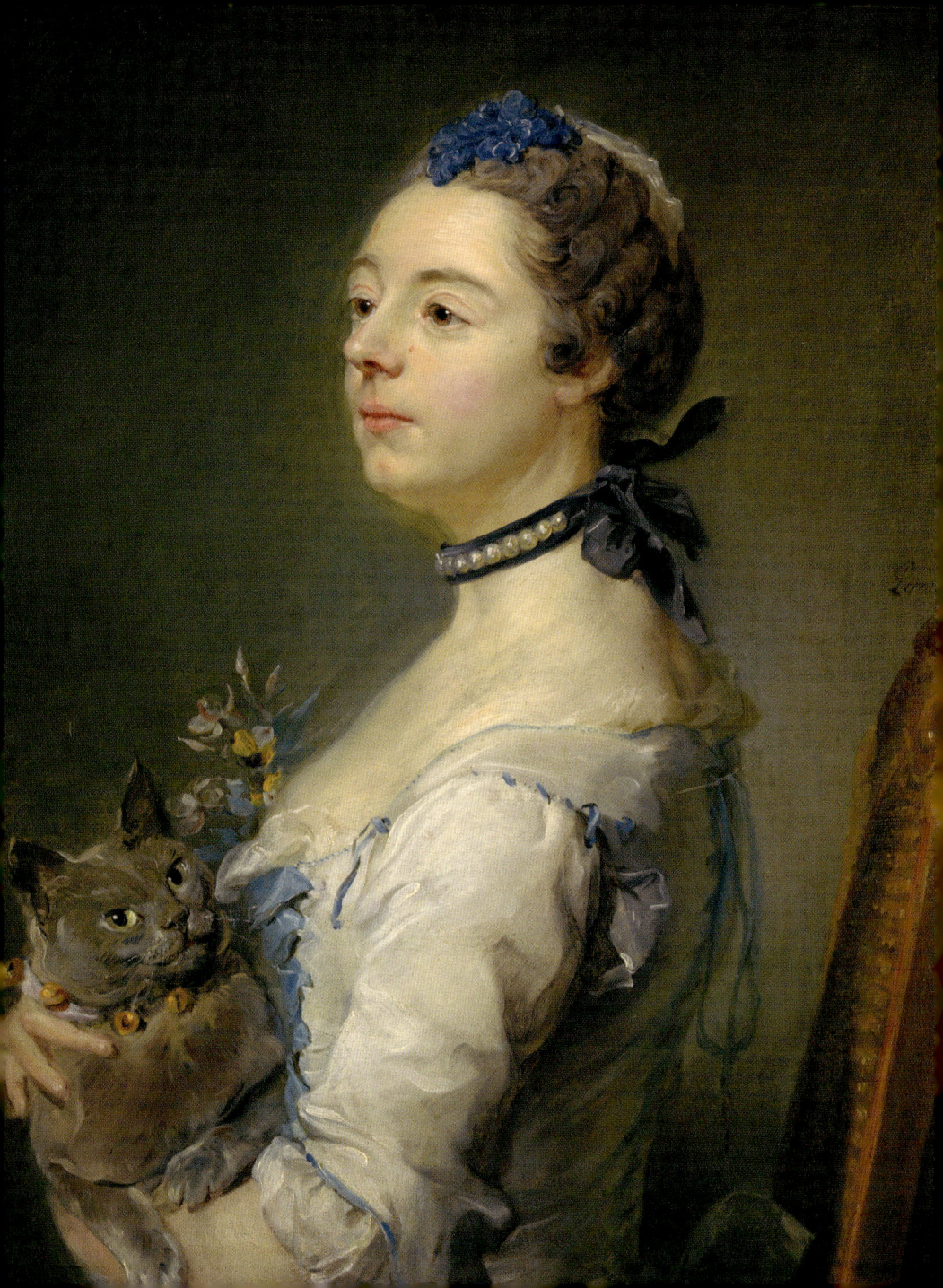

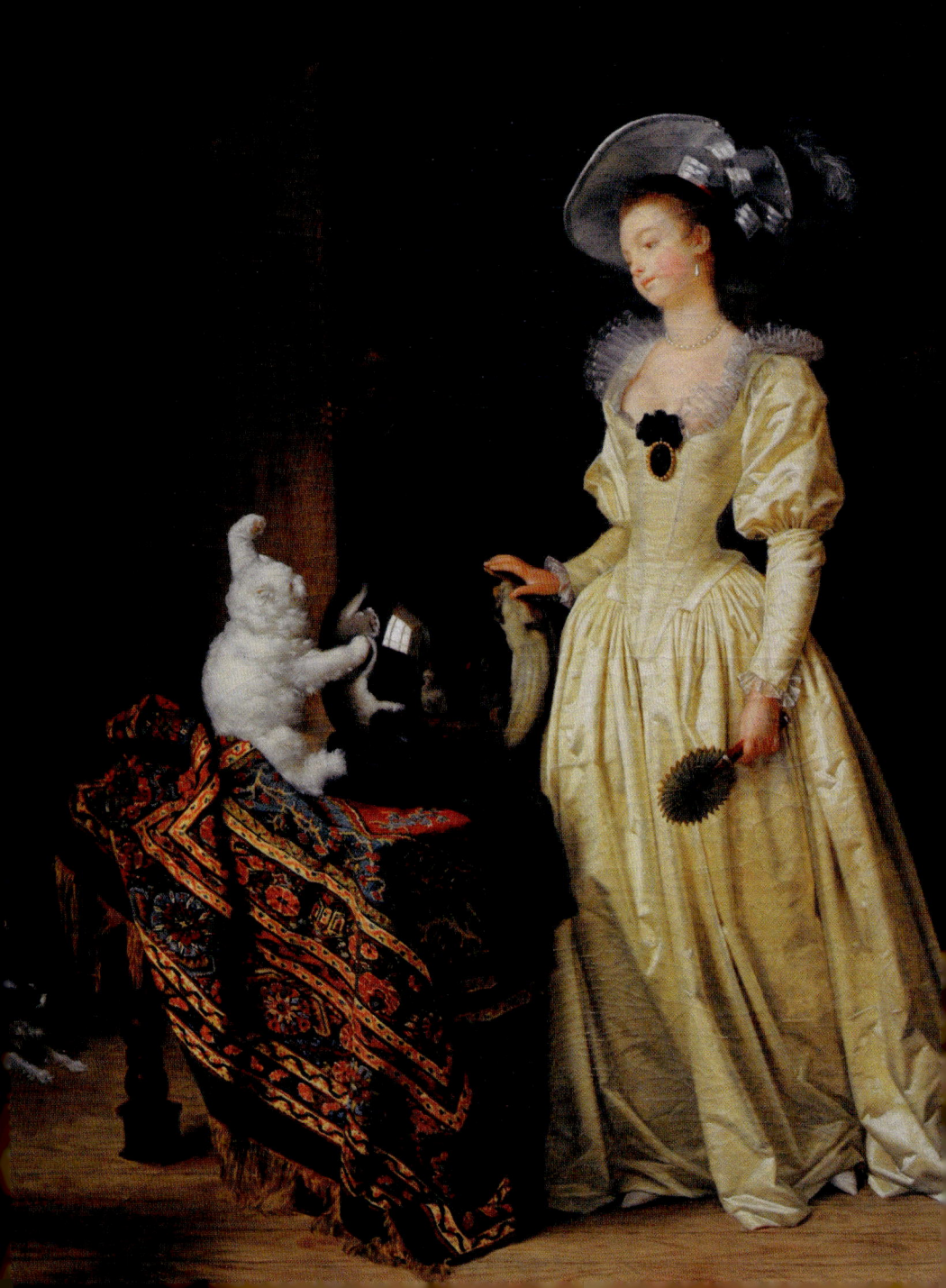

Reflected rival

In the years leading up to the French Revolution in 1789–99, many of the wealthiest French citizens realized that grand occasions and fashions would soon be replaced with more modest lifestyles. Artists, especially those who had been successful in the frivolous Rococo style, began painting genre scenes rather than more decadent situations. This painting reflects these new ideas. An elegant young woman in a dress of golden taffeta watches her fluffy white Angora cat, which is playing with a silver globe. A black cloth next to it suggests that it was previously covered. The cat attacks the globe as though it is angry with its "rival" in the reflection. Also reflected in the globe is a woman sitting at an easel in a small room with two other figures. Jean-Honoré Fragonard (1732–1806) and Marguerite Gérard (1761–1837) were related through marriage (Fragonard was married to Gérard's sister) and often worked in collaboration. Fragonard was one of the most famous and celebrated Rococo artists, and Gérard, who also became successful, carefully emulated his approach to detail and delicate brushwork. With its dark interior, elderly servant (also seen in the reflection), patterned carpet on the table, and the amusing anecdote being portrayed, this scene seems to follow the model of seventeenth-century Dutch genre painting.

17

JEAN-HONORÉ
FRAGONARD
AND
MARGUERITE
GÉRARD

The Angora Cat

c. 1783

Oil on canvas

26 × 22 in
(65 × 53.5 cm)

Wallraf-Richartz
Museum &
Fondation
Corboud, Cologne,
Germany

TURKISH ANGORA

Turkish Angora cats originated in central Anatolia (Ankara Province in present-day Turkey) some time during the fifteenth century. It is likely that the breed is descended from the African wildcat, but the long, silky hair is either the result of a natural mutation or an evolutionary modification that helped it to survive in harsh, snowy climates. Angoras have many similarities with Persians, and have been documented since the seventeenth century. Thriving on attention, the Turkish Angora has a friendly, sociable personality and appreciates constant companionship. Usually clever, they can be mischievous and playful, and are often more energetic than their quiet gentleness might suggest.

A golden age

Recovering from the turbulent invasions of the Japanese and the Manchus in the late sixteenth and early seventeenth centuries, the Joseon dynasty in Korea experienced a period of political stability and socio-economic prosperity in the eighteenth, now known as Joseon's Golden Age. The arts flourished, and new artistic themes and genres emerged. The dynasty was founded by Taejo of Joseon in 1392 and persisted until Korea was annexed by Japan in 1910. During its more than 500-year duration, its rulers encouraged Confucian ideals and doctrines, discouraged Buddhism, and allowed the development of a more relaxed and profitable exchange between parts of Asia and Europe. This hanging scroll by an unknown artist features traditional elements of Joseon art at its peak, when paintings of animals, birds and flowers were particularly popular. It includes elements shared with Chinese and Japanese art of the same period, such as a sensitive use of ink and colour, an asymmetrical composition, soft gradations of tone, minimal use of line and writing to accompany the image, as well as a cat and flowers in the detail shown here. The curves and controlled use of colour make it particularly decorative and calming.

ASIAN LEOPARD CAT

Domesticated about 5,000 years ago in Neolithic China, the Asian leopard cat (*Prionailurus bengalensis*) can be found in 21 countries in Asia. It varies so much in colouration and size that for a long time it was thought to be several different species and given many different names, including Jerdon's cat, Elliot's cat, Sumatra cat, Java cat and Chinese cat. This long-legged breed has a small head marked with two dark stripes running from the eyes to the ears and a short, tapered white muzzle. These cats prefer to be alone rather than with other cats, and they are active and curious.

18
UNKNOWN ARTIST
Cat under Chrysanthemums, Hen and Chicks under Flower
18th century
Ink and colour on paper
14⅛ × 10⅜ in (35.9 × 26.4 cm)
LACMA, Los Angeles, USA

Opposite: detail

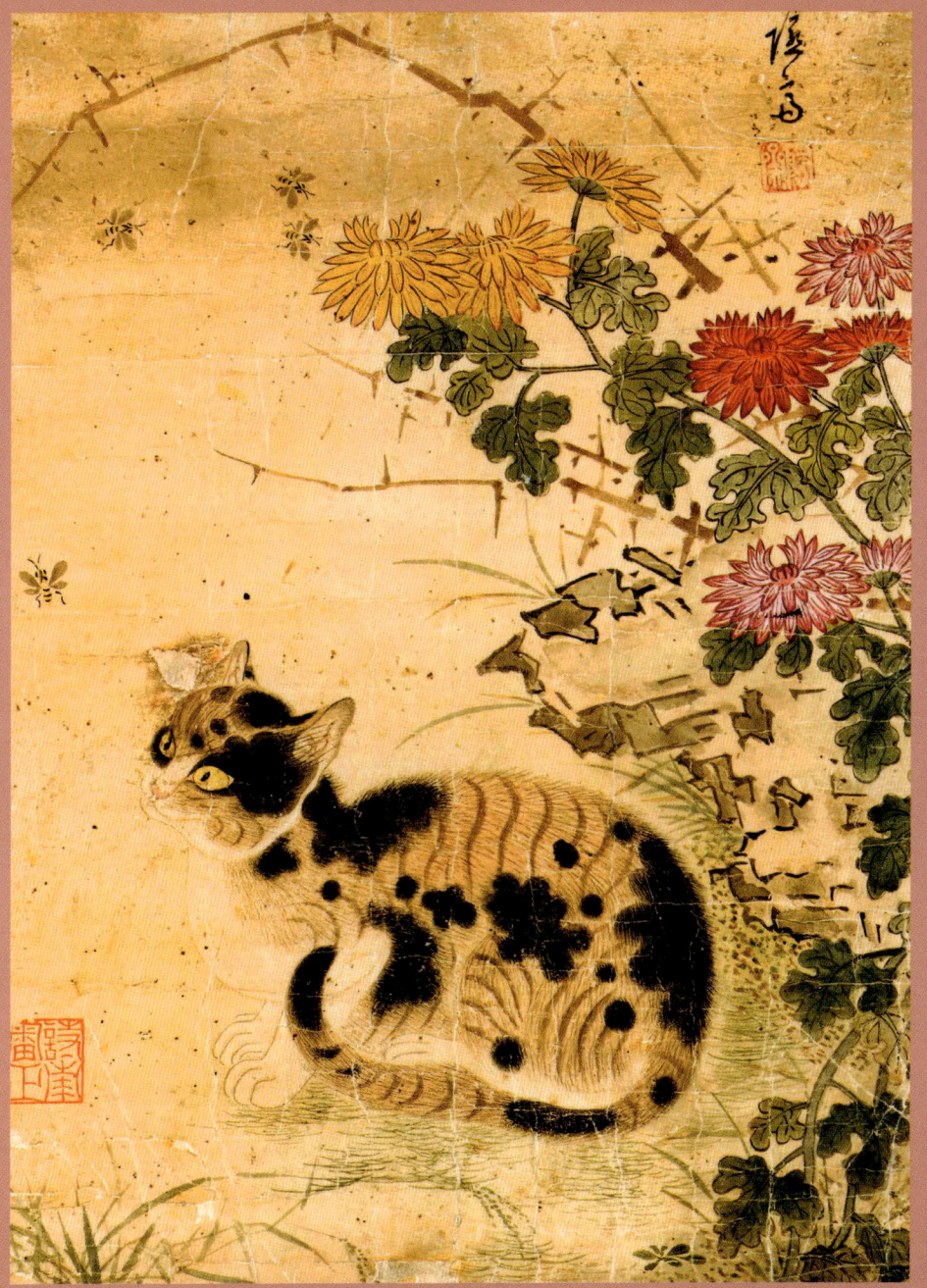

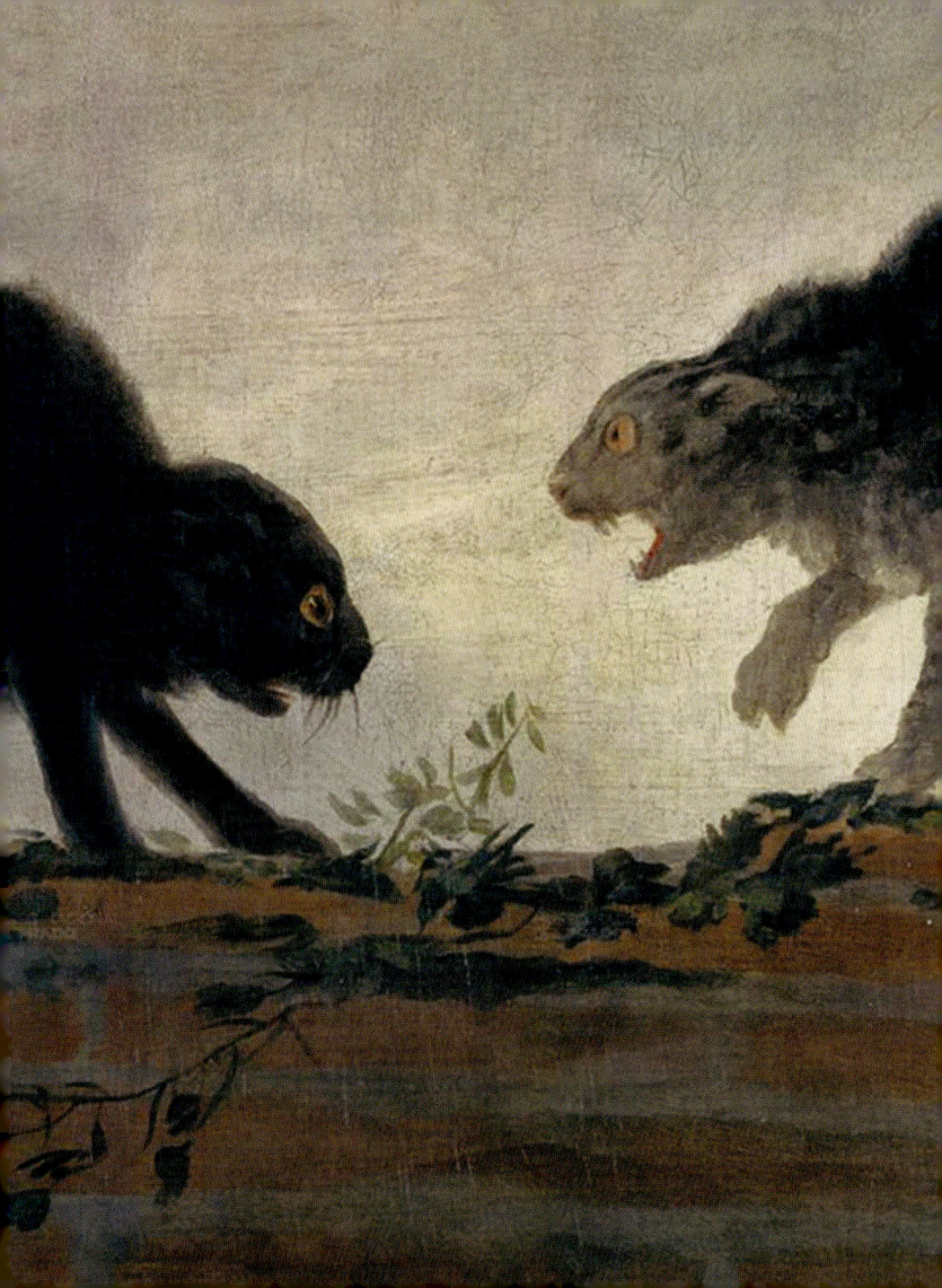

Conflict and discord

Designed to hang over a door, this painting depicts two cats facing each other on top of a brick wall. With their backs arched and their fur standing up, they are clearly about to fight. This was a cartoon (a design, drawing or painting made by an artist as a model for a finished work) created by the Spanish artist Francisco Goya (1746–1828) for the dining room of the Prince and Princess of Asturias in the Royal Palace of El Pardo, Madrid. Goya is often described as both a traditional artist and the first modern artist; his style followed that of the Renaissance, but his work expresses Romanticism's emphasis on subjectivity, imagination and emotion, and he also responded to the turbulent events that surrounded him. Set against a muted, overcast, atmospheric sky, this scene evokes discord or impending aggression. It could symbolize the tumultuous events that had occurred in Spain in recent years, suggesting that conflict is never far away. The work exemplifies Goya's ability to evoke a range of emotions and narratives through seemingly simple, everyday subjects, demonstrating his mastery of creating impact with visual storytelling.

19

FRANCISCO
DE GOYA

Cats Fighting

1786

Oil on canvas

22¼ × 77⅓ in
(56.5 × 196.5 cm)

Museo Nacional
del Prado, Madrid,
Spain

Opposite and
overleaf: details

SPOTTED TABBY

Tabby cats are among the best-loved felines, and of them the spotted tabby, which often resembles a miniature leopard, is one of the most popular. It has oval or round spots across its body, and tiger stripes on its face, legs or tail, and the most common colour combination is black spots on a brown base. Both pure-bred cats (including the Bengal, Egyptian Mau, ocicat and Savannah) and mixed breeds can have spots. Although the tabby is not a breed of cat, all tabbies share distinguishing characteristics and, in varying amounts, have what are called agouti hairs, those that are banded with alternating light and dark segments.

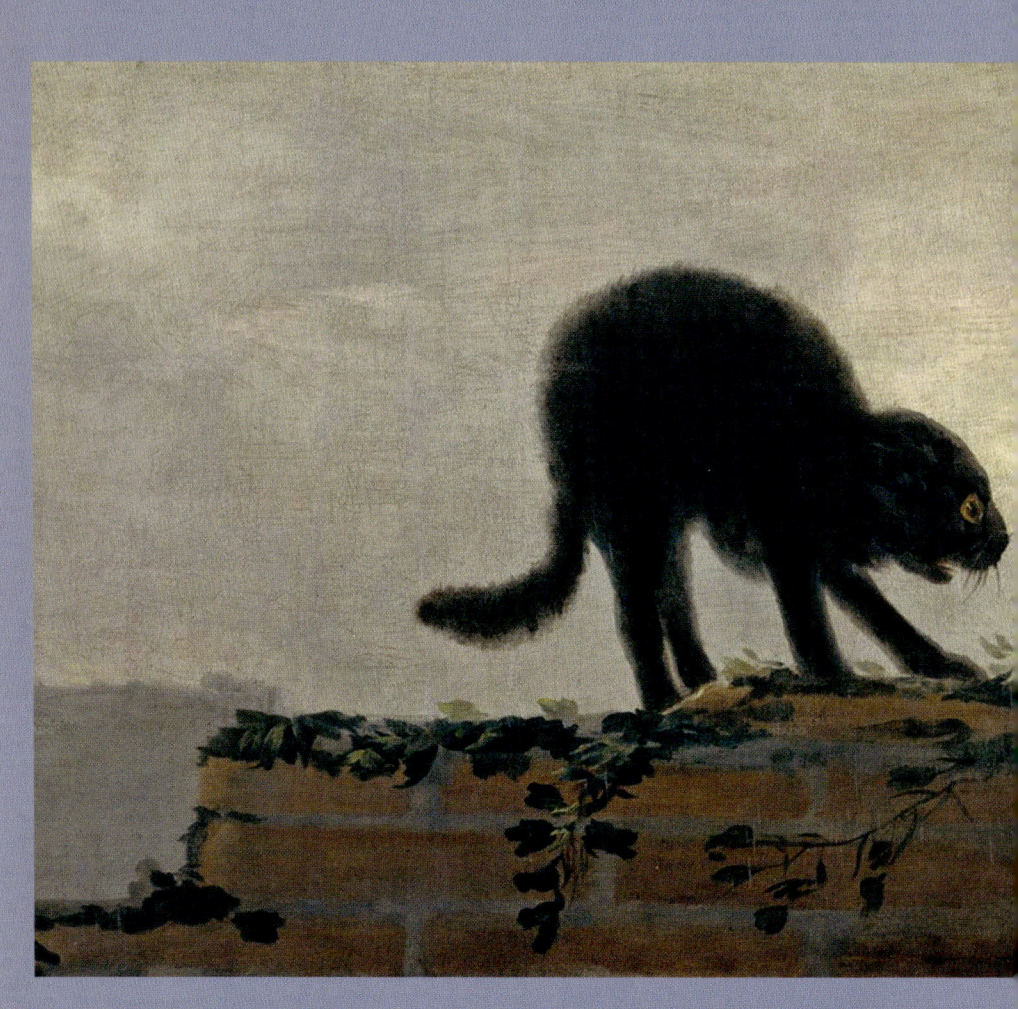

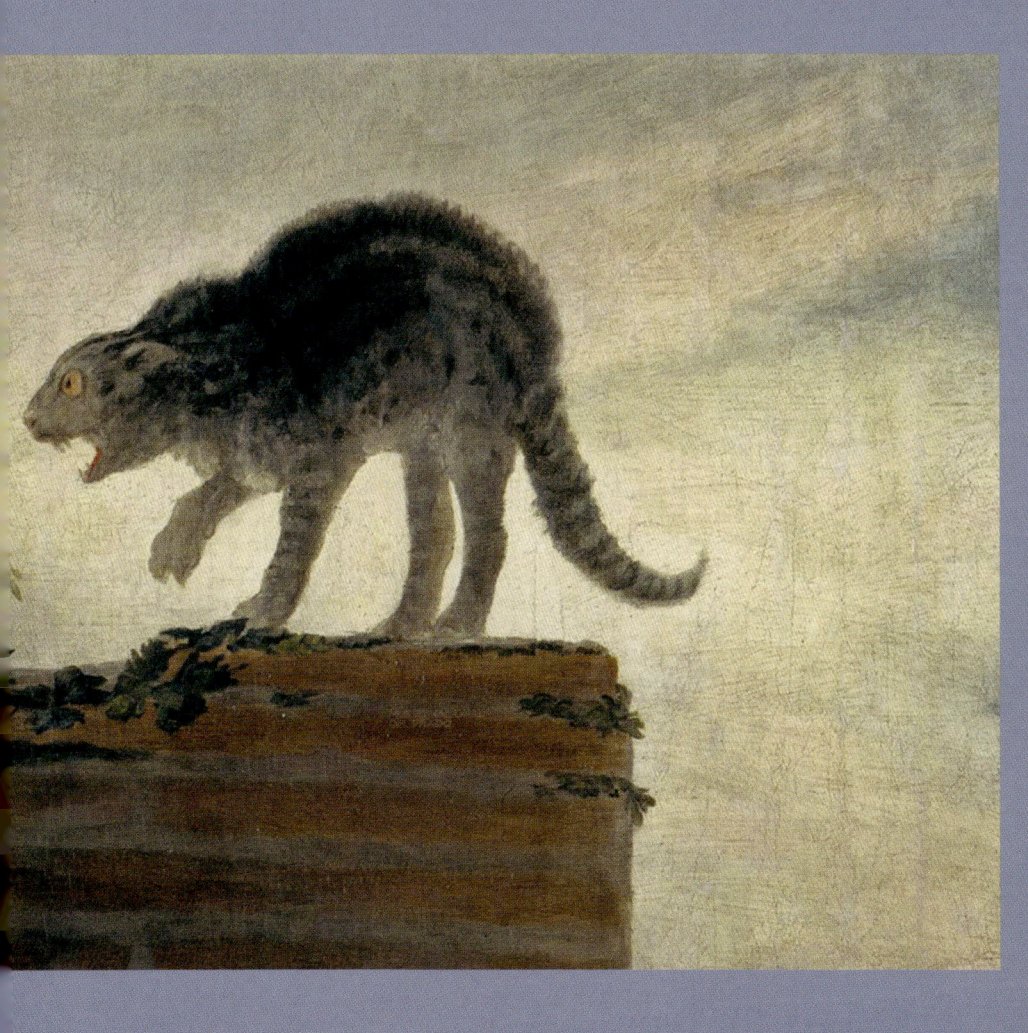

Blending cultures

Johann Zoffany (1733–1810) was a German Neoclassical painter who gained prominence in England, Italy and India. In 1760 he moved to England, where he soon won the patronage of King George III and Queen Charlotte, and became a founding member of the Royal Academy of Arts. He spent the years from 1783 until 1789 in India. This painting depicts one Colonel Blair, his family and an Indian child who may be adopted or working for them as an ayah (nursemaid). Wearing a flame-red-and-gold *dupatta* over her head, she holds a cat and looks directly at the viewer. Blonde-haired Maria Blair is next to her, and she holds the cat's paws, while the cat looks uncomfortable with the dog so near. The two children seem to be close friends, but the Indian girl may be responsible for helping with Maria's upbringing. The painting provides a glimpse into the domestic life of British families in India at the time. Ayahs were often crucial in British households, and many formed close bonds with "their" families, teaching them the local languages and introducing them to Indian customs. The cat carries several layers of symbolism. Associated with home and hearth, it suggests domestic comfort. In various cultures, cats have also been seen as symbols of protection and guardianship – which echoes the role of the Indian girl. The two girls sharing their pet may imply the blending of British and Indian cultures.

20
JOHANN ZOFFANY
Colonel Blair with His Family and an Indian Child
1786
Oil on canvas
38 × 53 in
(96.5 × 134.6 cm)
Tate Britain, London, UK

Opposite: detail

TUXEDO

Often called tuxedo or piebald cats, black-and-white cats are not a breed in their own right, and several pure and mixed breeds can be black and white, such as the Maine Coon, British and American shorthair, Scottish Fold and Turkish Angora. Bicoloured coats are formed by genetics, as pigment cells multiply and move randomly during the development of the embryo. Unlike calico and tortoiseshell cats, tuxedos can be male or female; they can also be long- or short-haired. For unknown reasons, black-and-white kittens and cats are friendly, non-aggressive and often more easy-going than those of other colours.

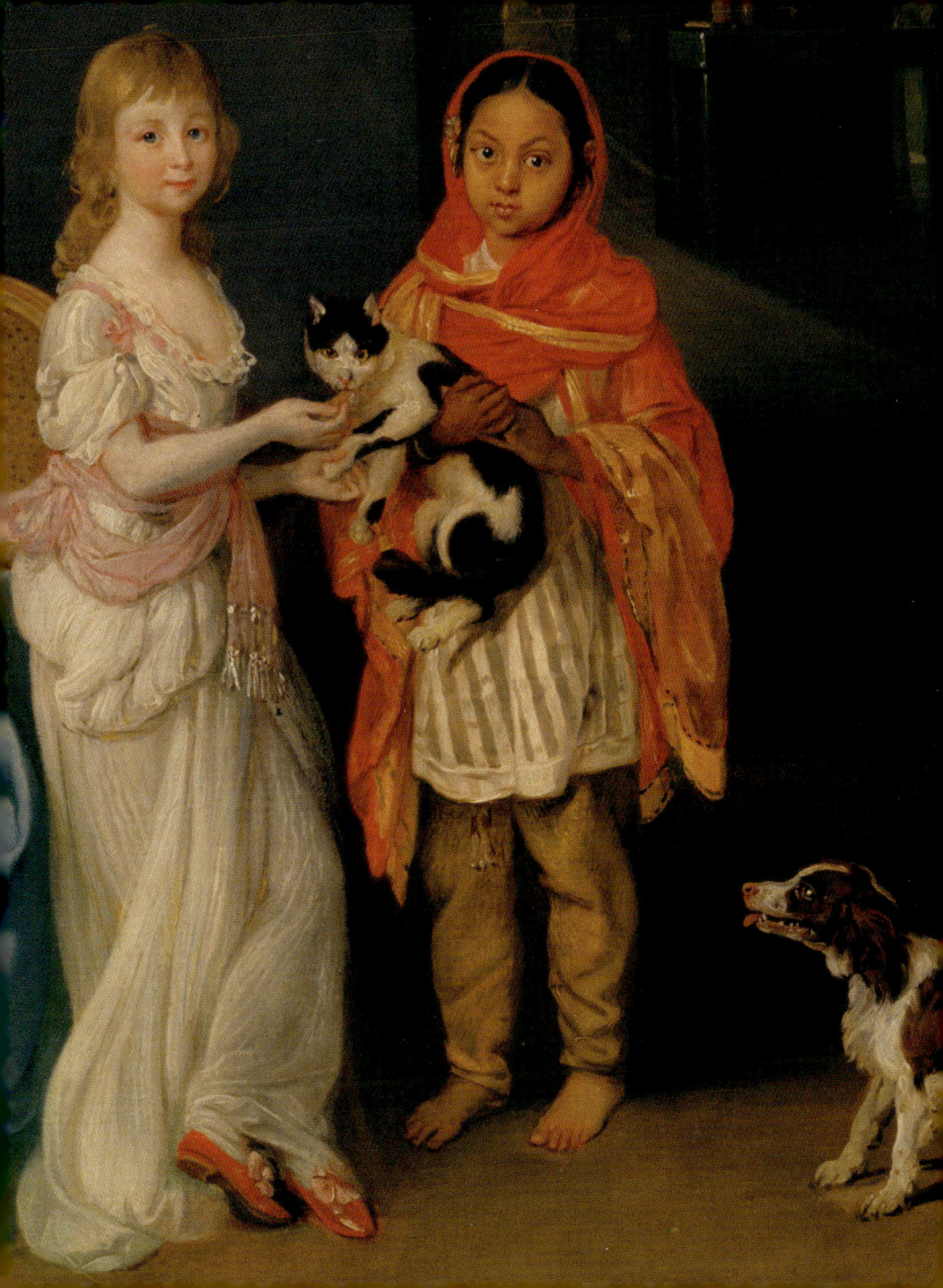

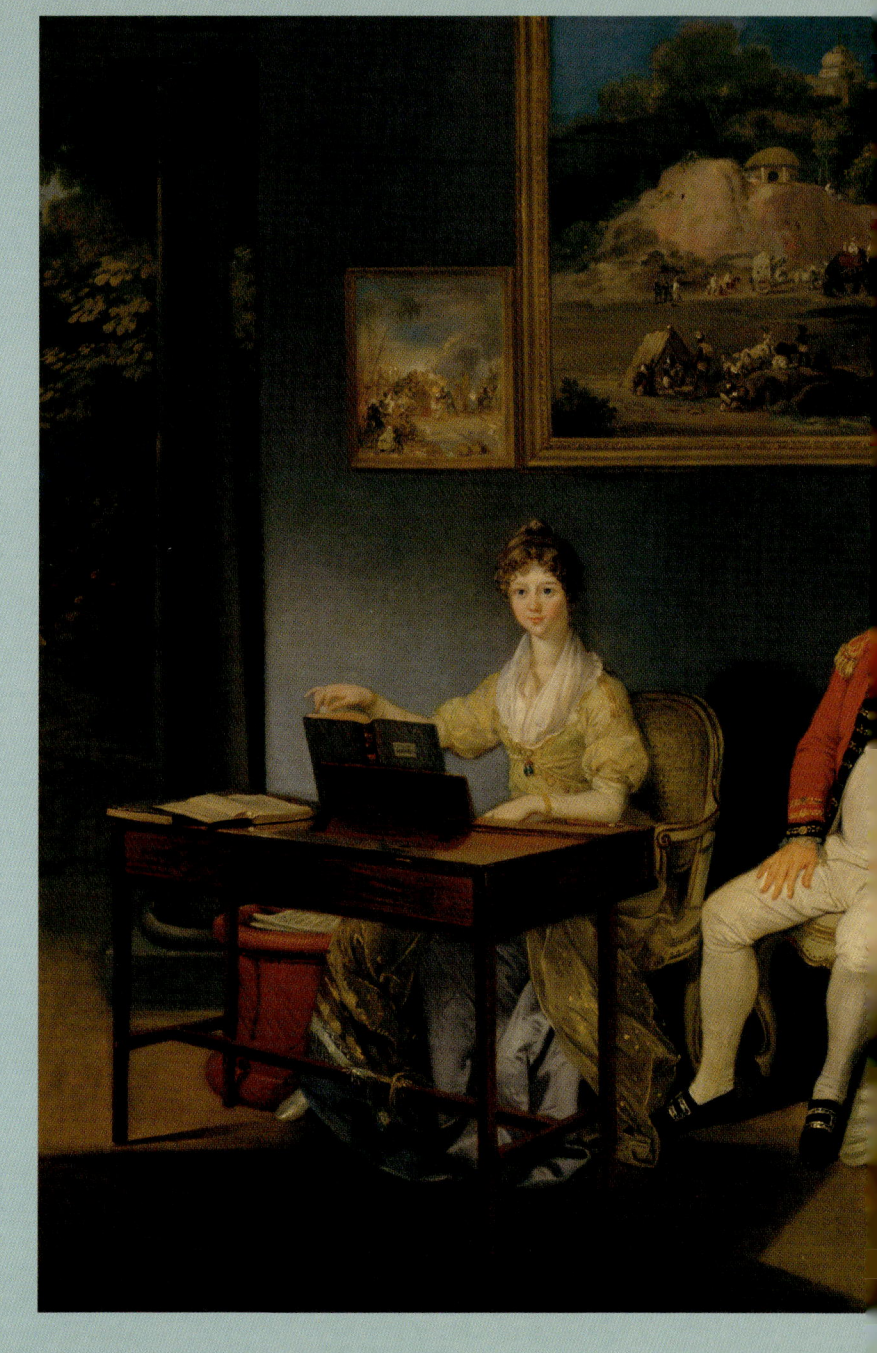

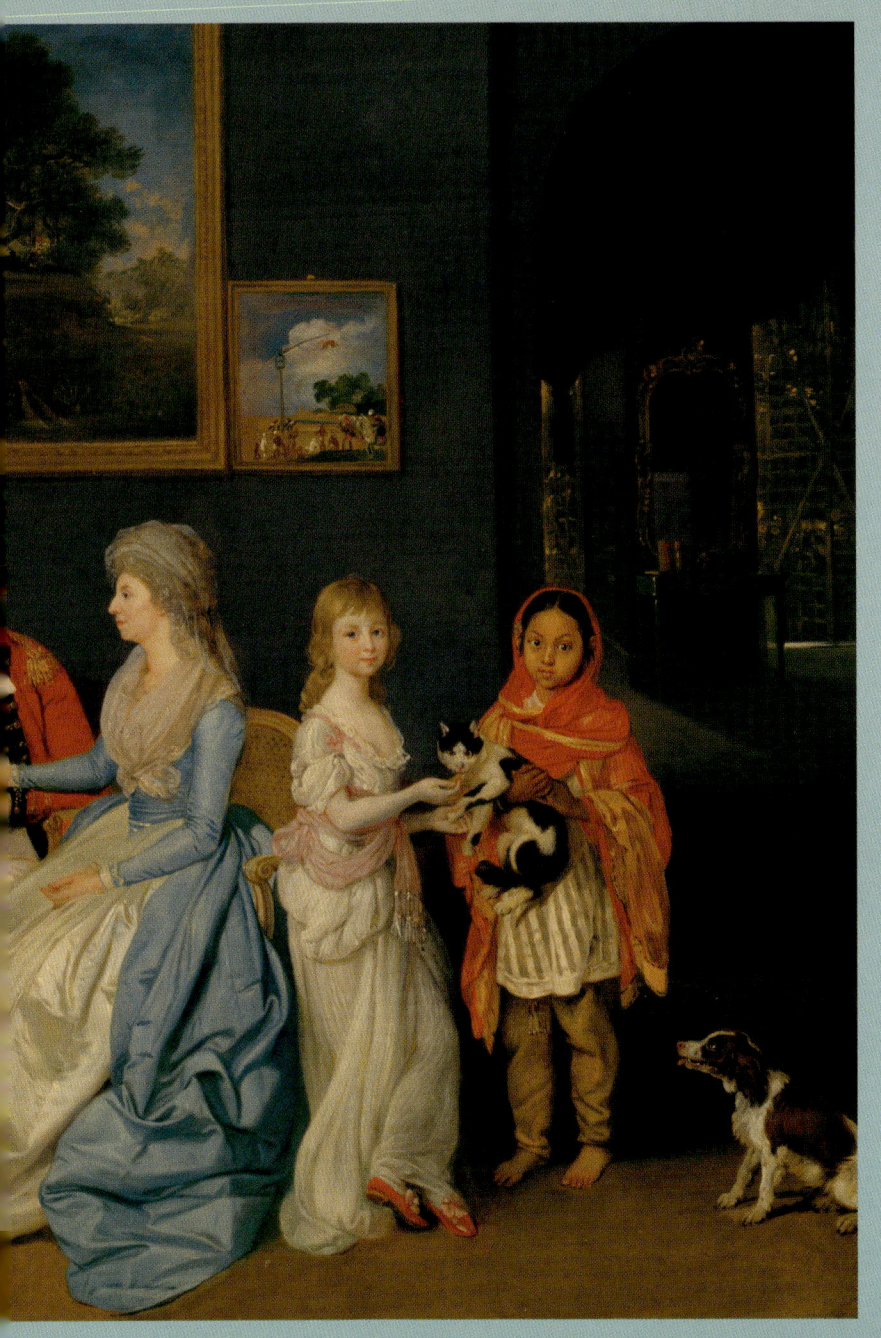

Innocence and warmth

Louis-Léopold Boilly (1761–1845), the creator of portraits and genre paintings that documented French middle-class life, lived and worked through turbulent times in France, from the Revolution that led to the deposing of royalty and founding of the Napoleonic Empire, to the Bourbon Restoration and the July Monarchy. His work introduced the term *trompe-l'œil* (fool the eye) to describe ultra-realistic imagery. He rose to prominence towards the end of the eighteenth century, when he became recognized for his incredibly lifelike portraits, of which this is an example. Gabrielle Arnault was the daughter of the French playwright Antoine-Vincent Arnault, and here, just four years old, she sits and holds her cat in her arms. By painting a plain background and the little girl's simple clothing, Boilly emphasizes her large, expressive blue eyes and delicate features, which convey artlessness and contemplation. Even at this young age, Gabrielle was recognized for her exceptional musical talent, particularly as a pianist, and from this time onwards, her skill was celebrated by many around her. Later, as Madame Donat d'Ariès, she became a prominent figure in society. Here, though, the cat helps to highlight the themes of innocence, youth and love. As in so many works of art, it also symbolizes domesticity, comfort and warmth.

21
LOUIS-LÉOPOLD BOILLY
Gabrielle Arnault as a Child
1815
Oil on canvas
8¼ × 6¼ in
(21 × 16 cm)
Musée du Louvre, Paris, France

LONG-HAIRED CATS

The result of a genetic mutation, long-haired cats are less common than short- or medium-haired cats, but there are many breeds within the category, including the American and Japanese bobtail, American Curl, Balinese, Birman, Himalayan, Javanese, Maine Coon, Norwegian forest cat, Persian, ragamuffin, Ragdoll, Siberian, Somali, Turkish Angora and Turkish Van. The fur of long-haired cats can be up to ten times longer than that of short-haired cats, and they have an underlying layer of soft, shorter hairs. Although most are fastidious about grooming, they usually need extra help from their owners to keep their fur silky, soft and smooth.

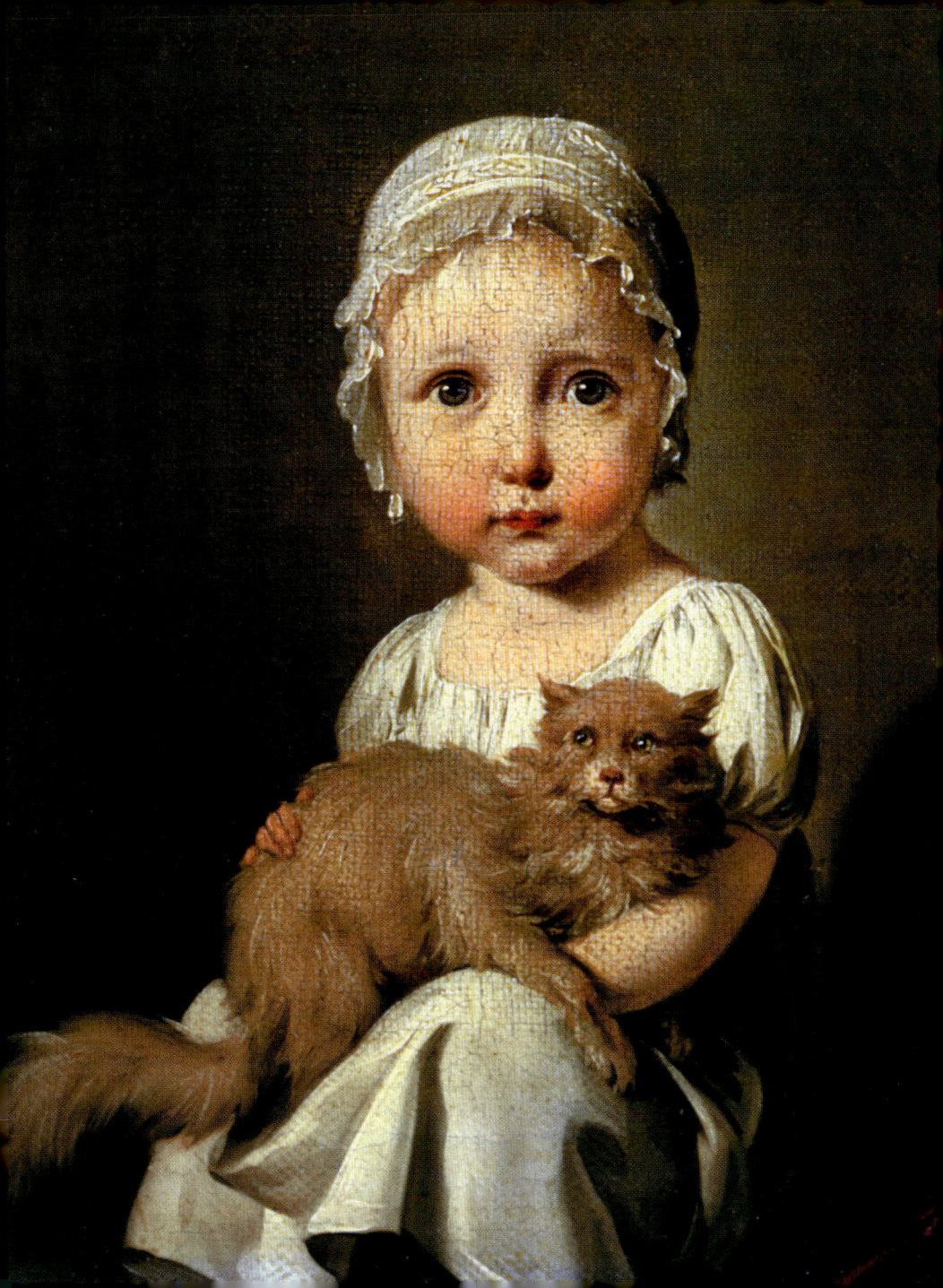

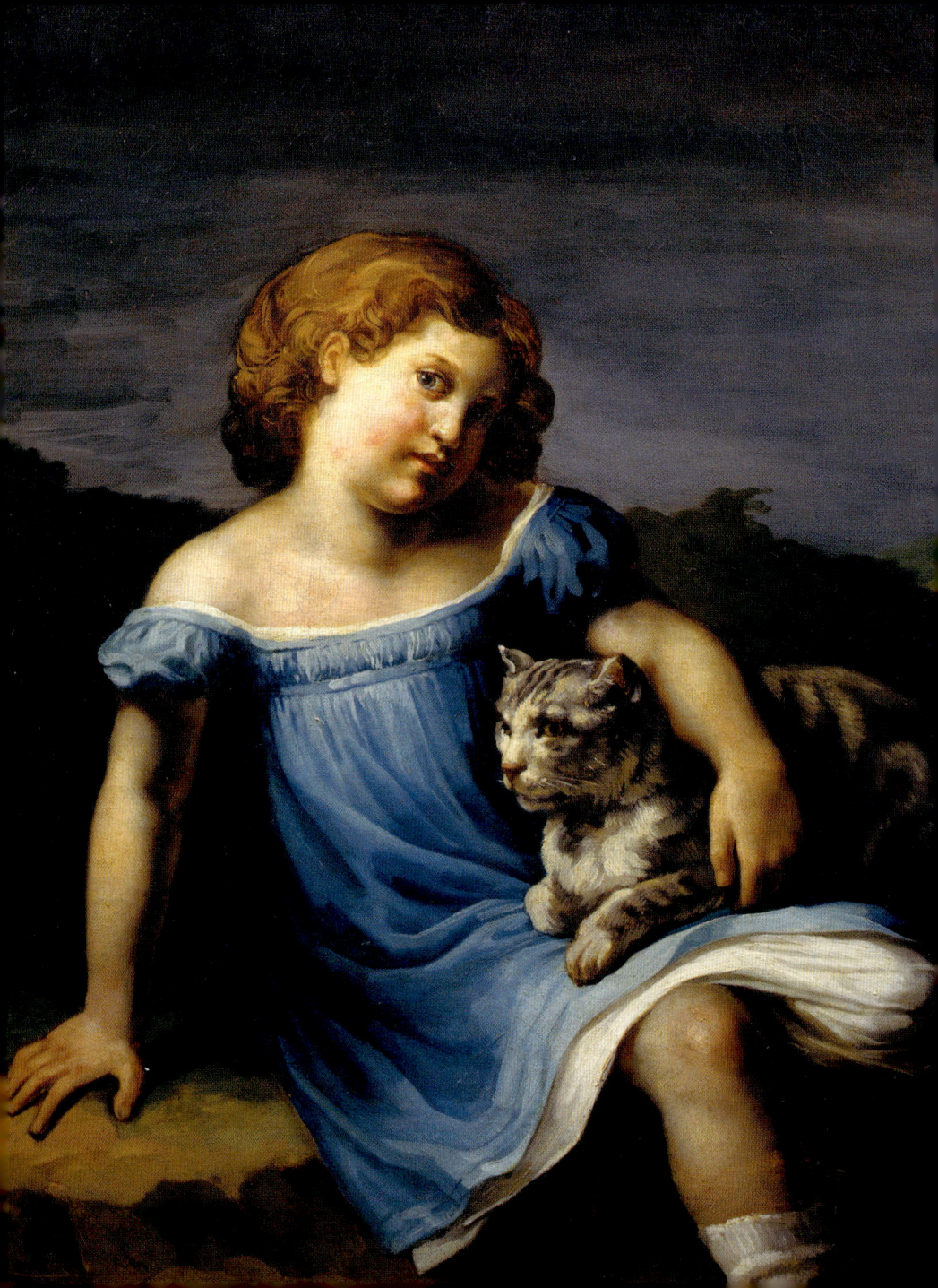

Comfortable relaxation

The French painter and lithographer Théodore Géricault (1791–1824) was a pioneer of the Romantic movement and, despite his short life, had a huge impact on the development of nineteenth-century French painting. In his art, he blended close observation, realism, and social and political awareness with emotion, and, although he was influenced by academic art, his brisk, energetic brushstrokes and contrasting light effects created a sense of atmosphere that broke from the smooth Neoclassical style. This portrait depicts Louise Vernet (daughter of the artist Horace Vernet), who later married Paul Delaroche, another artist. Géricault's skill in capturing the natural ingenuousness of a child is clear. With rosy cheeks and a resigned expression, Louise – aged just four or five – looks as though she has been interrupted while playing to sit for her father's friend. On her lap, she holds her large tabby cat, which seems relaxed and comfortable, while Louise appears keen to move away. The composition focuses on her face and upper body, while the background is simple, making sure the viewer's attention focuses on Louise. Géricault's use of chiaroscuro (dramatic contrasts of light and shade) creates depth, while his brushwork is neat, especially in the rendering of Louise's hair and clothing.

22
THÉODORE GÉRICAULT
Portrait of Louise Vernet as a Child
1818–19
Oil on canvas
23⅞ × 19⅞ in
(60.5 × 50.5 cm)
Musée du Louvre, Paris, France

MACKEREL TABBY

With their narrow tiger-striped pattern, mackerel tabbies are among the most recognizable of all tabby varieties. On the forehead is a distinct "M" shape that evolved during the ancient Egyptian period. The markings and coats of these cats are so luxurious that they were once compared to fine silk from the Attabiy district of Baghdad. This made its way into fourteenth-century Middle French as *tabis*, which later became "tabby". The mackerel pattern is commonly believed to have originated from the African wildcat, which has narrow patterns and spots. Mackerel tabbies are known for their curiosity and their bold sense of adventure.

Strength and individuality

Known best as an *animalière*, a painter of animals, the French artist Rosa Bonheur (1822–99) produced paintings and sculptures in a realist style and became renowned internationally for her ability to capture the essence and character of animals and the landscape around them. Her love of animals began when she was a child and her father gave her painting lessons. As well as providing live creatures for her to study, he encouraged her to copy images from books and, eventually, to reproduce the artworks in the Louvre. She later reflected, "I became an animal painter because I loved to move among animals." As she grew up, she kept many animals as pets, and in 1857 she was given permission to wear trousers in public so that she could visit abattoirs and study animals' anatomy. Her accuracy and meticulous attention to detail are clear in this painting of a powerful, majestic wild cat reclining in its natural habitat – even though, at first glance, it could be a domestic cat. With light brushstrokes, Bonheur captures the soft texture of the fur, the shining eyes and the relaxed pose. Her use of light, shadow and colour creates a lifelike image with great impact. The painting may also symbolize such concepts as strength, independence and the natural world itself.

23
ROSA BONHEUR
Wild Cat
1850
Oil on canvas
18¼ × 22 in
(46 × 56 cm)
Nationalmuseum,
Stockholm,
Sweden

WILD CAT

Also known as felids, wild cats are a diverse group of carnivorous mammals. They vary greatly in size, and their fur can range from short and sleek to long and shaggy, depending on the species, with colouration and patterning that include anything from solid to striped, spotted or mottled. With well-developed eyesight and keen hearing, they are great hunters, and tufts of fur on the tips of their ears can help with communication and possibly aid in camouflage. These animals can be found in a variety of habitats around the world, ranging from dense forest to open grassland and desert, and the various species have adapted to thrive in specific environments.

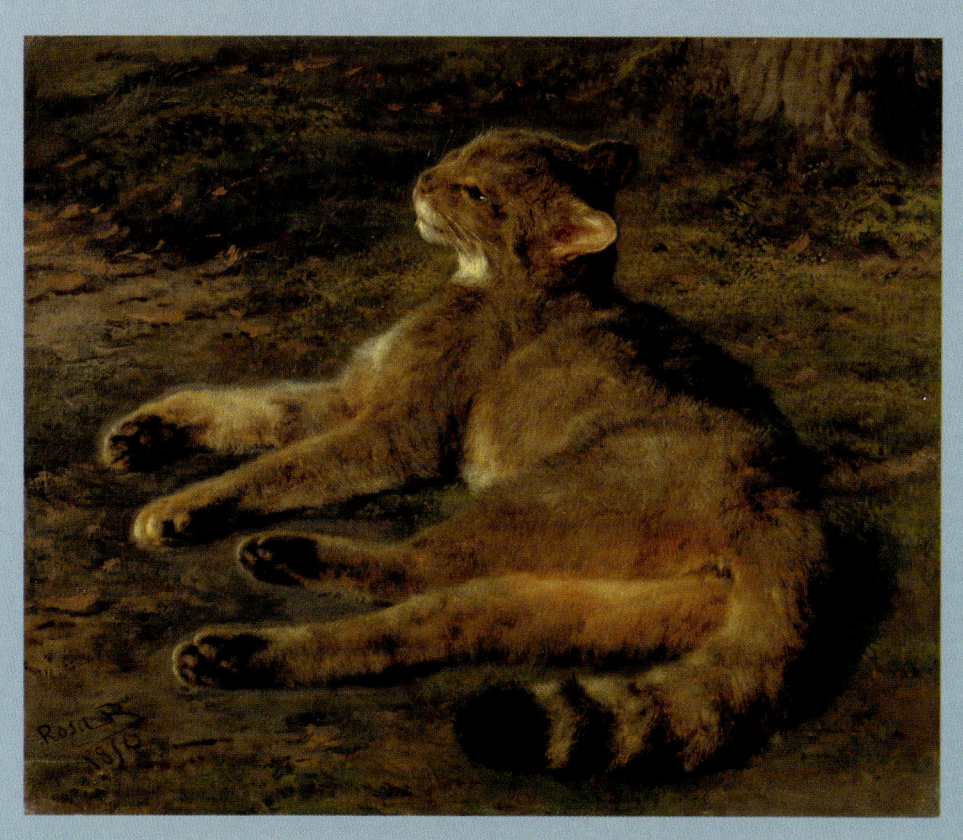

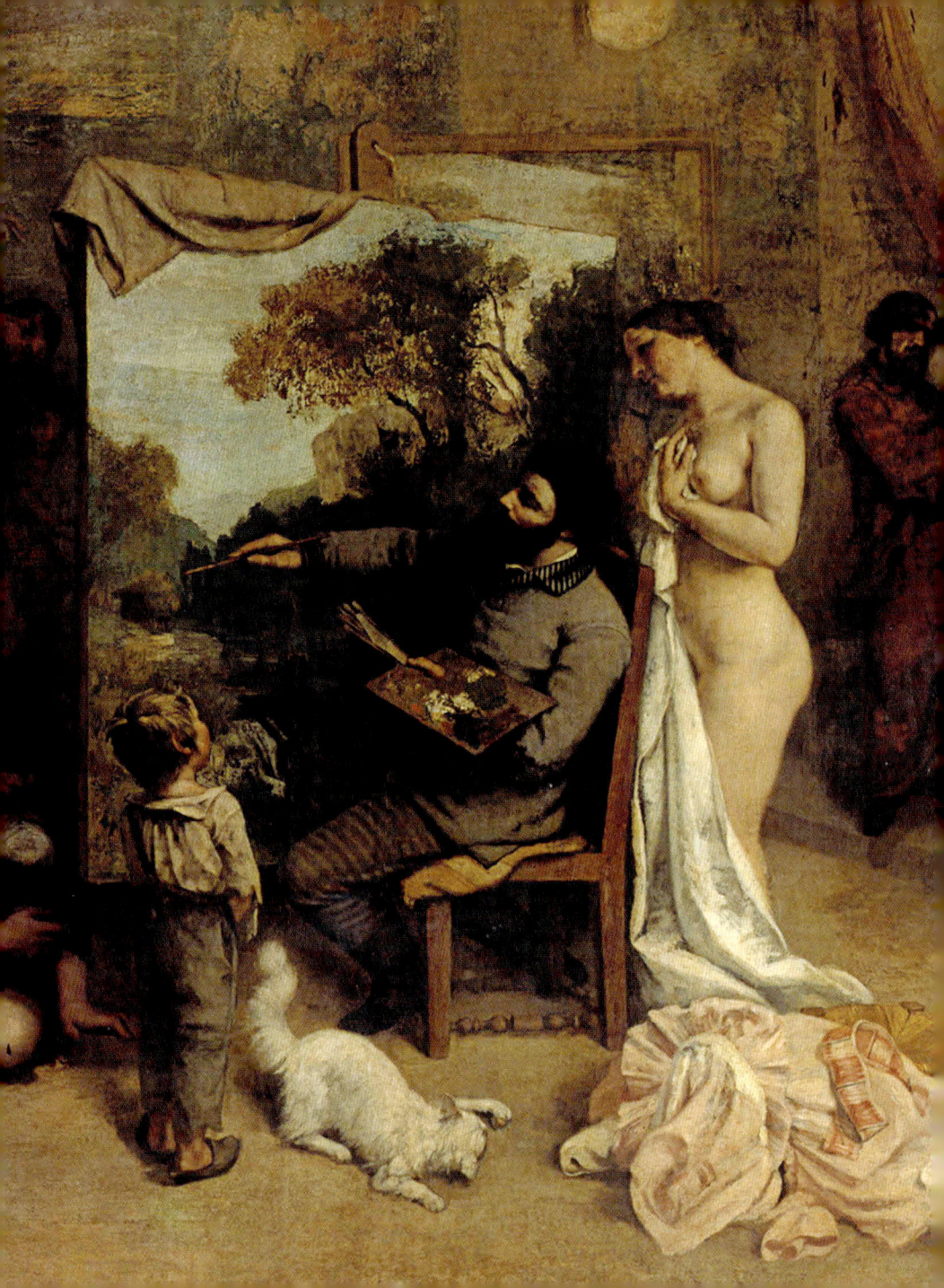

Challenging convention

Gustave Courbet (1819–77), leader of the French Realist movement, rejected academic convention and Romanticism, and often depicted the poor on the grand scale that was traditionally reserved for paintings of religious or historical subjects. He painted this large, complex work to represent aspects of society and his life. Its subtitle – *A Real Allegory Summing Up Seven Years of My Artistic and Moral Life* – is apposite, since every figure in it represents characters from his earlier paintings, gathered around him in his studio as he paints a landscape. They include people from all levels of society, a nude representing academic art, a child, a dog and a white cat. At the left-hand side of the painting are people of everyday French life. The crucified figure may be a symbol of the "death" of the art of the French Royal Academy. On the right-hand side are several of Courbet's friends, who either played a role in his artistic career or inspired him in some way. The Angora cat might symbolize independence or freedom; it could also refer to *Les Chats* (1869), a book by Courbet's friend the art critic and novelist Champfleury; or – because white is the opposite colour to the conventional lucky black cat – it might symbolize Courbet's anti-traditionalist position.

24

GUSTAVE
COURBET

The Artist's Studio

1855

Oil on canvas

142 × 235 in
(361 × 598 cm)

Musée d'Orsay,
Paris, France

Opposite: detail

CATS IN ARTISTS' STUDIOS

In the late nineteenth century many artists kept cats, particularly in the bohemian area of Montmartre, Paris. Their studios – in which they generally lived as well as worked – were cramped, and they found solace in the company of cats, which required little care and embodied the spirit of unpredictability, resilience and mystery. Théophile-Alexandre Steinlen (page 129) famously produced an image of a black cat for the poster advertising Le Chat Noir, Montmartre's most famous cabaret and a gathering place for avant-garde artists, writers and musicians. Cats were associated with magic, independence and defiance, making them the perfect emblem for an anti-establishment artistic movement.

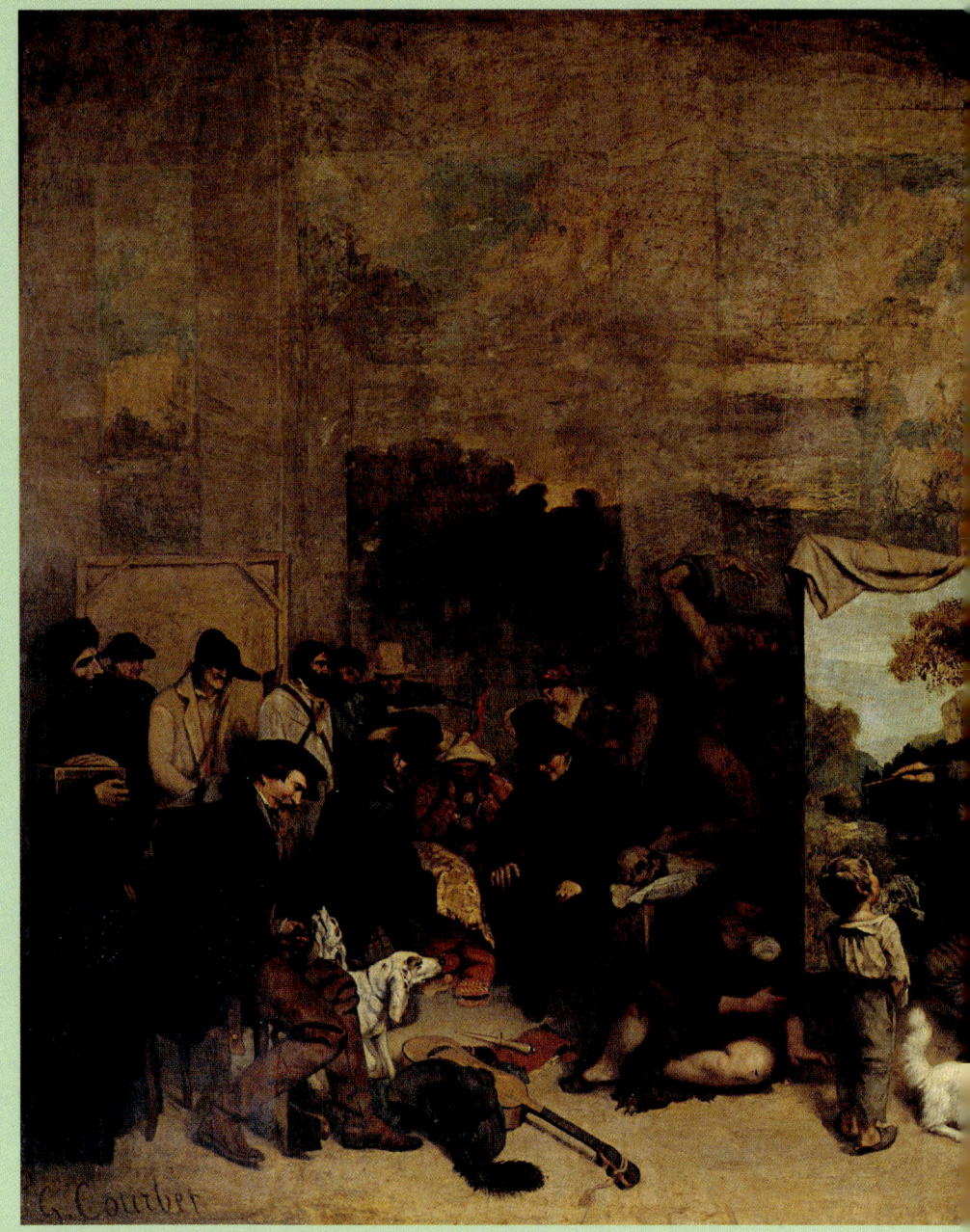

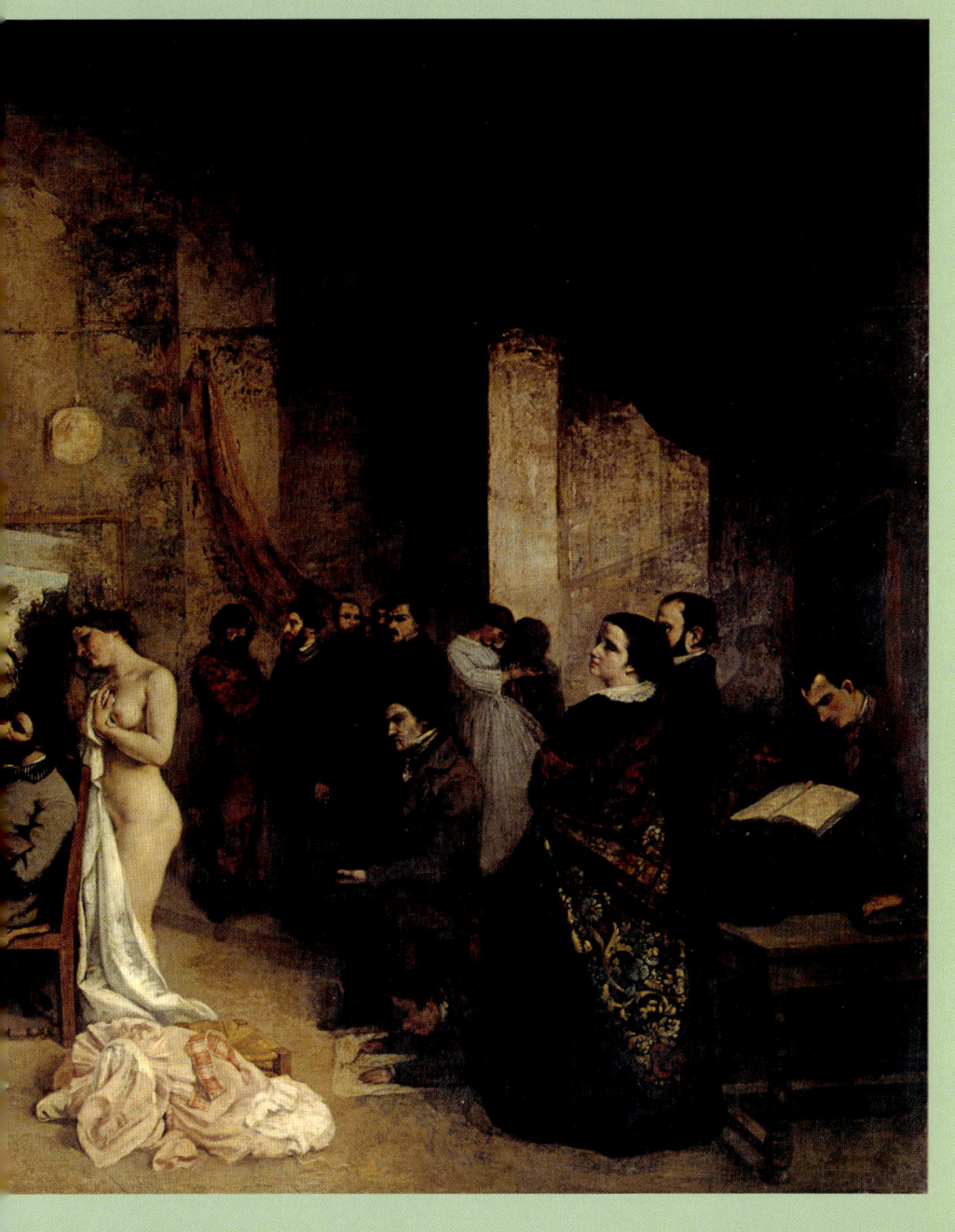

Just the two of us

After training as a lawyer and spending four years articled as a solicitor's clerk, Robert Braithwaite Martineau (1826–69) became a painter. He studied at the Royal Academy schools in London, then with the Pre-Raphaelite artist William Holman Hunt. Martineau was particularly inspired by the art of the Pre-Raphaelite Brotherhood, and he adopted the group's emphasis on realism, bright colours, meticulous detail, emotional depth and detailed storytelling. *A Girl with a Cat* is an intimate portrait of a young girl in a garden holding a cat in her arms. She leans her head on her cat's soft fur, and the composition draws the viewer's eye straight to her. In turn, she gazes directly at the viewer, creating a sense of intimacy and connection. The cat, which is not young, is clearly used to such displays of affection and appears relaxed and trusting, emphasizing the bond between the girl and her pet. Martineau captures the scene with the exceptional technical skill for which he became known. His smooth, almost imperceptible brushstrokes, rich palette of colours and skilful lighting convey the textures of red brick, shiny beads, a latticed window, colourful flowers, thick fur, patterned cotton, delicate skin and silky hair. Corresponding with Victorian taste, the painting may symbolize innocence, innocent love or companionship.

25
ROBERT
BRAITHWAITE
MARTINEAU
A Girl with a Cat
1860
Oil on panel
12½ × 9 in
(32 × 23 cm)
Johannesburg
Art Gallery,
Johannesburg,
South Africa

EUROPEAN SHORTHAIR

Evolving from the domestic cats brought to Europe by the ancient Romans, the European shorthair was officially recognized as a breed in the twentieth century. Known for its robust health, adaptability and affectionate personality, it is a natural breed of domestic cat and one of Europe's oldest and most widespread. This friendly, loving, agile, medium-to-large cat is often compared to the British and American shorthair breeds, but it has a more athletic build and a greater diversity of coat patterns. The eyes can be of any colour, the face is well rounded, and the fur is short, dense and glossy. With their balance of independence and affection, these cats make excellent family pets.

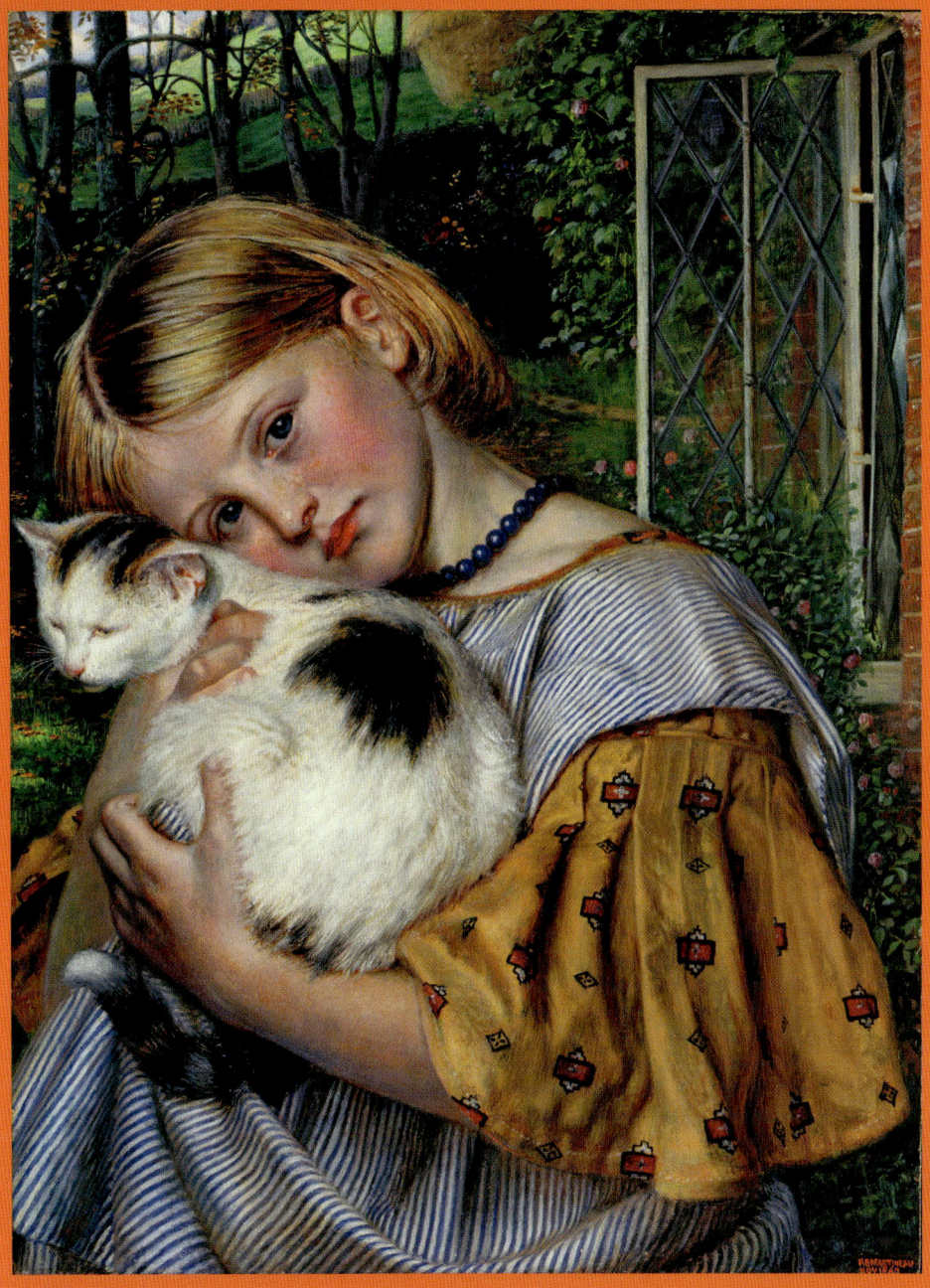

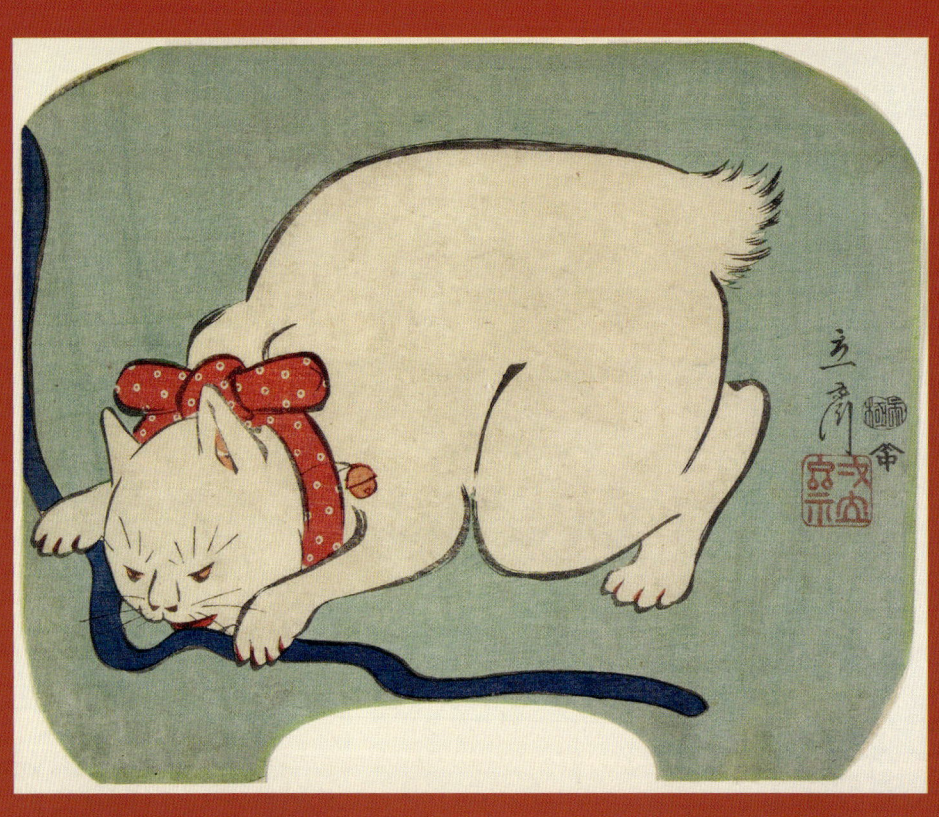

Fun and games

Utagawa Hiroshige II (1826–69), an artist living in Japan during the Edo period (1603–1868), inherited the name Hiroshige II after the death of his master, also Utagawa Hiroshige, in 1858. He also married Hiroshige's daughter Tatsu, and his art resembles that of Hiroshige I so closely that scholars have often confused them. However, this unusual woodblock print reflects the younger artist's unique approach, showing his use of bold outlines, angular and pared-down composition, dynamism and close observation. A fluffy white Japanese bobtail cat crouches to pounce on a piece of blue string, its bottom in the air, having fun. The energetic pose adds movement and liveliness to the image, which is an example of *ukiyo-e*, a genre of Japanese art that flourished from the seventeenth to the nineteenth century. The term translates as "pictures of the floating world", and *ukiyo-e* artists produced paintings and woodblock prints of various subjects, including the everyday, landscapes, female beauties, kabuki actors and sumo wrestlers. A cat playing is universally appealing, relevant and ordinary, while the use of woodblock printing (*nishiki-e*) with ink and colour on paper was also typical of the style. The artist's skill is evident in the careful rendering of the cat's fur and the texture of the string.

26

UTAGAWA
HIROSHIGE II

*A White Cat
Playing with
a String*

1863

Ink and colour
on paper

8⅜ × 10½ in
(21.3 × 26.7 cm)

Minneapolis
Institute of Art,
USA

JAPANESE BOBTAIL

A domestic cat breed with a tail that looks more like a rabbit's than a cat's, the Japanese bobtail has existed in Japan for centuries. It probably derived from populations of kinked-tailed cats that were prevalent throughout Southeast Asia and southern China and that arrived in Japan from China or Korea in 600–700 CE. They were given to Buddhist monks who wanted to keep rats from eating the rice-paper scrolls they used for temple records. In 1602 the Japanese authorities decreed that all cats should help to deal with the rodents that were threatening the nation's silkworm population. The Japanese bobtail is considered a lucky breed, and owning one is said to bring wealth and happiness.

Disturbed by a visitor

Born in Paris to a wealthy family, Édouard Manet (1832–83) initially enrolled in the Navy and the Marines before studying art with the French history painter Thomas Couture. Breaking with the artistic rules of the time, his revolutionary approach became hugely influential. This painting is based on Titian's *Venus of Urbino* (1538). Yet rather than a modest young woman, as in Titian's work, the main figure here is a prostitute, and she looks boldly and directly at the viewer. The name Olympia was used in eighteenth- and nineteenth-century France to refer to prostitutes, and she is adorned with telling trinkets: a black choker, a golden bangle, pearl earrings and an orchid tucked behind her left ear. Dangling from her feet are dainty slippers. The sheets on her bed are crumpled, and near her feet, almost imperceptible against the dark background, a black cat arches its back, tail up, amber eyes wide, seemingly disturbed by a visitor. Behind Olympia and the cat is a maid who tries to show her mistress a bouquet of flowers, perhaps from a previous client. Manet painted in loose brushstrokes that shocked the public and critics when the painting was first exhibited, but it helped to change the course of art.

BOMBAY

Although the Bombay cat breed was not officially recognized until 1970, the cat in this painting could be a precursor to it. This breed of short-haired, solid black cats with bright copper-golden eyes is named after the Indian city of Bombay (now Mumbai), suggesting the territory of the Indian black leopard. The breed was first developed in the late 1950s through Burmese and chinchilla Persian crosses, or European Burmese and black domestic shorthair crosses, to create a cat resembling a miniature black panther. These sleek-coated felines even have black whiskers and skin, including their paw pads, noses and mouths.

27
ÉDOUARD MANET
Olympia
1863
Oil on canvas
51⅓ × 74⅞ in
(130.5 × 191 cm)
Musée d'Orsay, Paris, France

Opposite: detail

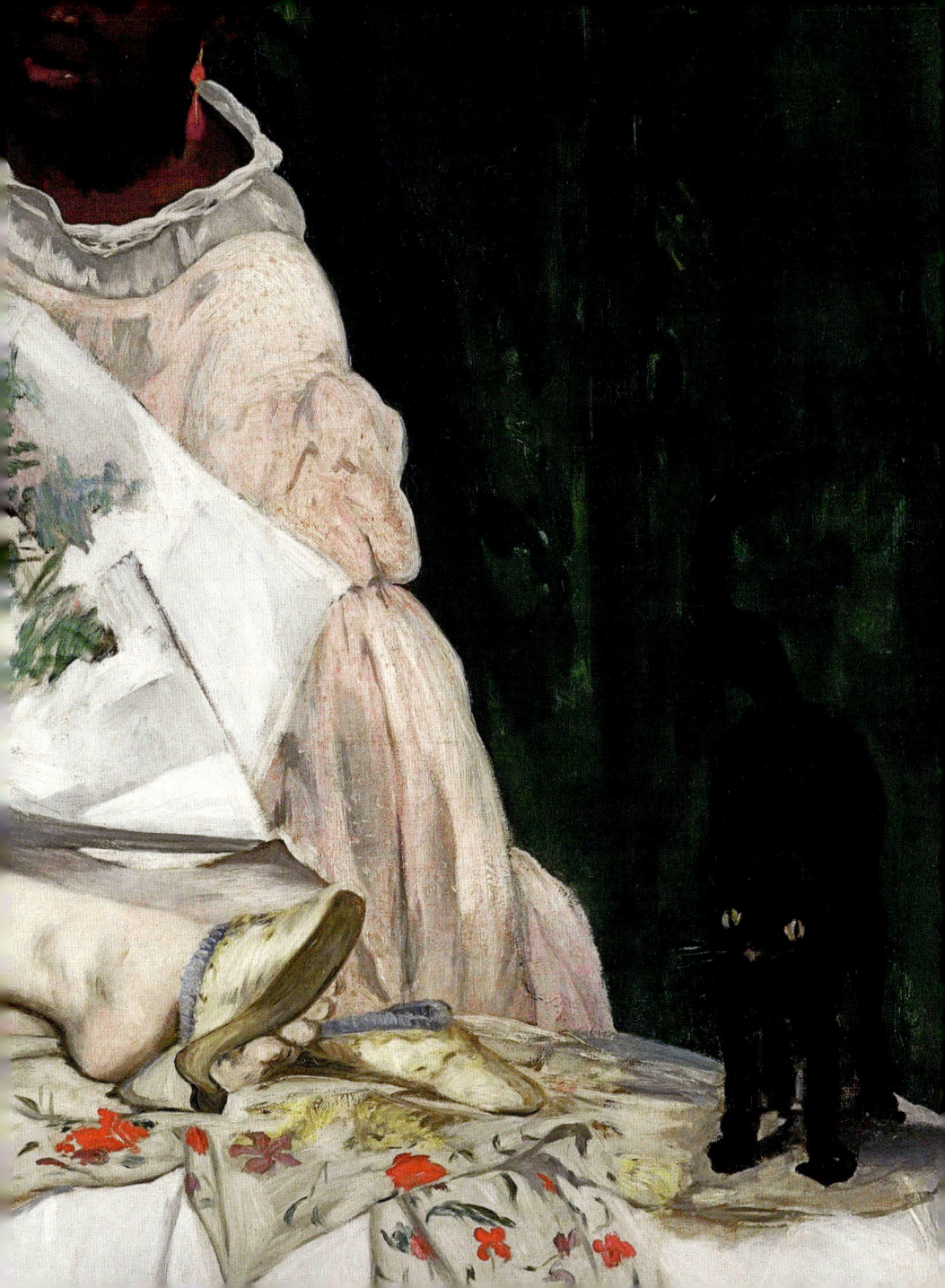

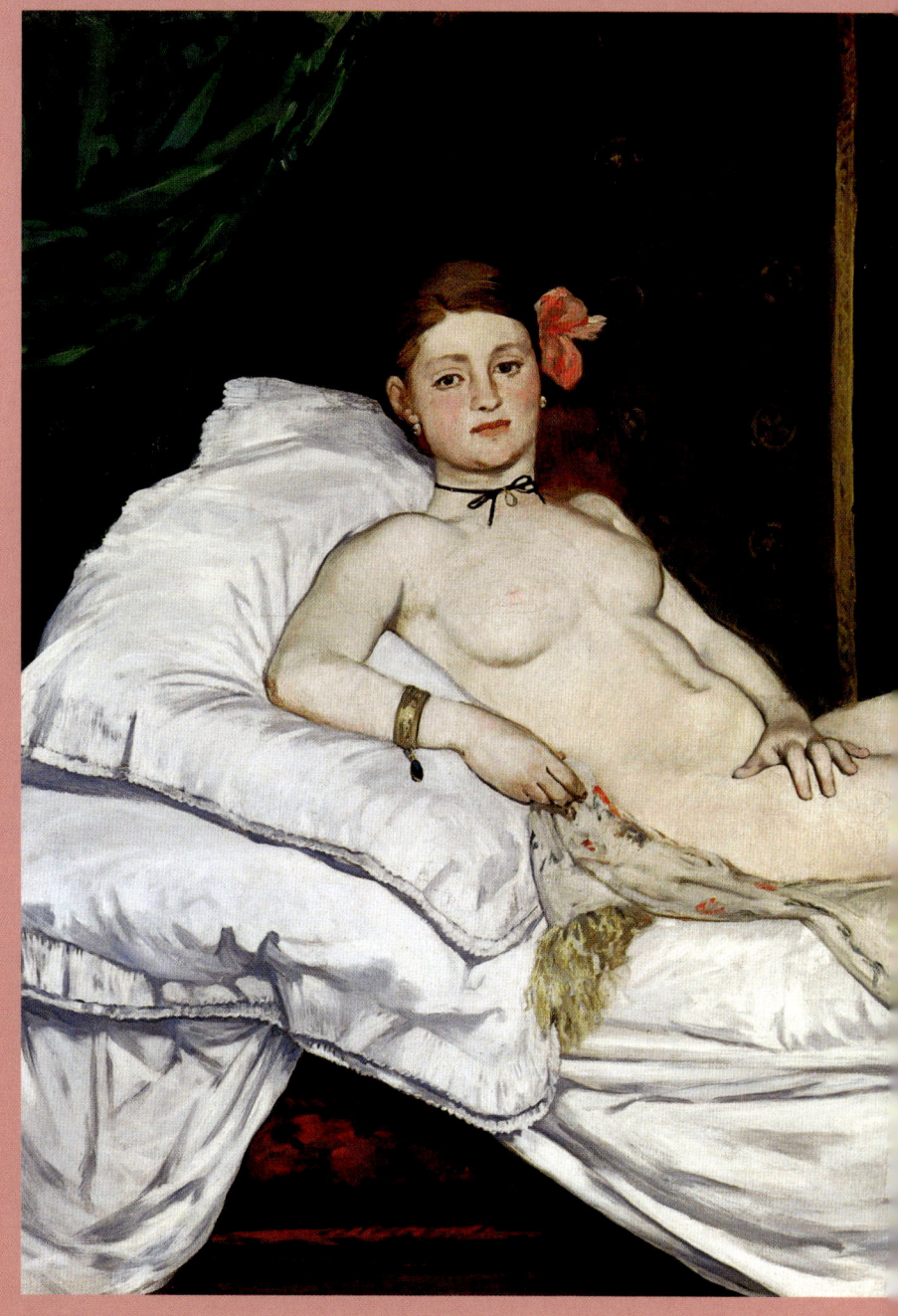

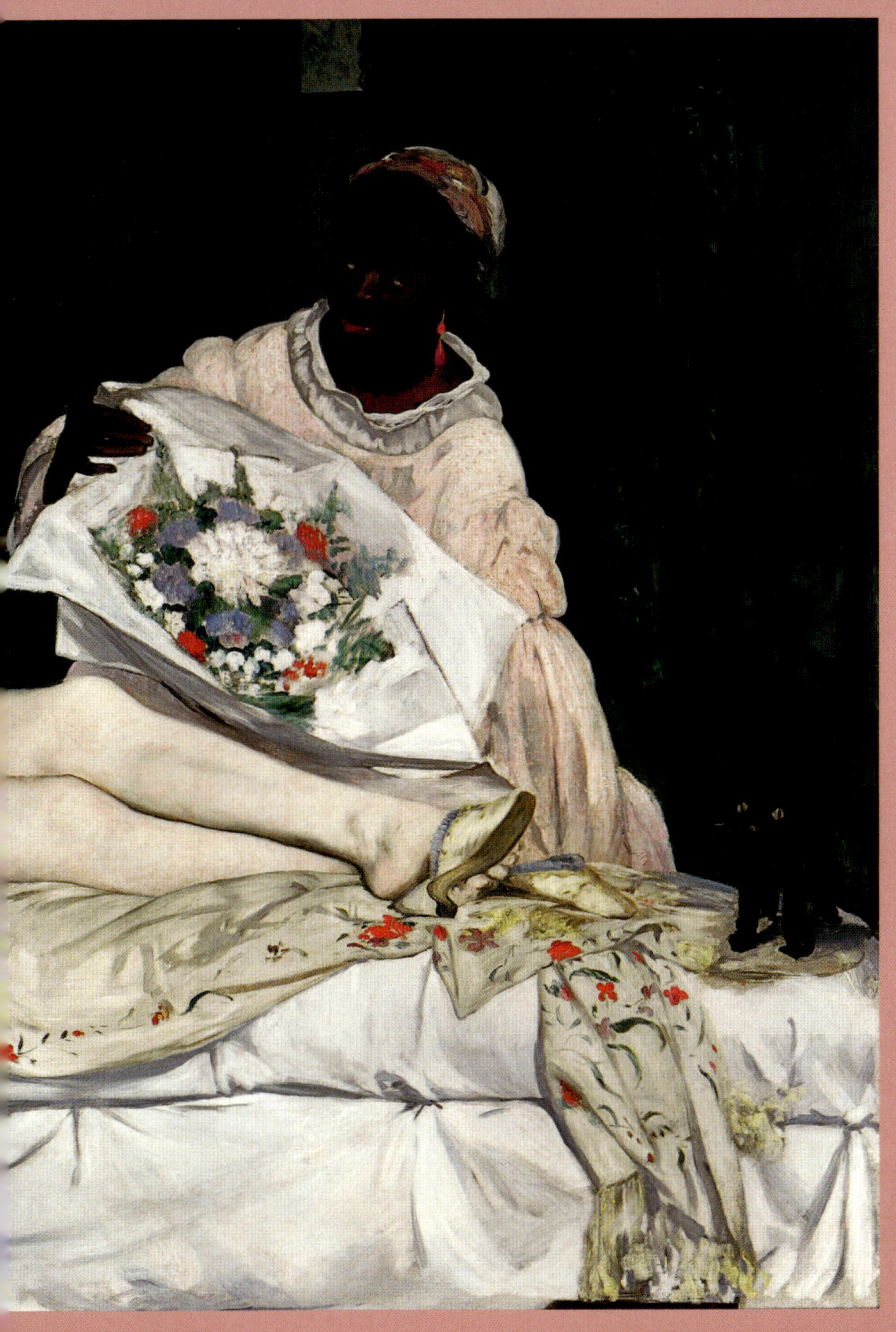

Diligence and contemplation

One of the founders of the Barbizon School of painting near Fontainebleau in rural France, Jean-François Millet (1814–75) produced images of landscapes and peasants, often conveying these humble people as industrious, devout and mild. During a period of strong class consciousness and fear of revolution in France, anyone who celebrated the poor was regarded with suspicion by the wealthy. Nonetheless, Millet's unromanticized imagery helped to propel new ideas in art, and his approach influenced and inspired many later artists. While most members of the Barbizon School focused on landscapes painted *en plein air*, Millet preferred to depict the life of the poor working within those landscapes. Here, a young woman churns butter. She is composed and diligent, undertaking her role with fortitude. Because she is absorbed, she seems not to notice the large, long-haired cat rubbing its cheek affectionately against her leg. Using soft colours and often loose, sensitive marks, whether in oil paints or in pastels (as here), Millet depicted peasants as many earlier artists had portrayed historic, aristocratic or biblical figures or heroes. Here, the woman's pose and expression suggest introspection and concentration, imbuing the scene with an atmosphere of calm acceptance.

28

JEAN-FRANÇOIS MILLET

La Baratteuse

c. 1866

Pastel and black pencil on brown paper and canvas stretcher

48 × 33½ in (122 × 85.5 cm)

Musée d'Orsay, Paris, France

NORWEGIAN FOREST CAT

Similar to the Maine Coon, the Norwegian forest cat – which may be the breed shown here – is known for its thick, water-resistant fur and strong, muscular build. In this artwork, it is light ginger with white, but these cats come in many different colours. The breed originated in northern Europe and is adapted to an extremely cold climate, with a double coat of long fur over a woolly undercoat. It was a natural outdoor working cat on Scandinavian farms, and its strength and skill in climbing and hunting display this aspect of its history. Like the Maine Coon, cats of this breed mature slowly and may not reach full stature until they are four years old.

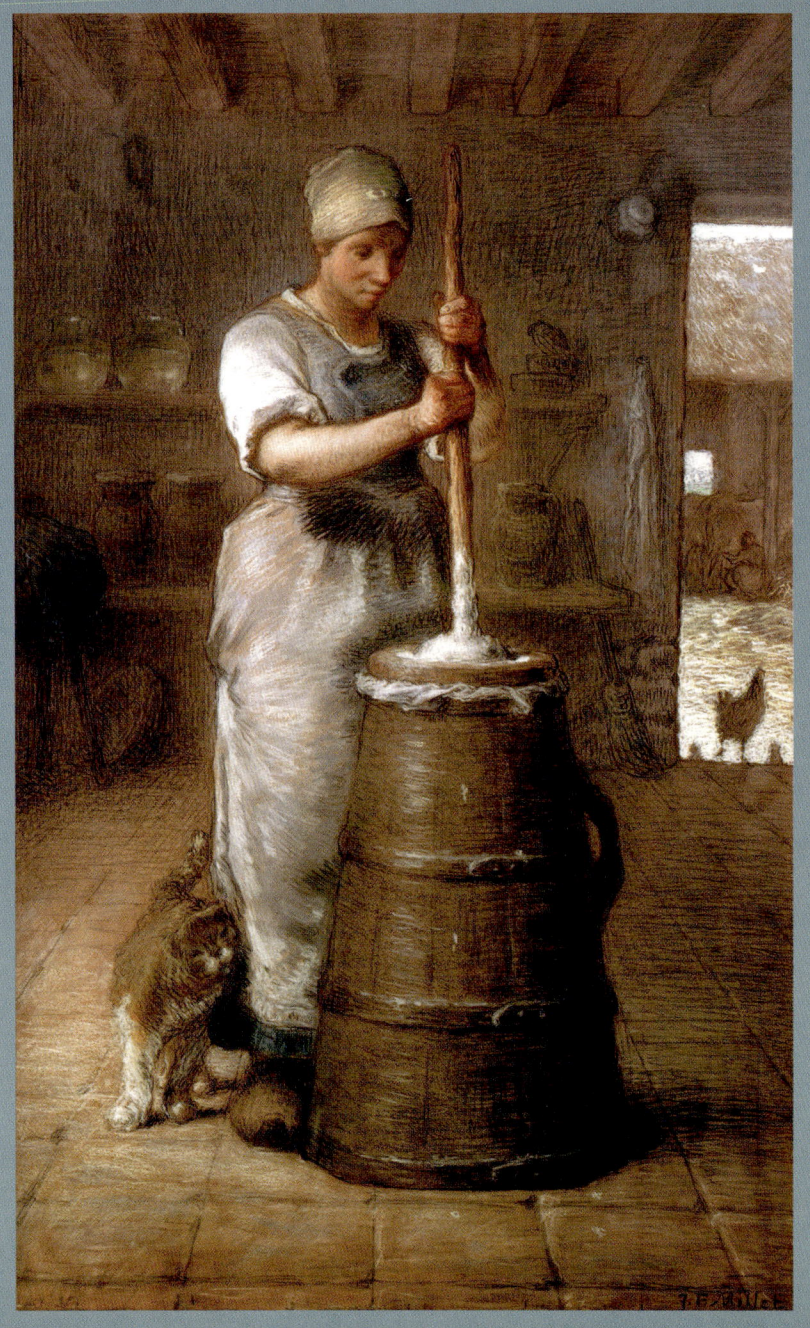

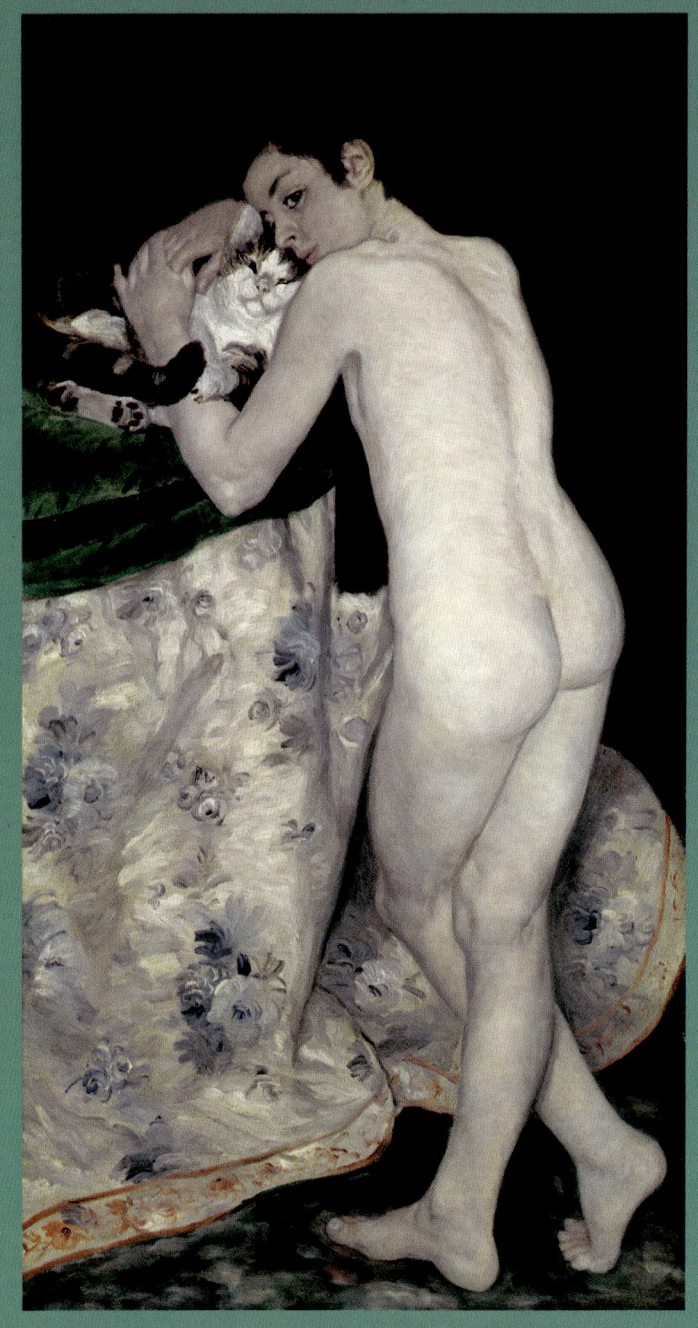

Enigmatic

Known best for his paintings of Parisians enjoying the bustling life, times, modernity and leisure pursuits of the late nineteenth century, the French Impressionist artist Pierre-Auguste Renoir (1841–1919) initially went out into the countryside to paint *en plein air* with his friend Claude Monet. He exhibited with the Impressionists from 1874, but later in his career he began exploring the use of cleaner lines and smoother paint application. He and Monet were essential in the development of the Impressionist style in the late 1860s as they explored ways of capturing optical sensations and light effects in paint. A nude boy was an unusual subject for Renoir, and he made at least four preparatory drawings for this painting to explore the effects of light and shadow on the boy's skin, on the cat and on the expanse of patterned fabric. It captures a brief moment in time. Renoir's short, neat brushstrokes and subtle blending of colours create a sense of depth. While nothing like his more expressive Impressionist paintings, the work draws attention to the dynamic relationship between humans and animals. However, the identity of the boy seen from the back cuddling his cat is not known, and his sidelong glance at the viewer remains enigmatic.

29

PIERRE-AUGUSTE RENOIR

Young Boy with a Cat

1868–9

Oil on canvas

43¾ × 26¼ in (124 × 67 cm)

Musée d'Orsay, Paris, France

PIEBALD CAT

Bicoloured cats, also known as piebald or magpie cats, are common in many breeds. The term "piebald" originates from "pie", part of magpie (a bird with similarly contrasting black-and-white colouring), and "bald", a white patch or spot. So a piebald cat has a coat featuring a white base with patches of another colour, such as black, tabby or grey. The amount of white varies hugely, from tiny areas to almost entirely white cats with just a few spots of colour, giving every piebald cat its own distinctive appearance.

Individualities

A Swedish artist who painted wildlife rather than photographing it, Bruno Liljefors (1860–1939) is esteemed today as one of the genre's most influential figures. This painting of Rapp the dog and Johan the cat was probably a commissioned portrait of a wealthy family's pets, and it was an unusual subject for Liljefors, who rarely painted domesticated animals. Nonetheless, he seems to have captured the characters of both the serene cat and the faithful, cautious dog. Influences of Impressionism and Japanese *ukiyo-e* art, encountered during a stay in France, can be seen in the balanced composition, light palette and loose brushwork. Yet the artist still applies his findings through the lens of acute observation, conveying the individual characteristics of both animals. Liljefors, who was recognized during his lifetime for his understanding of animals, believed in portraying them as unique beings rather than generic representations of their species. He once said, "We generally regard animals in the way that an inhabitant of Mars suddenly transformed to Earth would regard human beings. He would only notice the different races, types, castes and not the individuals. Neither do we see the animal individuals, but it is just these which I try to predict. I paint animal portraits."

30
BRUNO LILJEFORS
Rapp and Johan
1886
Oil on canvas
27¾ × 33½ in
(70.5 × 85.1 cm)
Private collection

RUSSIAN BLUE

A breed with a short, dense coat in colours that vary from a light shimmering silver-blue to a darker slate-blue, the Russian blue may have originated in the port of Arkhangelsk, Russia. These cats are also sometimes called Archangel blues, since it is generally believed that sailors took them from the Archangel Isles to Great Britain and northern Europe in the 1860s. Most Russian blues have bright green eyes. The unusual double coat of these cats consists of two layers: a dense, soft undercoat for warmth with longer guard hairs on top, which provide insulation, water resistance and protection. The guard hairs are silver tipped, which gives them a silvery sheen or lustrous appearance, while the tail may have a few almost unnoticeable stripes.

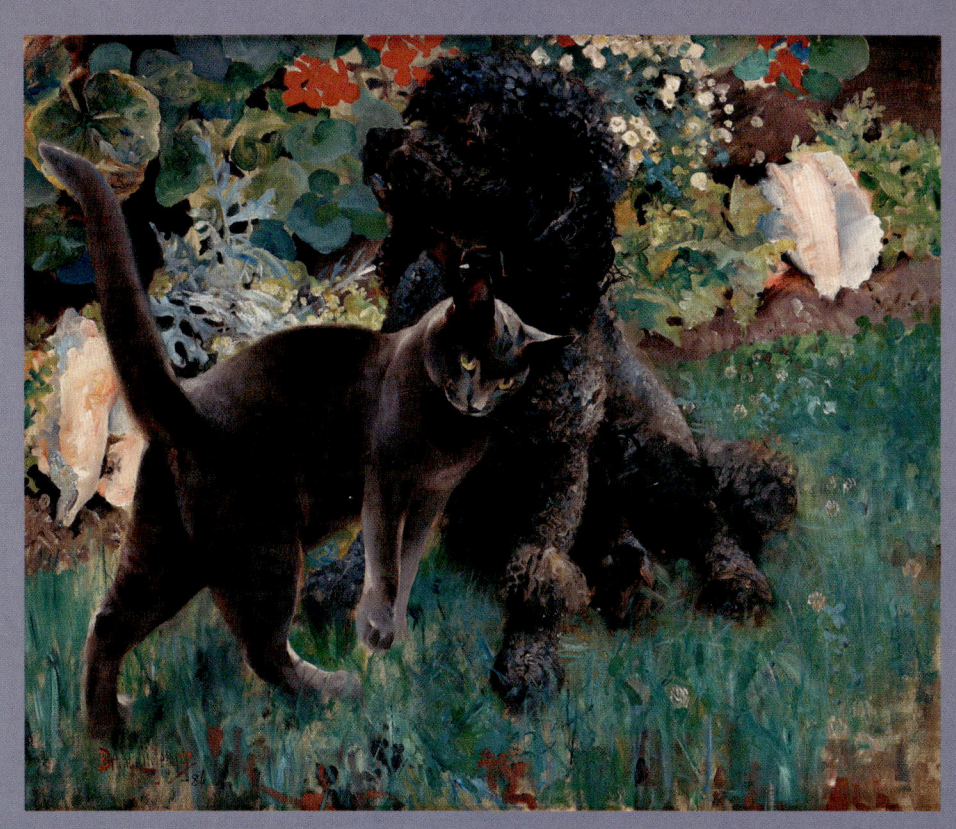

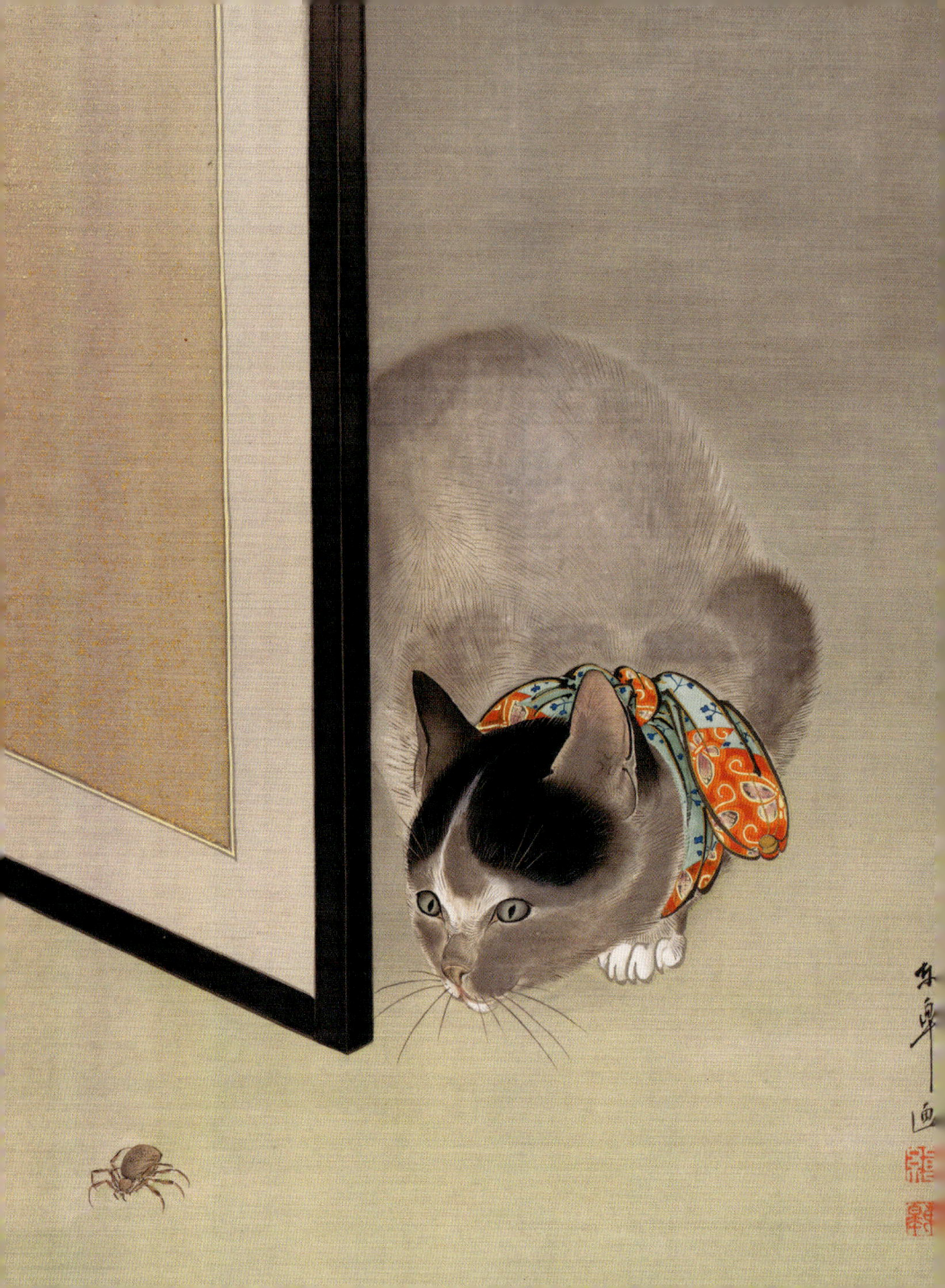

Curiosity and grace

Known for his traditional Japanese woodblock prints, Ōide Tōkō (1841–1905) was born in Edo (now Tokyo) and became part of the Nanga (Southern painting) or Bunjinga (Scholar or Literati painting) School. Influenced by Chinese art, Nanga artists – most of whom lived in Kyoto and Osaka – generally considered themselves to be intellectuals and poets as well as painters. They usually produced small paintings, such as hanging scrolls and fans, but some also created screen paintings. This is a traditional Japanese woodblock print, which involved carving images into blocks of wood, then inking and printing them on paper. In a serene moment, a cat crouches, peering around a screen to watch a spider. The spider is possibly unaware of the cat, but the cat is fascinated by the spider. Since Tōkō created the image in close-up, it seems especially intimate. The focus of the scene is on the interaction between cat and spider, rather than on details. The cat is a generic feline, not a specific breed, making the image about cats' universal qualities, such as curiosity, grace and contemplation. The cat and the spider might symbolize such themes as inquisitiveness, patience and the connection between all living beings, and the image itself may be about balance, nature's harmony and the appreciation of everyday wonders.

31
ŌIDE TŌKŌ
*Cat Watching
a Spider*
c. 1888–92
Album leaf; ink
and colour on silk
14¾ × 11 in
(37.5 × 27.9 cm)
The Metropolitan
Museum of Art,
New York, USA

JAPAN AND CATS

Perceived as vessels of good luck in Japan, cats are revered creatures that are interwoven into the country's history and folklore. In stories and art, they are often conveyed as sacred guardians. Many homes and businesses have a welcoming cat sculpture, a *maneki-neko*, outside the door to greet all who enter. These sculptures honour a mythical cat that was said to wave to people passing by, directing them to safety. The country also has many cat shrines, temples and large sculptures, such as the Azusamiten shrine in Tachikawa, Tokyo, which is dedicated to cats. Although cats are beloved in Japanese culture, no domestic cat breeds originated there.

Bold and animated

The American artist Julian Alden Weir (1852–1919) was a member of the Cos Cob Art Colony in Connecticut and a founding member of a loosely allied group of American artists called The Ten. After studying art in the USA, he enrolled in 1873 at the École des Beaux-Arts in Paris, where he worked under the painter Jean-Léon Gérôme and became good friends with the artist Jules Bastien-Lepage. When he first saw Impressionist painting in France, Weir declared, horrified: "I never in my life saw more horrible things ... They do not observe drawing nor form but give you an impression of what they call nature. It was worse than the Chamber of Horrors." Influenced by Bastien-Lepage, Édouard Manet (page 92) and several other European artists, Weir continued to paint in a naturalistic style until the 1880s, when he began warming towards Impressionism after all. In 1889 he stayed on the Isle of Man, a small island in the Irish Sea between Great Britain and Ireland, and the homeland of the Manx people and cats. There, even more than his usual paintings, he produced numerous etchings – bold, sketchy, linear works like the one shown here. This print of two Manx cats relaxing on a chair with a kitten below is created with light, expressive lines and marks.

MANX CATS

Famous for not having a tail, Manx (or Manks) cats are usually exceptionally loyal and, unlike most cat breeds, fairly easy to train. Most have golden eyes and rounded heads and bodies. They come in all coat colours and patterns, although totally white ones are rare. Manx cats were first documented in the eighteenth century, and their history is interwoven with folk tales and myths, but their lack of a tail actually arises from a genetic mutation. Most have absolutely no tail, while some have a small stub, hence their colloquial nickname "stubbin". Prized as skilled hunters, these cats have often been kept on farms and ships to reduce the rat population.

32
JULIAN ALDEN WEIR
Manx Cats – Isle of Man
1889
Etching on paper
4 × 5⅝ in
(10.3 × 14.4 cm)
Smithsonian American Art Museum, Washington, DC, USA

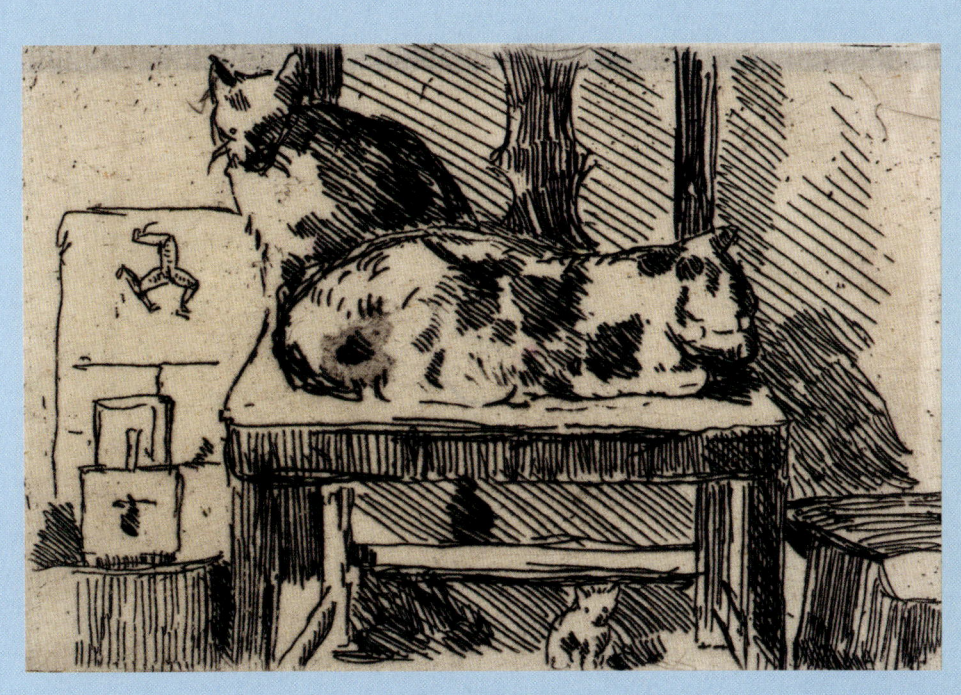

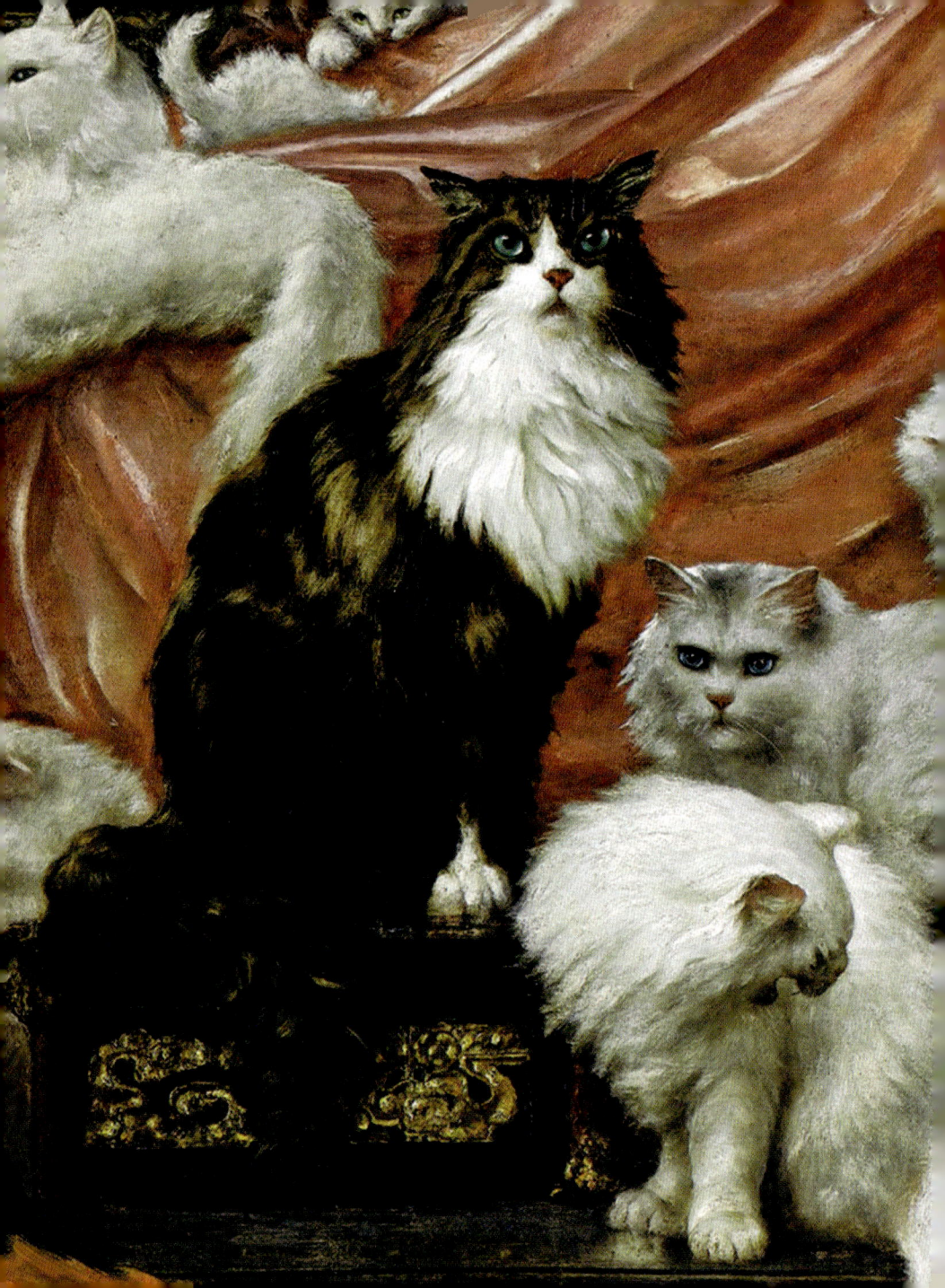

Proud and playful

Here are 42 Turkish Angora and Persian cats belonging to the nineteenth-century American millionaire Kate Birdsall Johnson, painted by the Austrian artist Carl Kahler (1856–1906). After accepting Johnson's commission, Kahler spent three years studying the animals' poses and learning their habits, then months making preparatory sketches and paintings. In the finished work, he depicted the cats larger than life size. A large Persian named Sultan – which Johnson had bought in Paris for a huge price – sits proudly in the centre. Surrounding Sultan are the many other cats, playing, hissing, climbing, cuffing, stretching, reclining, sitting and scratching. Several look directly out of the canvas, while others are preoccupied, such as stalking a moth. Both individuals and family groups are portrayed from various angles. Kahler was born in Linz, Austria, and studied at the Academy of Fine Arts in Munich, Germany. He soon became known as a portrait and animal painter. Johnson lent the painting for display at the 1893 Chicago World's Fair, and the following year it was bought by the collector Ernest Haquette for his Crystal Palace Saloon in San Francisco. Although both Kahler and the Saloon perished in the San Francisco earthquake of 1906, the painting survived.

33
CARL KAHLER
My Wife's Lovers
1891
Oil on canvas
6 × 8½ ft
(1.8 × 2.6 m)
Private collection

Opposite: detail

PERSIAN

Persian cats have been cherished for thousands of years, and probably originated in the deserts of Persia, which encompassed several present-day countries, including Iran. They have long coats of various hues, and large, almond-shaped eyes, which also vary in colour. A medium-sized to large breed, they have round, flat faces and the angle of their small mouths tends to make them appear grumpy, even though they are sweet-natured and gentle. Not a particularly active or energetic cat, the Persian is generally more beautiful than athletic. Its fur is so long and silky that it should be brushed regularly to avoid matting. Because of its sumptuous, exotic appearance, the breed has traditionally been popular with royalty and the nobility.

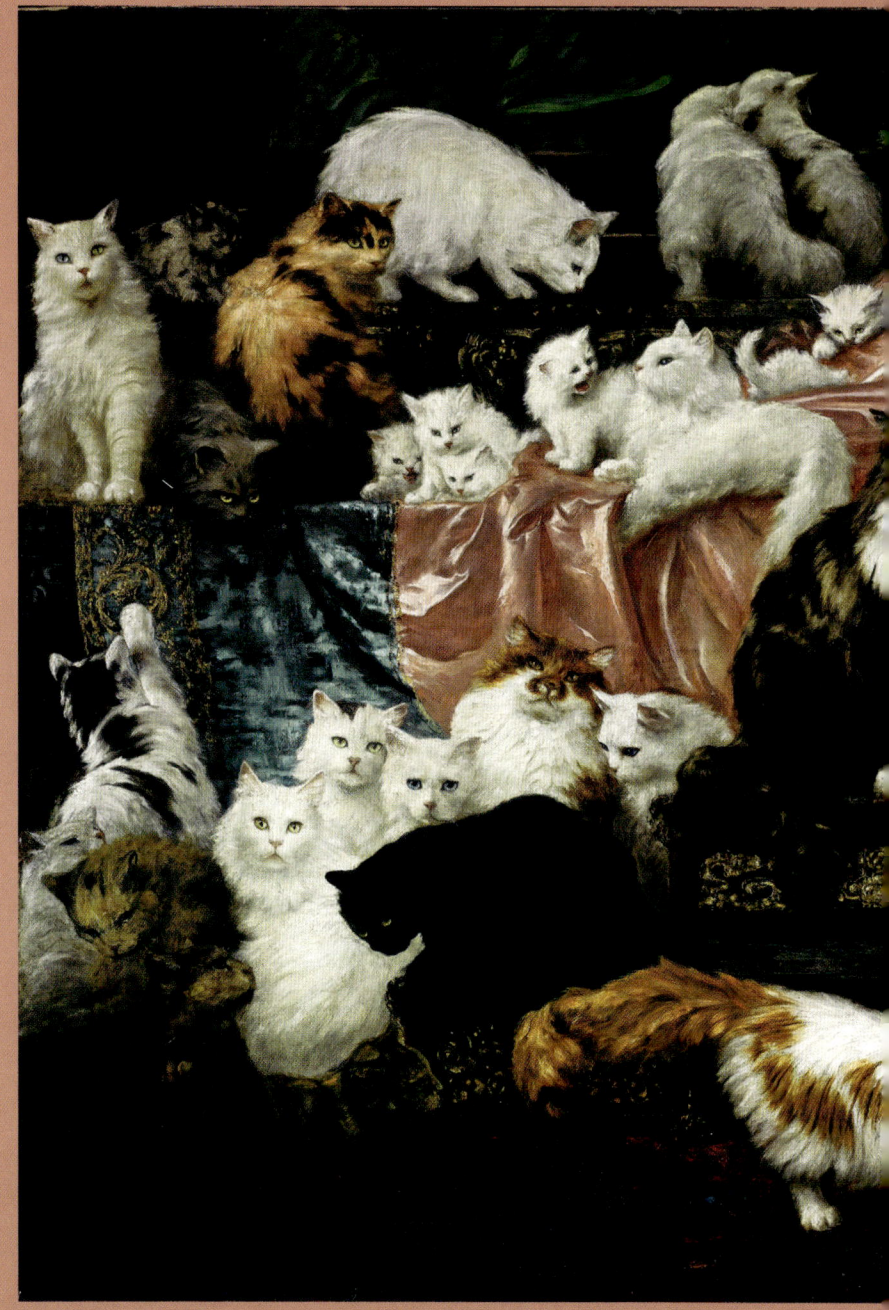

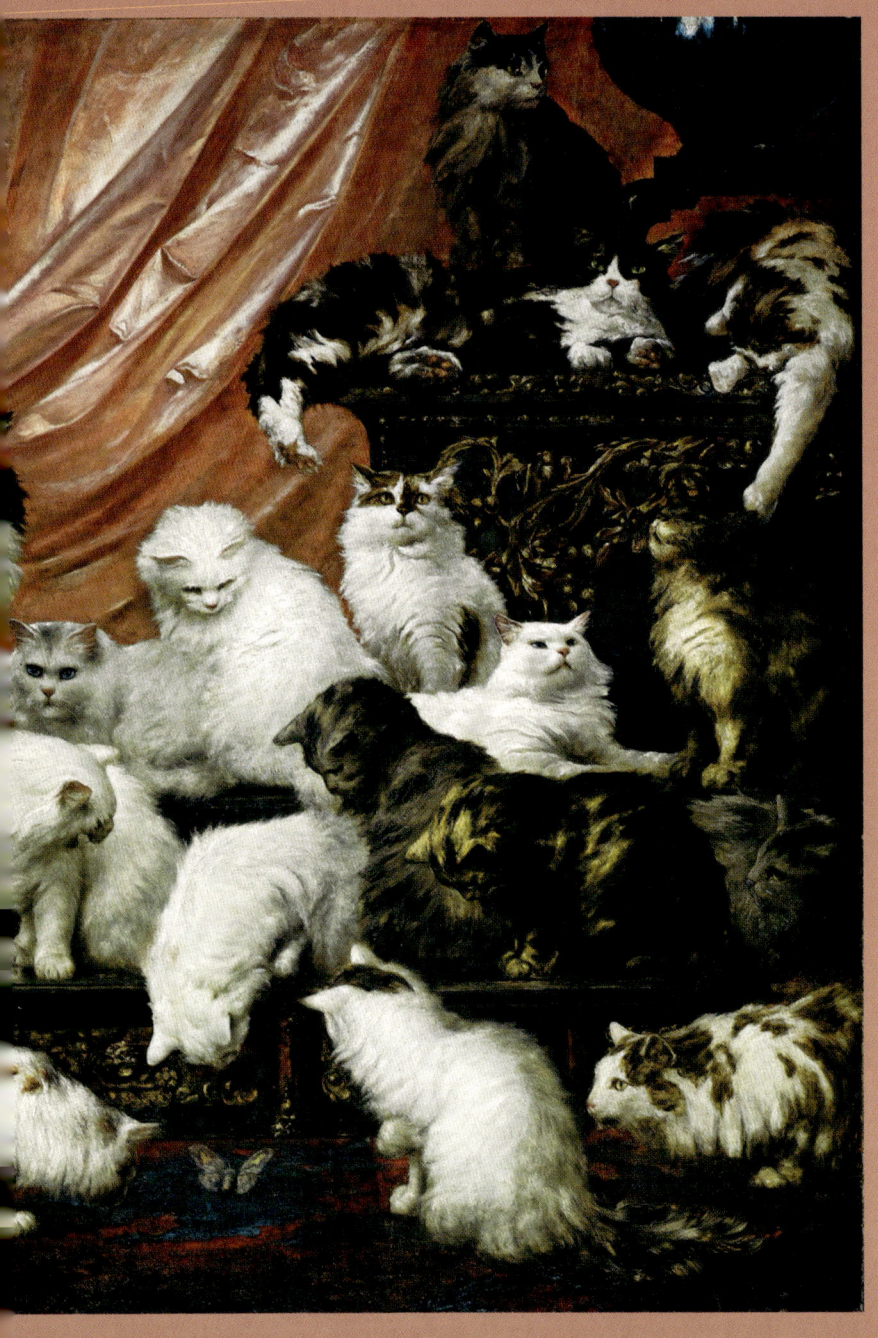

A quiet moment

Although she exhibited in the second Impressionist exhibition, in 1876, which came just two years after the first and was still seen as rebellious and shocking, Berthe Morisot (1841–95) had already achieved success at the age of 23 with acceptance to the prestigious Paris Salon. Even after she joined the avant-garde group of Impressionists, she remained one of the major French painters of the late nineteenth century. As a woman, she had not been allowed to study art in the same way as her male counterparts, neither could she paint the same subjects, so most of her paintings reveal her explorations of the subjects that were available to her: usually private, intimate aspects of feminine life that men could not share. Here, a young woman reclines comfortably, holding her cat on her lap and looking confidently at the viewer. Painted in the summer of 1892, the scene seems relaxed and calm. The sitter – the professional model Jeanne Fourmanoir, who posed regularly for Morisot and for Renoir (page 99) – looks contented and was probably chatting to the artist as the cat purred. Through free, swirling brushstrokes, Morisot creates a sense of movement. Light falls softly on the young woman and her cat, and with light brushwork, Morisot captures the textures of flowing hair, gleaming pearls and soft fur.

34
BERTHE MORISOT
La Jeune Fille au Chat
1892
Oil on canvas
21⅞ × 18¾ in
(55.5 × 46.6 cm)
Private collection

BLUE CATS

Blue cat coats evolved from a dilution of the gene for a black coat. Only four cat breeds are always blue, while there are others that are sometimes blue. The Russian blue has a plain blue coat and bright green eyes, while the Chartreux has blue-grey fur and copper-coloured eyes. The Nebelung (German for "creature of the mist") is blue-grey with green eyes, and finally, the Korat from Thailand is dark blue, described there as "rain-cloud grey". The British shorthair used to be called a British blue because of its blue fur and copper-coloured eyes. However, the Burmese, Oriental and American shorthair cats can also have blue coats.

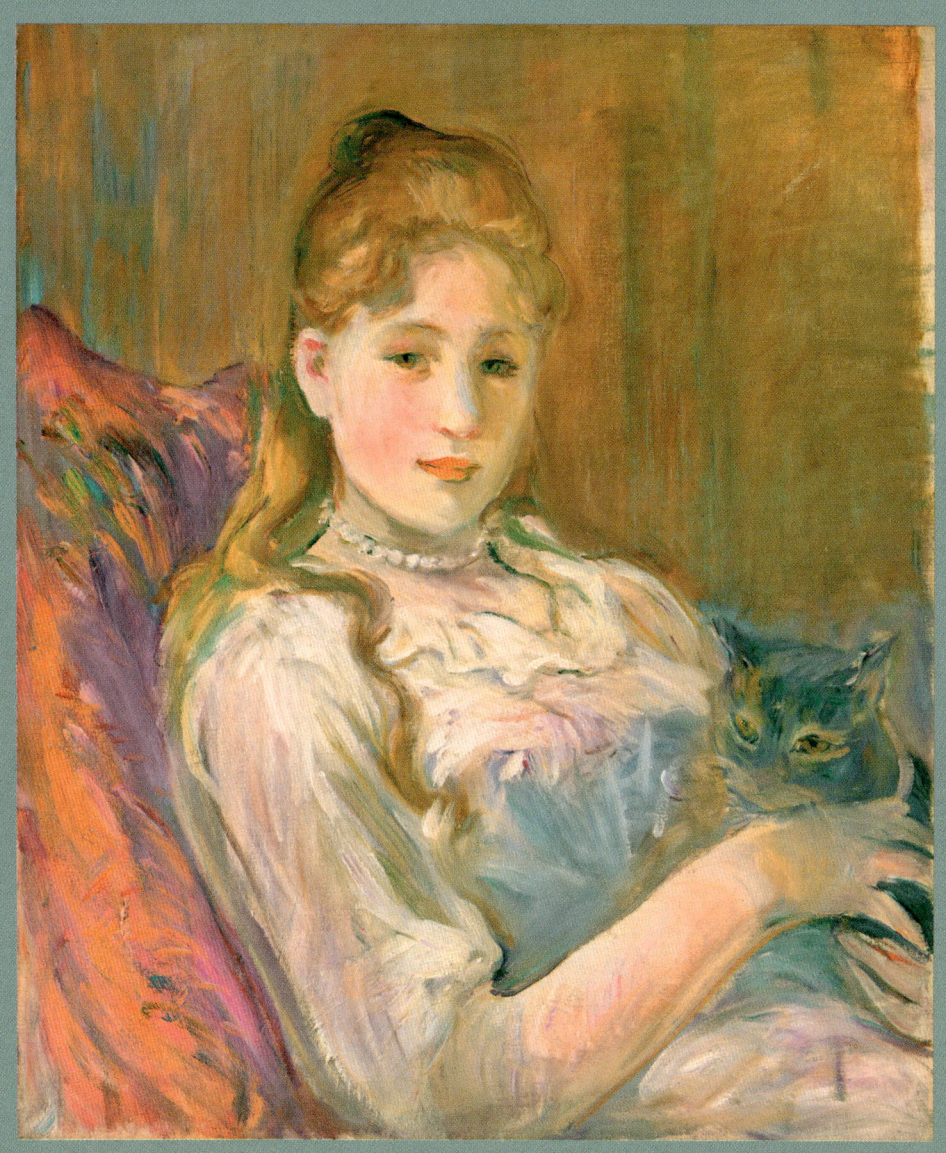

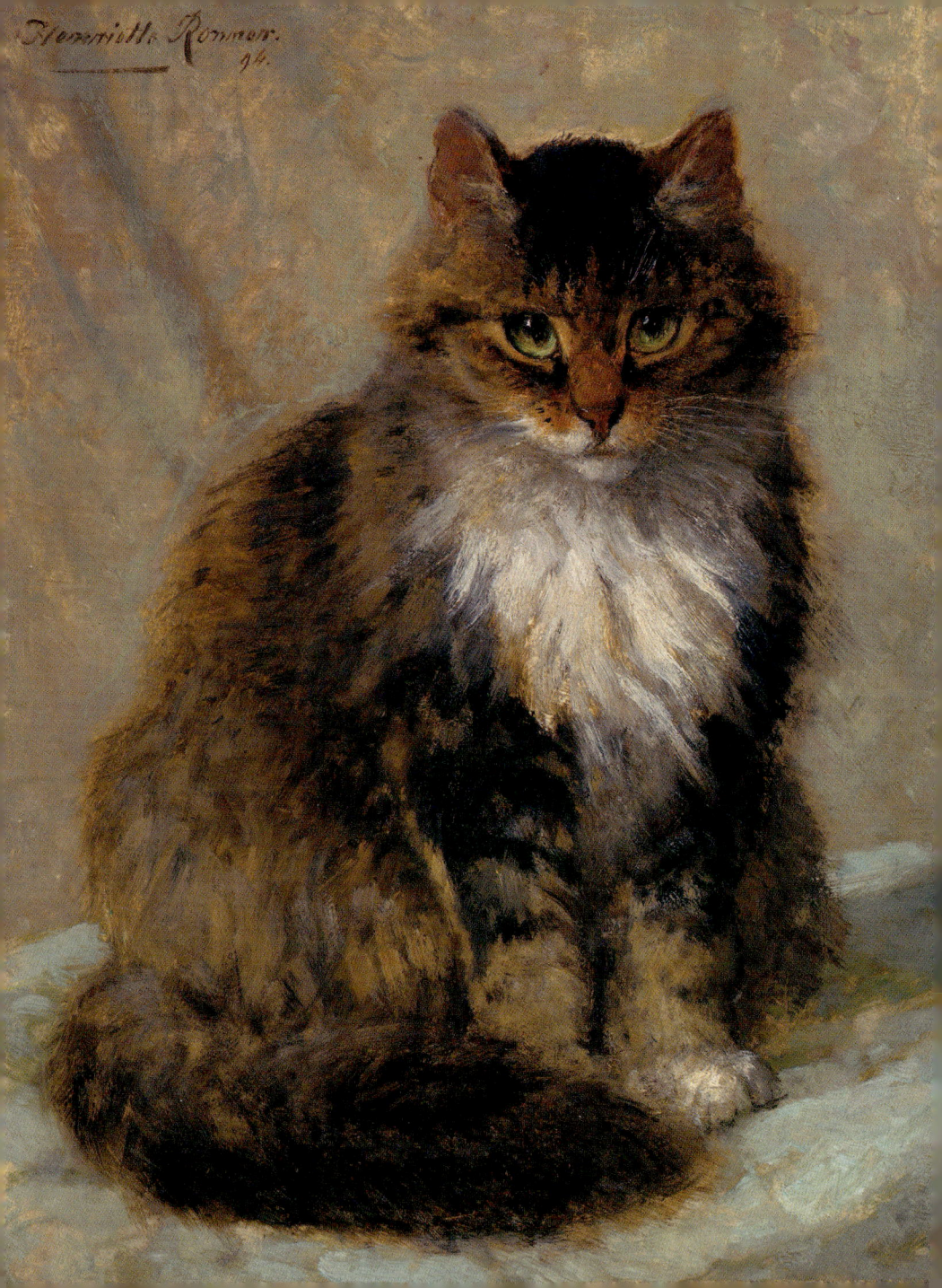

Fluffy and friendly

With dry, free brushwork applied in the direction of the cat's fur, the popular Dutch-Belgian artist Henriëtte Ronner-Knip (1821–1909) painted this portrait – probably a commission – of a noble-looking Maine Coon. Belonging to the late Romantic school, Ronner-Knip focused on conveying strong emotions using rich colours and bold brushstrokes, and she specialized in portrayals of domestic pets in middle-class homes. In this, she was extremely successful, receiving national awards in Belgium, France, the Netherlands, the United Kingdom and the United States, and her work was collected by the royalty and nobility of the late nineteenth and early twentieth centuries. Cats were her favourite subjects, and her images of them convey their charm and character. This large, fluffy cat looks directly at the viewer, its shining green eyes calm but watchful, apparently aware and astute. Ronner-Knip built up the portrait by applying layers of moist, opaque paint first, then dragging drier, thinner paint over the top. In this way, she conveys the density of the cat's fur and the dark tabby pattern. She prepared fastidiously for all her paintings. First she made careful, detailed sketches, then she modelled each animal in papier-mâché, and finally she created the painting using her sketches and models as references.

35
HENRIËTTE
RONNER-KNIP
The Maine Coon
1894
Oil on panel
15¾ × 12½ in
(40.5 × 32 cm)
Private collection

MAINE COON

The double-layered coat and bushy tail of the Maine Coon help the breed to survive in the coldest conditions. Maine Coons are large, long-haired cats, and one of the oldest natural breeds in North America. As the name indicates, they originated in the state of Maine, descendants of cats introduced to America by settlers. The breed evolved to be quite large and hardy, with a thick, shaggy, protective coat. One of the largest domesticated cat breeds, they are recognized for their dense, long fur and tufted ears, as well as their gentle, easy-going personalities. Intelligent, friendly, sociable and playful, they often express themselves audibly with meows and soft squeaks.

Guardian or protector

Associated with the Post-Impressionist and Symbolist movements, the French painter, sculptor, printmaker, ceramicist and writer Paul Gauguin (1848–1903) is recognized for his experimental use of colour and form in painting, and his search for beauty and purity in the world. Initially working as a stockbroker, he became an artist in his forties and soon began travelling regularly to the South Pacific, where he developed a style that blended direct observation with mystical symbolism. This painting, with its title that translates as "Not Working", depicts two young Tahitians sitting in a hut smoking, while Gauguin himself is seen through the window, painting. The work, which symbolizes the relaxed, contemplative lifestyle of Tahiti, displays Gauguin's use of bold colour, flat shapes and simplified forms, and his interpretation of Indigenous cultures. The white cat has been interpreted as a symbol of mystery, spirituality and connection to the natural world, perhaps also otherworldliness. Gauguin sought to depict the essence of traditional Tahitian beliefs and customs, and the connection between humans and the natural world. His inclusion of the cat helps to convey the calm and tranquillity of what he saw as a mysterious, exotic society.

KHAO MANEE CAT

The animal depicted here may be the pure-white Khao Manee ("white jewel") cat. The breed, which developed in Thailand hundreds of years ago, also has jewel-like eyes of blue, green or gold, or of two different colours. These cats have short, silky fur and a friendly character. In about 1350 CE the *Tamra Maew*, also called *Treatise on Cats* or *Cat Book Poems*, was written: a collection of illustrations and poetic descriptions of cats, featuring more than 20 ancient Thai cat breeds. In it, the Khao Manee was described as being a breed that would bring good fortune, and odd-eyed Khao Manees were considered especially lucky.

36
PAUL GAUGUIN
Eiaha Ohipa or Tahitians in a Room
1896
Oil on canvas
26 × 30 in
(65 × 75 cm)
Pushkin State Museum of Fine Arts, Moscow, Russia

Overleaf: detail

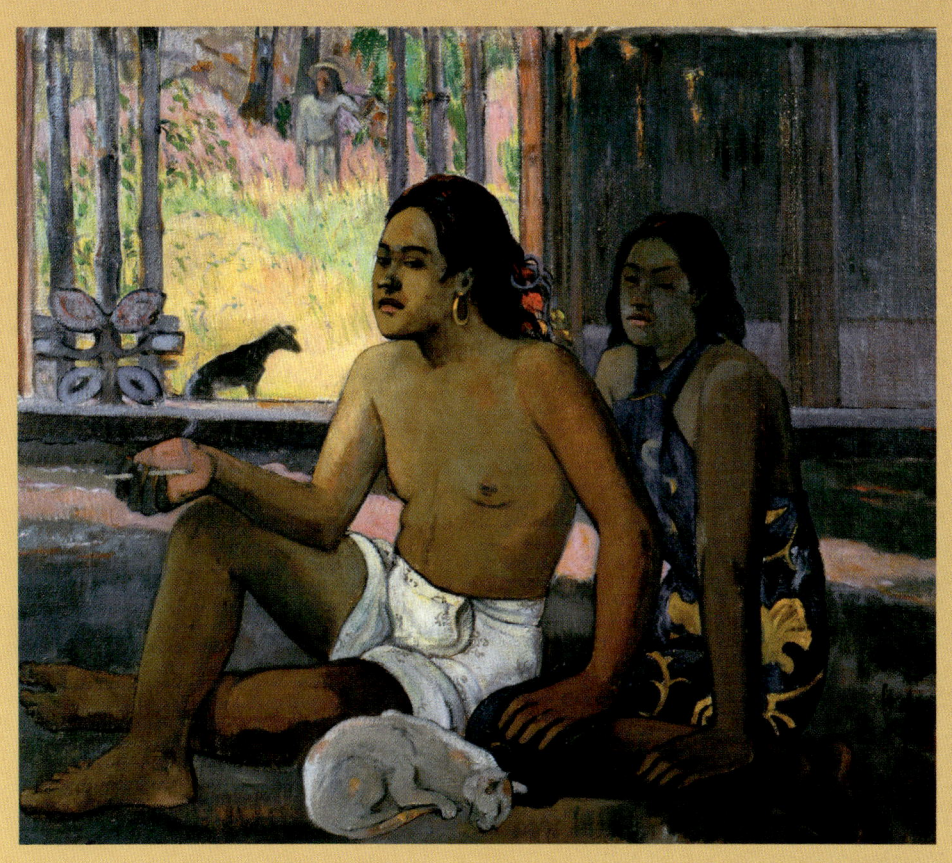

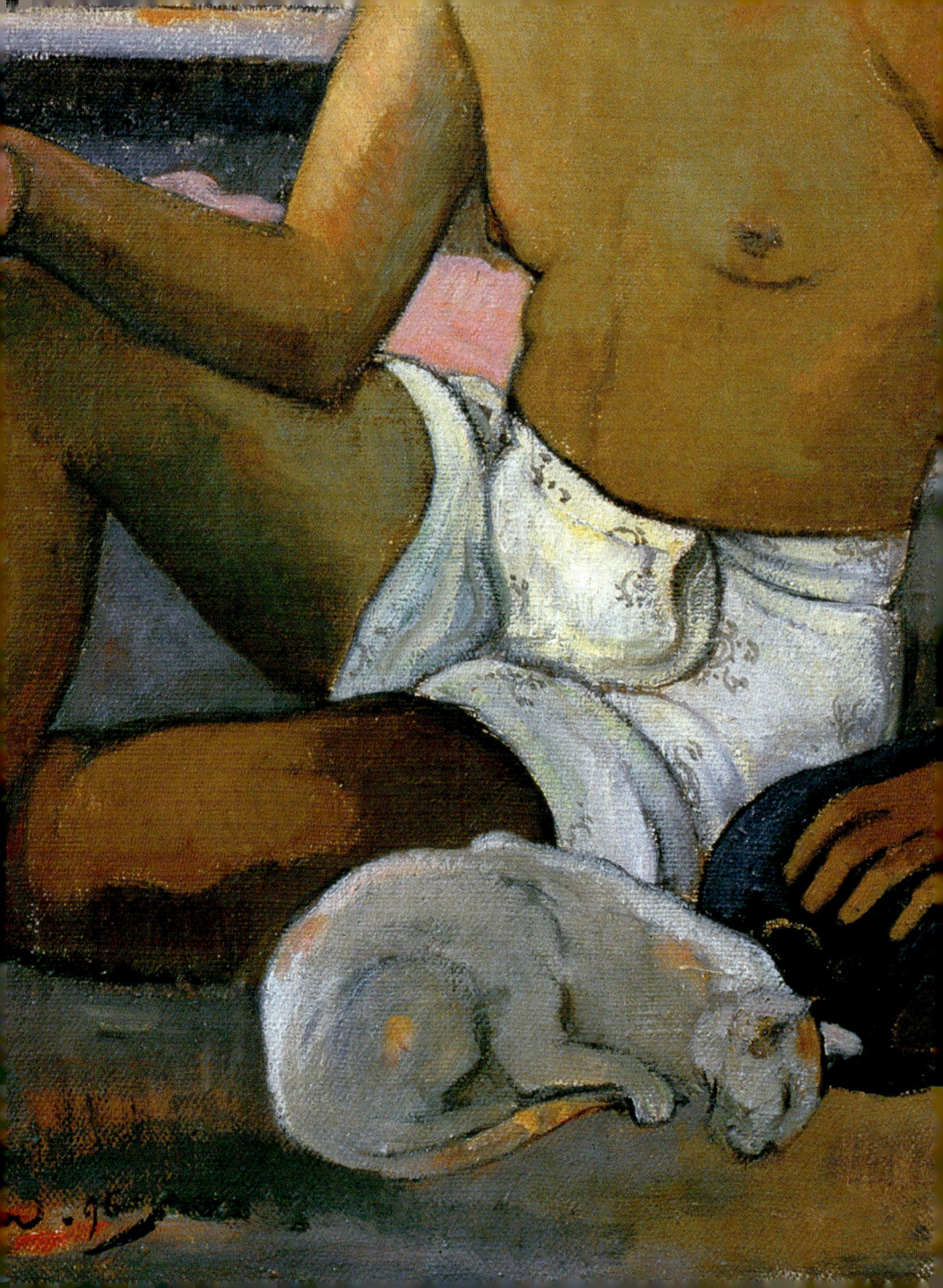

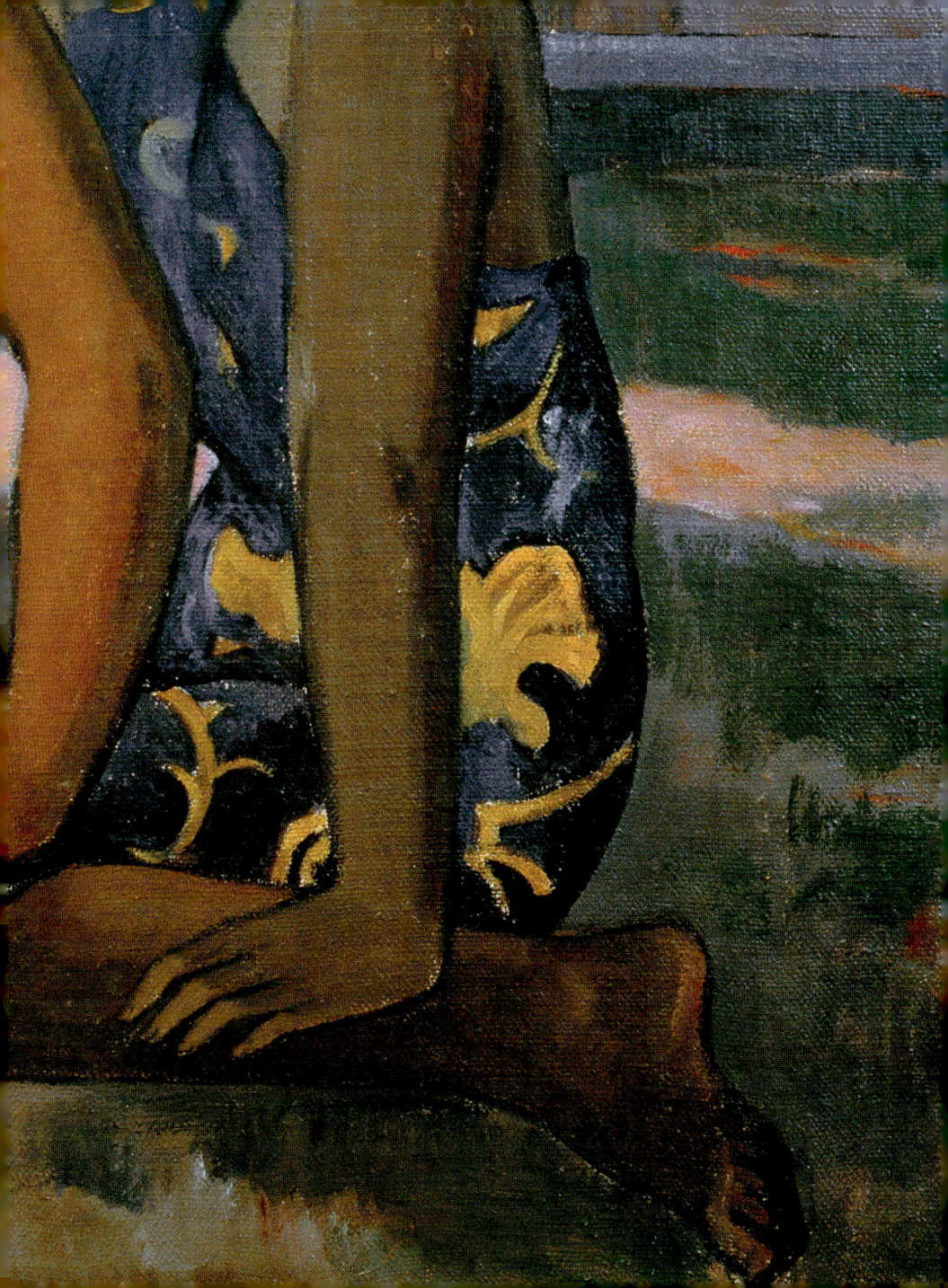

Free spirit

Gathered around a still-life painting – *Fruit Bowl, Glass and Apples* of 1879–80 by Paul Cézanne – are several key figures from the once secret brotherhood known as Les Nabis (Hebrew for "prophets", reflecting the group's belief in the transforming power of art), including the painter of this work, Maurice Denis (1870–1943). The image celebrates Cézanne, and the group stands in the shop of Ambroise Vollard, a Parisian art dealer who supported Cézanne and several other relatively unknown avant-garde artists of the time. Paintings by Gauguin (page 114) and Renoir (page 99) can be seen in the background. The artists pictured here include Odilon Redon, Paul Sérusier, Édouard Vuillard, Pierre Bonnard (page 133), and Denis and his wife, Marthe. Below the easel is a tabby cat, which may represent independence, mystery, aloofness, a free spirit or an enigmatic presence – or all these qualities. The inscrutability of the reasoning behind it adds depth and ambiguity to the image. The inclusion of the cat could also be another reference to Cézanne, who was fond of animals. Alternatively, cats are known for their vigilance and keen observation, so its presence here could symbolize concentration or intuition.

37
MAURICE DENIS
Homage to Cézanne
1900
Oil on canvas
71$\frac{2}{3}$ × 95$\frac{7}{8}$in
(182 × 243.5 cm)
Musée d'Orsay, Paris, France

Opposite: detail

TORTOISESHELL

Not a breed but a description of a colour combination, the tortoiseshell cat has mottled black and orange fur, usually in asymmetrical patterns. The name refers to its resemblance to the patterns on tortoises' shells. A cat that is predominantly white with tortoiseshell patches is described as tricolour, tortoiseshell-and-white or calico, but the black-and-orange markings are unbroken on a "proper" tortoiseshell cat. These cats usually look dark overall, with flecks of lighter colouring in their fur, which is generally thick. Tortoiseshell cats are almost always female. The type can be found in several pure-bred cats, such as the Cornish Rex, Maine Coon, Persian and Japanese bobtail, but many non-pure-bred cats are also tortoiseshell.

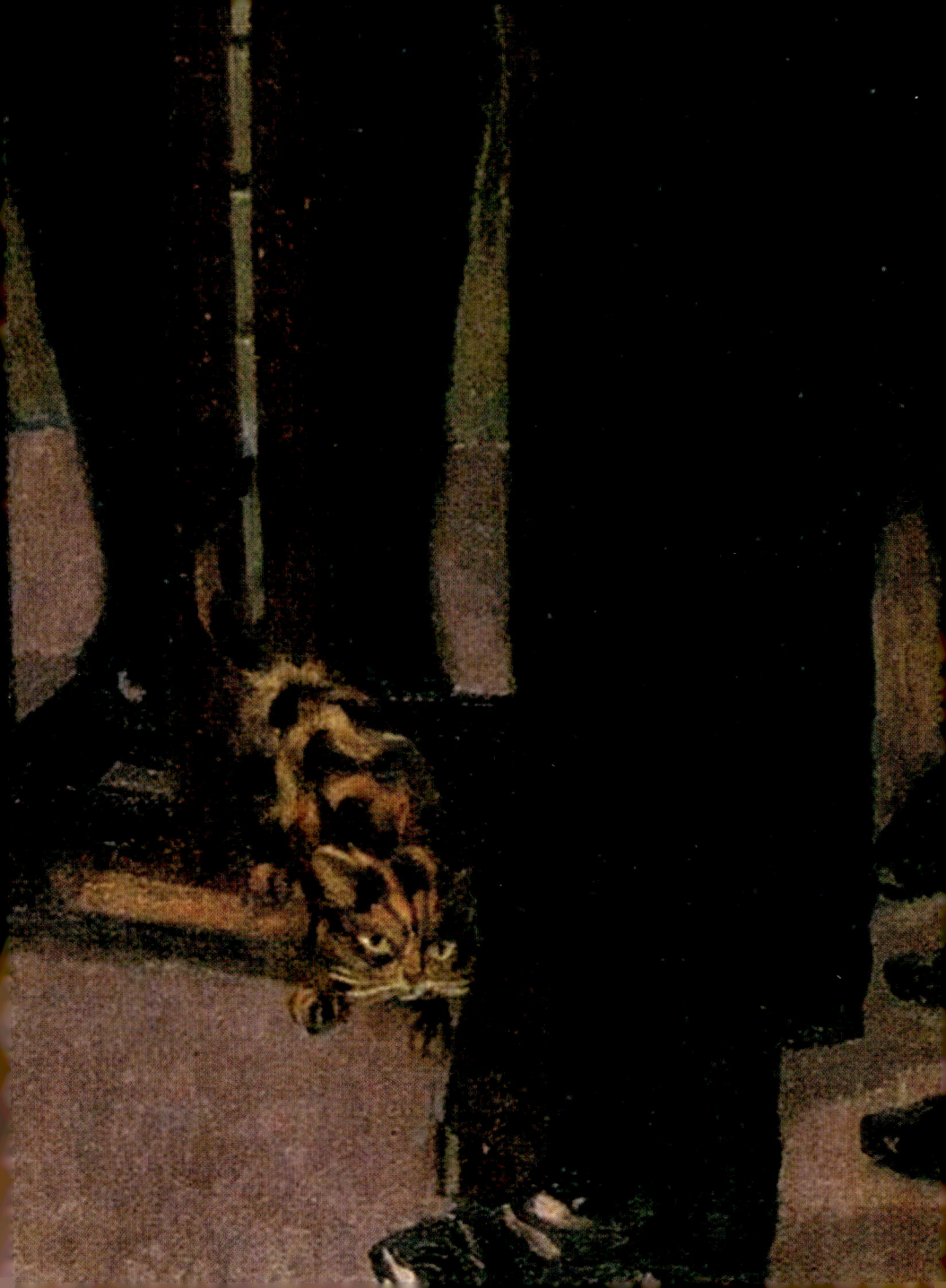

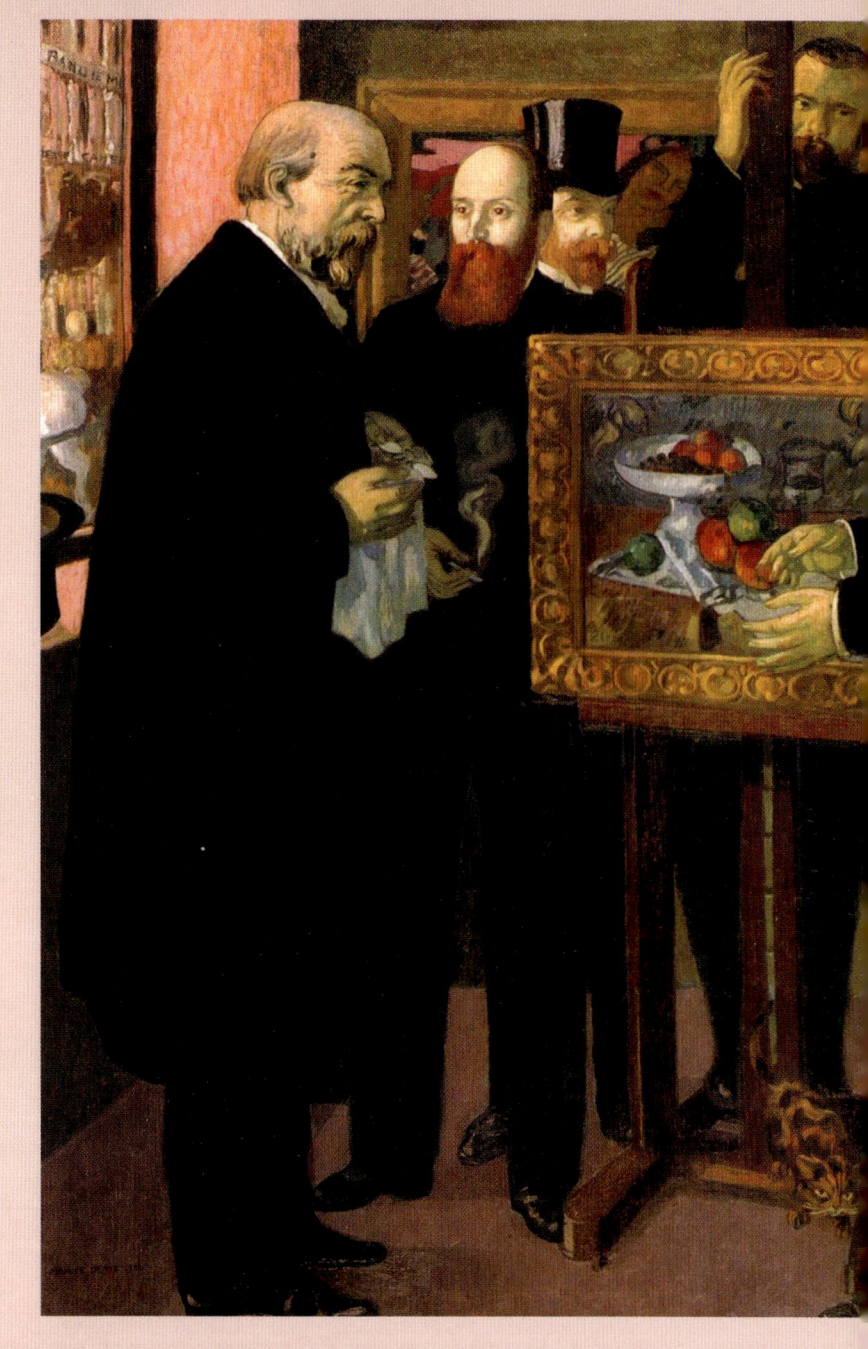

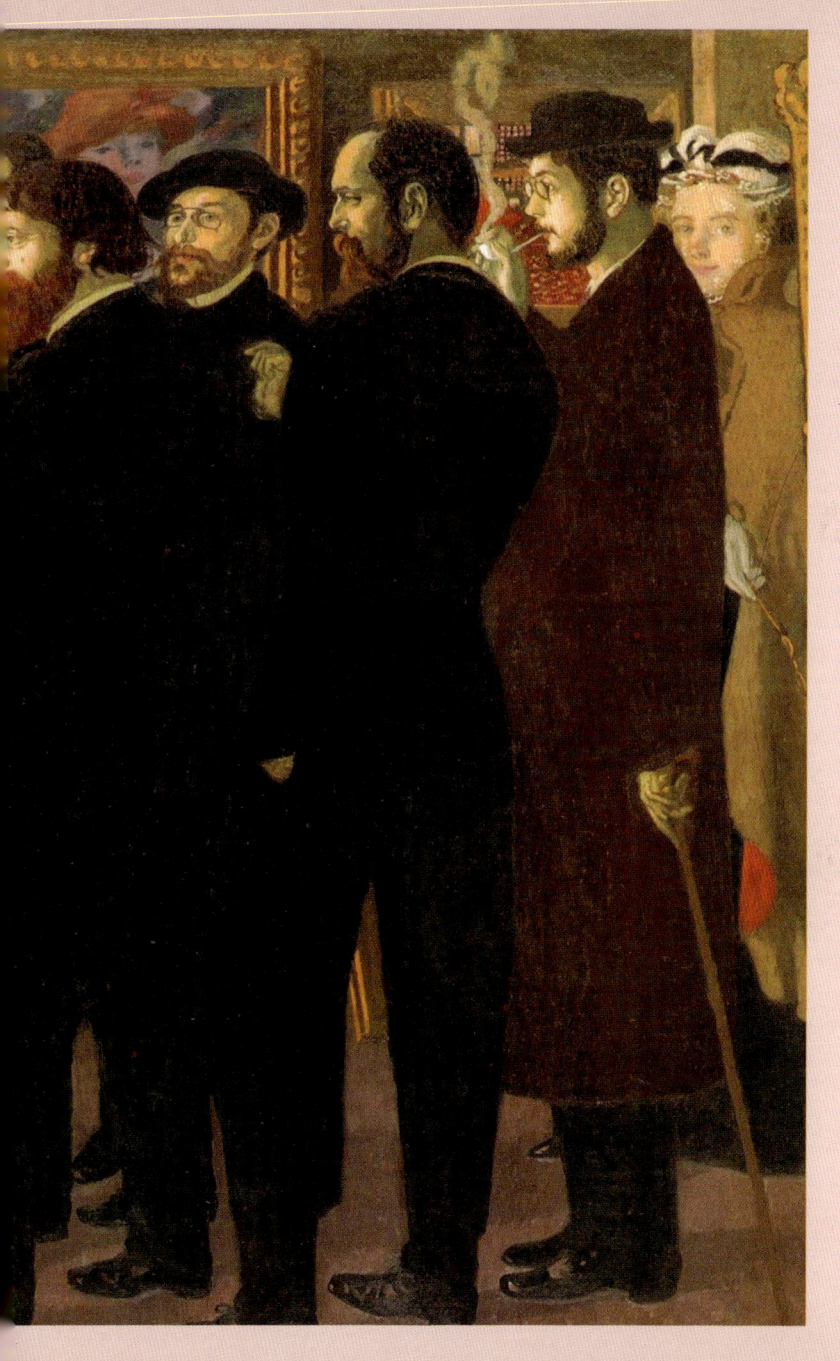

Beneath a plum tree

At the age of 15, Hishida Shunsō (1874–1911), who was born in Nagano Prefecture, Japan, moved to Tokyo and there studied under some of the most significant teachers of the time, including Kanō School artists Yuki Masaaki and Hashimoto Gahō, and with other students who also became famous. Under Gahō, Shunsō helped to develop *nihonga*, a style of painting that responded to changes in Japanese society during the Meiji period (1868–1912). Japan had recently opened its trade borders to the rest of the world for the first time in more than two centuries, and *nihonga* artists aimed to preserve the heritage of Japanese painting while also updating it for the changing, modern times of international exposure and artistic influence. Shunsō developed his art further during his travels to America, India and Europe in 1903–5. He also became known for his many images of cats. Here, using the *sumi-e* or ink diffusion technique, he depicts a cat crouching beneath a plum tree on a still day in early spring. Above the animal are a few delicate white plum blossoms; behind is the solid, gnarled bark of the old tree. Soft light falls on the cat's fur as it dozes quietly. The artist's refined, asymmetrical composition carefully amalgamates elements of realism and adornment.

38
HISHIDA SHUNSŌ
Cat and Plum Blossoms
1906
Colour on silk
46½ × 19⅔ in
(118 × 49.8 cm)
Adachi Museum of Art, Yasugi, Japan

Overleaf: detail

BIRMAN

Also known as the sacred cat of Burma, the Birman is a large cat breed with creamy fur, dark points on the ears, face, front legs and tail, and blue eyes. Semi-long-haired, it is fairly muscular, and there are many folk tales that describe how it obtained its unique markings. It is likely that the first of these cats were companions of temple priests in northern Burma (now Myanmar). In about 1919 two of the cats were taken from there to France, either given to someone as a reward or smuggled out. The name is derived from *Birmanie*, the French form of "Burma".

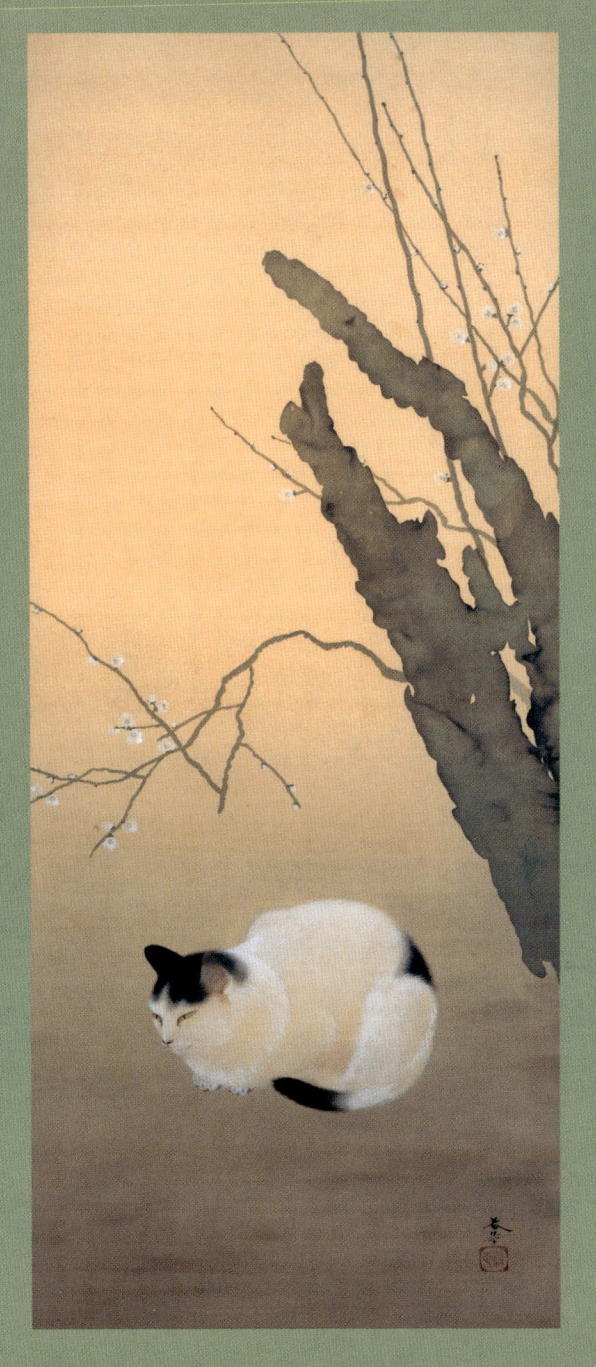

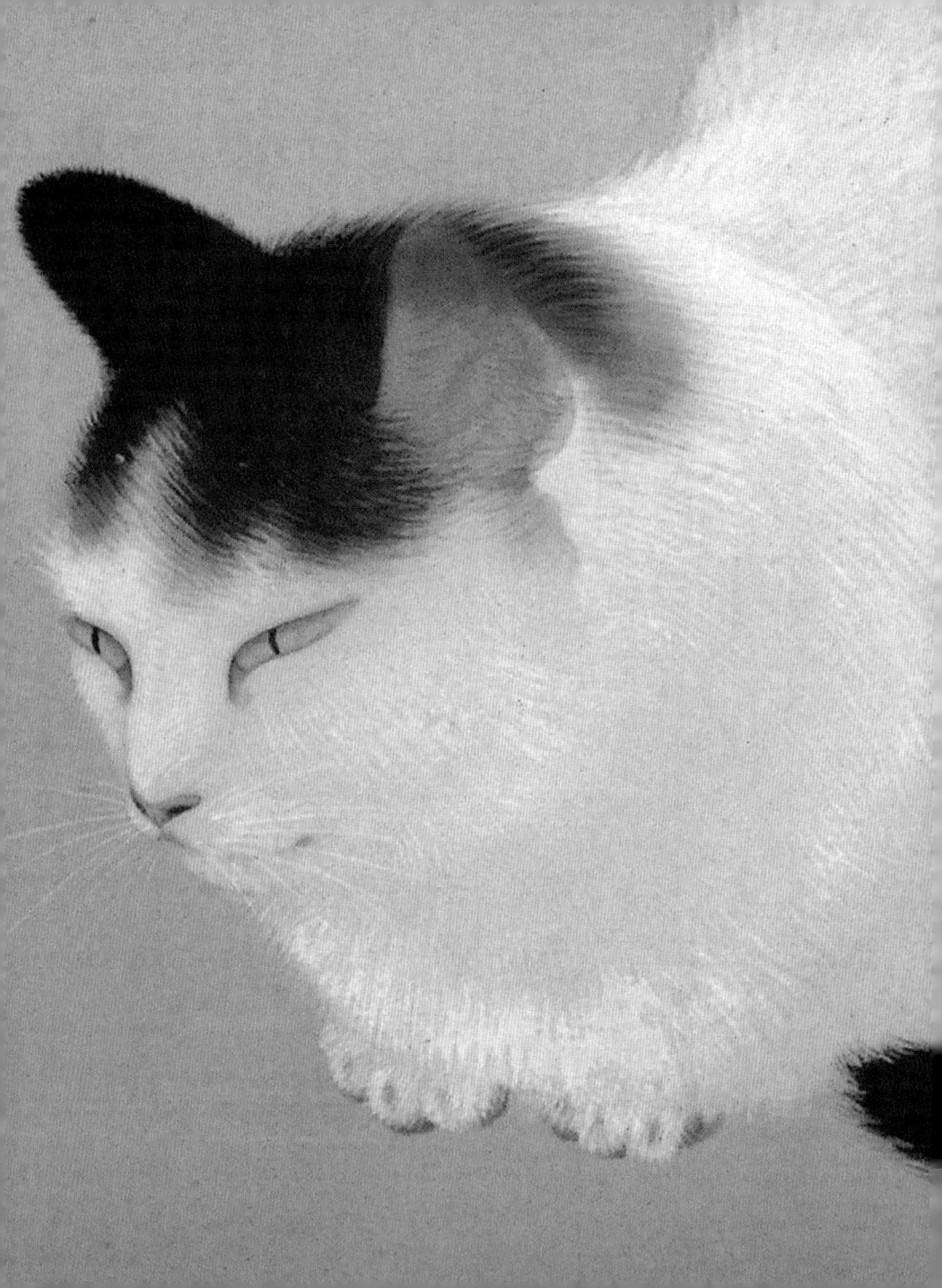

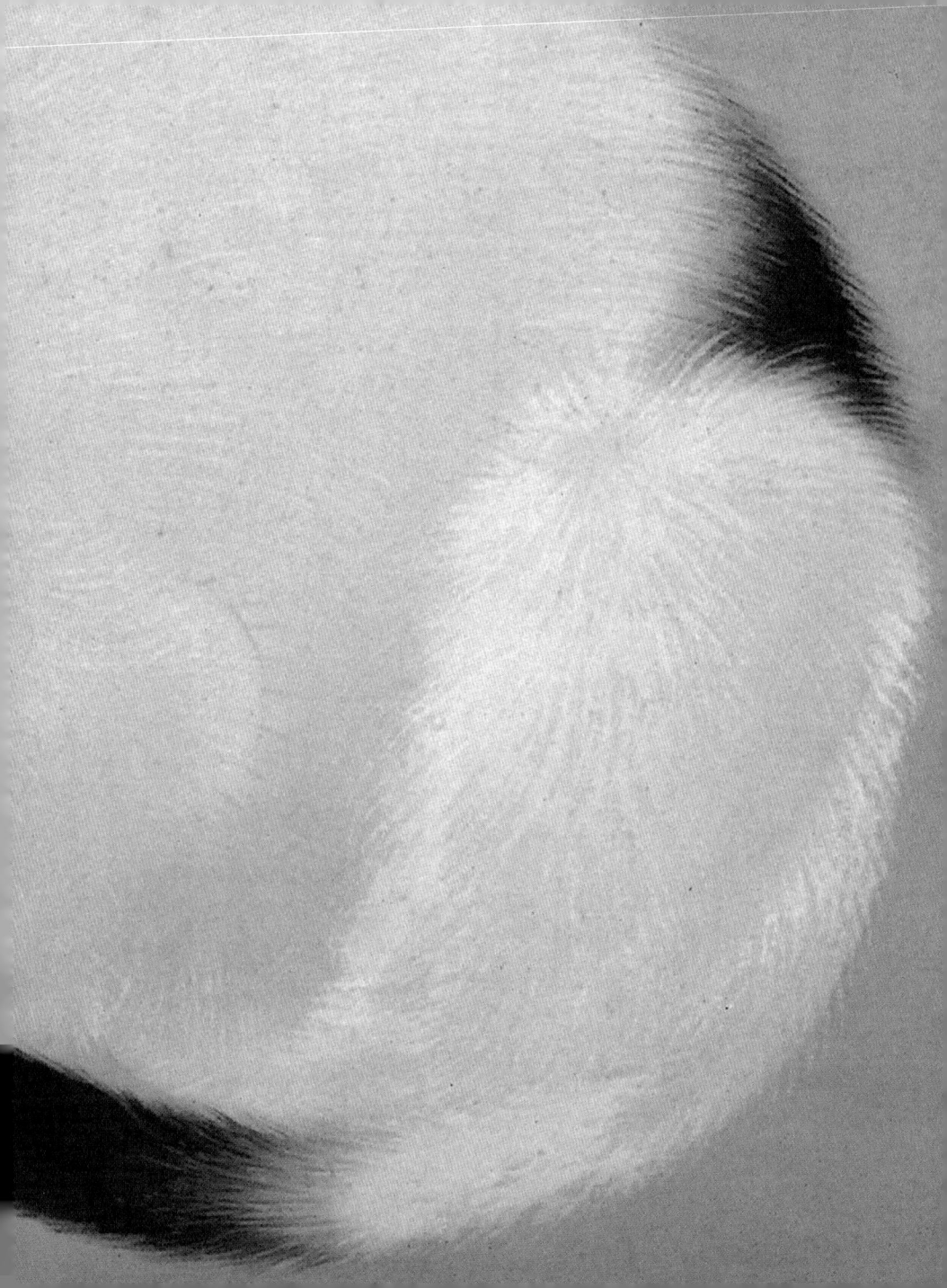

Emulating motherhood

American-born Mary Cassatt (1844–1926) travelled to France for her artistic training and remained there for most of her life and career. She was recognized there by such contemporaries as Edgar Degas (1834–1917), and she became the only American artist to exhibit with the Impressionists in Paris. As a female artist of the time, her subjects included portraits of women and portrayals of mothers and children. She combined the light colour palette and loose brushwork of Impressionism with compositions influenced by Japanese art, and she worked in a variety of media. This painting conveys her astute psychological insight and use of vibrant paint marks and colours to create the visual effect of various textures. Cassatt was well known in her local area to the northwest of Paris, and often used the same models, including children from the village of Le Mesnil-Théribus, Oise. From 1901, little blonde Sara sat for her often. Sara's sweet face, delicate features and reportedly happy disposition made her a favourite model for Cassatt, who spent time planning her compositions to make them look as spontaneous as possible. More than merely an image of a child with a kitten, this painting has links with one of Cassatt's common themes, maternity. In her gentle, caring embrace of the kitten, Sara emulates a mother's affectionate cradling of a baby.

39
MARY CASSATT
Sara Holding a Cat
1908
Oil on canvas
16¼ × 13 in
(41.3 × 33 cm)
Private collection

GINGER CATS

Although not a breed, ginger cats are known for their distinctive colouring, which can be in shades of orange, red, amber and gold. Even if it is not immediately clear, with their tiger-like appearance, all ginger cats are tabbies. The ginger gene "O" is responsible for producing the red pigment phaeomelanin, and this masks all other colours. Ginger cats can be moggies (alley cats) or pure-bred cats, including Persian, Munchkin, American bobtail, British shorthair, Maine Coon and Abyssinian, and their personalities come not from their colouration, but from the breed(s) from which they descend. Some 80 per cent of ginger cats are male.

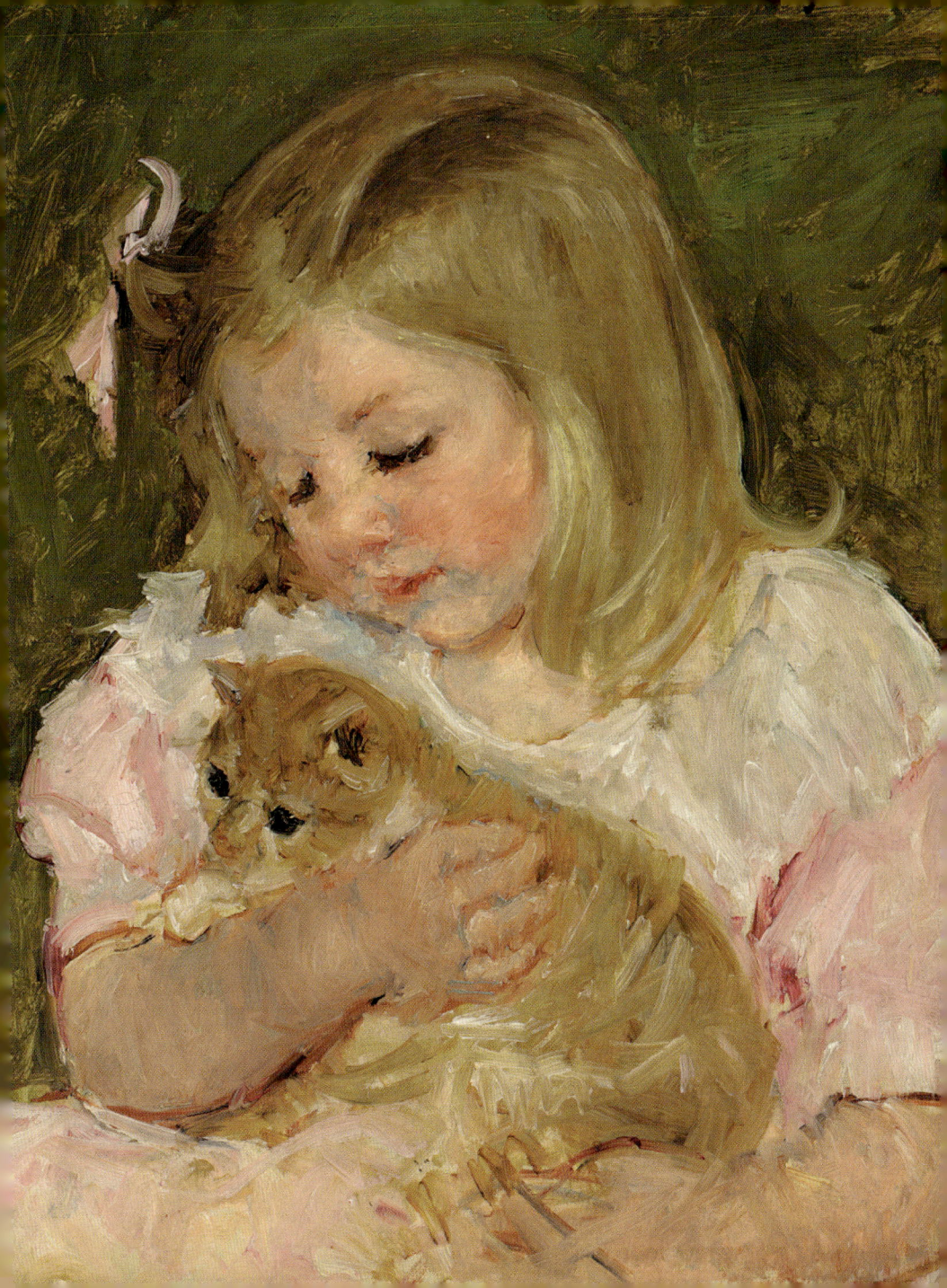

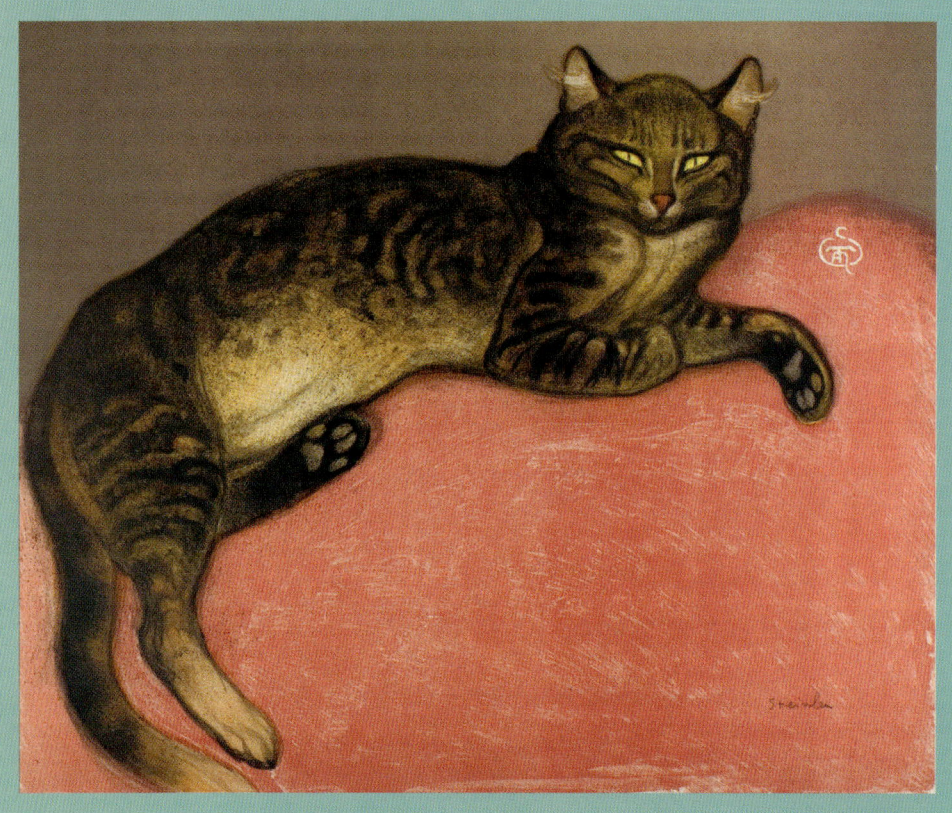

Golden eyes

Théophile-Alexandre Steinlen (1859–1923) was born in Switzerland and studied at the University of Lausanne before taking a job as a trainee designer at a textile mill in eastern France. At the age of 21, he moved to Montmartre in Paris. There, he befriended other artists at the bohemian venue Le Chat Noir, leading to commissions to paint posters for the cabaret owner Aristide Bruant and other commercial enterprises. Over the course of his career, Steinlen created many paintings, but he produced far more lithographic posters and illustrations for many left-wing publications. Cats were always an important subject for him; he loved them and always fed the strays in Montmartre. They appear in many of his advertising posters, and he also produced a huge number of drawings and prints of cats in moments of leisure. At the time, cats were symbolic of bohemianism and, more specifically, bohemian women. The fact that many Parisian cats lived in Montmartre, free of bourgeois domestication, was perceived as a metaphor for the bohemian lifestyle, or the rejection of the bourgeois social norms of that period. Even though this is a lithograph, Steinlen has created a sense of texture in the fabric of the cushion and the fur and markings of the cat, conveying the tonal qualities of a cosy evening.

40

THÉOPHILE-ALEXANDRE STEINLEN

Winter: Cat on a Cushion

1909

Lithograph in six colours (red, ochre, yellow, black, grey-brown, brown) from two stones, with scraping on stone, on ivory wove paper

19½ × 23¼ in (49.4 × 58.9 cm)

The Art Institute of Chicago, USA

BENGAL CAT

The Bengal originated as a cross between the Asian leopard cat and a domesticated cat, and was first mentioned in the late nineteenth century. Several breeds were used in its continued development, including the Egyptian Mau, ocicat, Abyssinian and Burmese, as well as various domestic shorthairs. Today, a true Bengal cat is the product of two pure-bred Bengal cats, rather than of any other breeds. Bengals are playful and active, affectionate, curious and lively, and they love to climb. With a golden shimmer to their coats, their markings can be large or small spots, dart shapes or marbling, and most have gold, green or yellow eyes.

A gesture of love

The Italian artist Giovanni Boldini (1842–1931) lived and worked in Paris for most of his career. His flowing style gained him the nickname "the Master of Swish", and he was acclaimed for his lively portraits of some of the most distinguished individuals of the time. Although he had studied painting in Florence, he became influenced not by the academic style taught there, but rather by the looser approach of Impressionism. As the most fashionable portrait painter in Paris, he was awarded the prestigious Légion d'Honneur in 1889. In 1910 he painted this portrait of the daughter of the Chilean diplomat Matías Errázuriz and his aristocratic wife, Josefina de Alvear. While the parents bought and commissioned art, left the world the National Museum of Decorative Arts in Buenos Aires, and moved about between Argentina and France, little is known about their two children, Matías and Josefina. Here, Josefina, who was fondly called Pepita, is about 11 years old. She holds the family pet in a gesture of love, even though the cat looks rather uncomfortable. Despite the cool, minimal palette and Boldini's loose brushstrokes, Josefina's smile and the emotional bond she shares with her pet give the impression of warmth, affection and playfulness.

41
GIOVANNI
BOLDINI
*Portrait of Josefina
Errázuriz de Alvear
Holding a Cat*
1910
Oil on canvas
74 × 41½ in
(188 × 105.3 cm)
Private collection

BRITISH LONGHAIR

The British longhair was developed in the United Kingdom at the end of the nineteenth century from British shorthair and Persian cats. However, the breed was rare before the First World War, making it just the kind of pet that the prosperous Errázuriz de Alvear family might buy. With rounded head and eyes, fluffy paws and an elegantly plumed tail, the breed is large, with a well-muscled body and a thick, double coat comprising a velvety undercoat and soft, silky upper layer. Although British longhairs are extremely calm cats, they are uncomfortable if picked up, as is clear from this painting. They come in many colours (the most popular being blue) and various patterns.

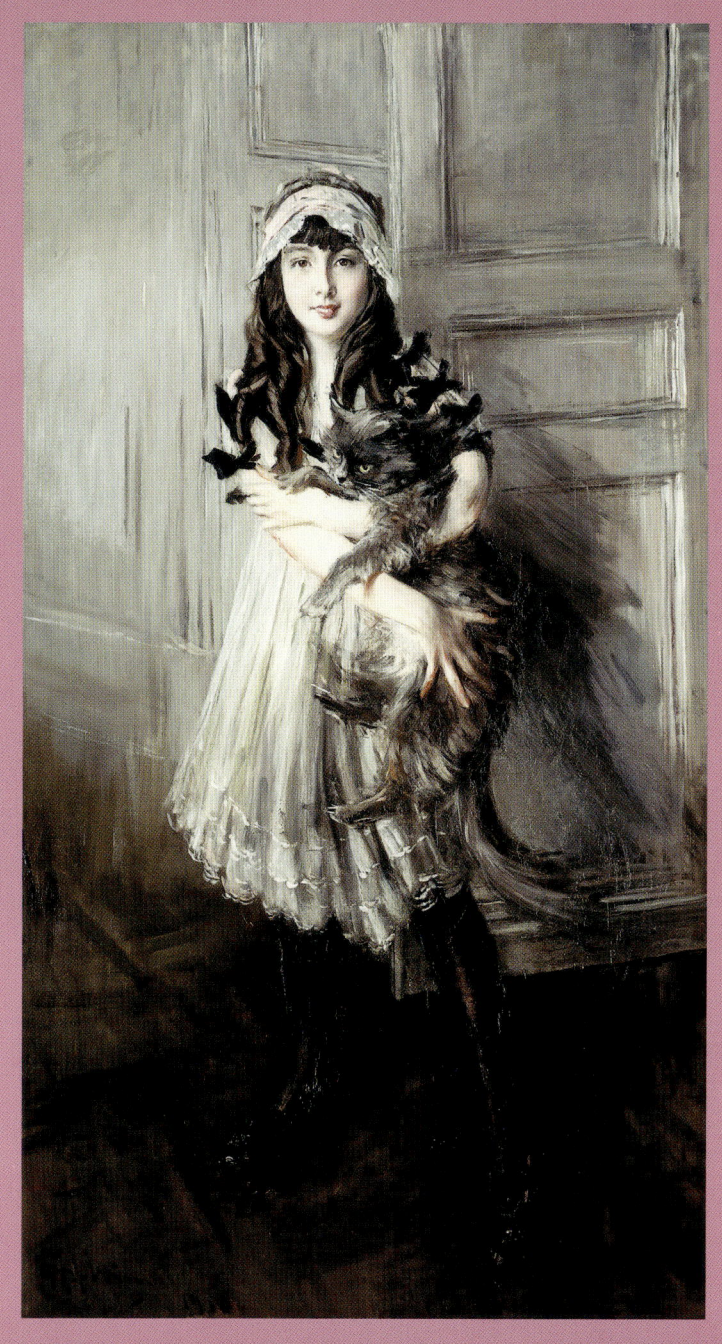

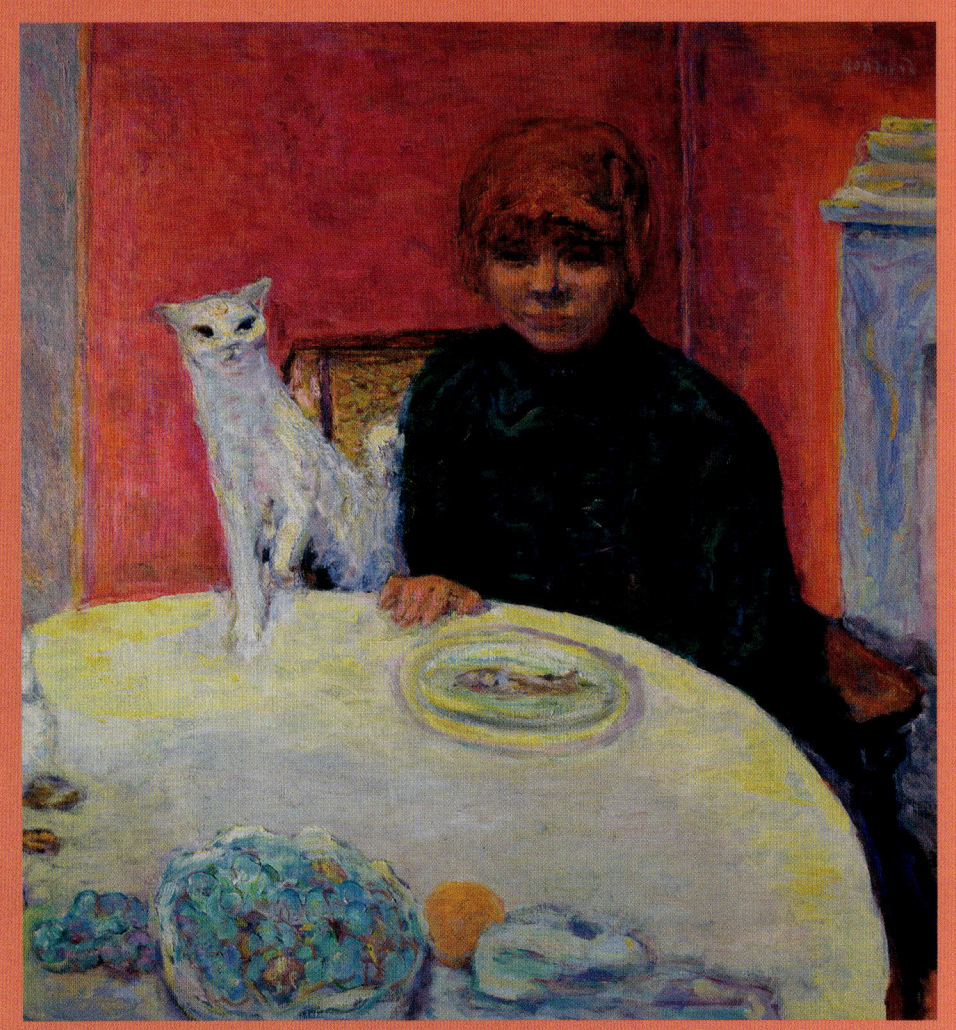

Sharing the moment

Painted in the same year as the white cat by Franz Marc (page 134), *Woman with a Cat* is sometimes known as *The Demanding Cat*. It is by the French painter, illustrator and printmaker Pierre Bonnard (1867–1947) and depicts Maria Boursin, his mistress at the time, who became Martha Bonnard when they married 13 years later. Her pet cat climbs on to a table that is arranged for a meal. Bonnard was a founding member of the Post-Impressionist group of artists called Les Nabis (see page 118). Members of this group rejected the naturalism of Impressionism in favour of symbolism, believing that art should convey deeper meanings and emotions. They therefore emphasized the artist's subjective experience, seeking to evoke emotions and ideas through their use of colour, form and composition. Although Les Nabis had gone their separate ways more than a decade before Bonnard made this painting, he still adhered to some of the group's ideas. Set in the corner of a room with only part of the round table in view, this work also shows the influence of Japanese art, with the high viewpoint, flat areas of colour and diagonally arranged composition.

42
PIERRE
BONNARD
Woman with a Cat
1912
Oil on canvas
31 × 30½ in
(78 × 77.5 cm)
Musée d'Orsay,
Paris, France

DOMESTIC SHORTHAIR

Making up the majority of pet cats worldwide, the domestic shorthair is a mixed breed with short fur in various colours and patterns. Usually a medium-sized cat, it is sometimes confused with the American shorthair, which is a distinct pure-bred cat. The genetic diversity that is a result of their mixed backgrounds means that domestic shorthairs tend to be healthier than many pure-bred cats. The white domestic shorthair has a long and varied history, since white cats have been cherished for centuries in many different cultures. In this breed, a white coat is usually caused by the dominant white (W) gene, which can mask other colours.

Bright colours

The German painter and printmaker Franz Marc (1880–1916) was one of the central figures of German Expressionism and a founding member of *Der Blaue Reiter* (The Blue Rider), a journal and group of artists. Many of his brightly coloured paintings feature animals. In the 1930s the Nazis labelled Marc's work degenerate as part of their suppression of modern art, and although his career was cut short by his early death, his art had a huge impact on the Expressionist movement in general. His images of brightly coloured animals often convey profound messages about spirituality, the world and the fate of humanity. Colour was extremely important for him. Not only did he understand its potential to affect mood, but also he developed a specific theory of colour symbolism. Blue was associated with the masculine, yellow with the feminine and red with the physical, often violent world. In this painting, a stylized, abstracted white cat is set against a colourful background. The animal is simplified and the background made up of vivid hues and dynamic shapes that convey movement and energy. The vibrant colours may evoke vitality, joy and harmony, or symbolize purity, innocence and simplicity.

43
FRANZ MARC
The White Cat (Cat on a Yellow Pillow)
1912
Oil on cardboard
19¼ × 23⅝ in
(49 × 60 cm)
Kunstmuseum Moritzburg, Halle, Germany

WHITE CATS

While partially white cats are fairly common, pure white is one of the rarest coat colours among solid-coloured cats. Most pure-white cats are not albino, and it is a misconception that all white cats are deaf, although some are, especially those with blue eyes. All-white cats are not linked to a specific breed, but many different breeds can present completely white coats, including the British, American and Oriental shorthairs, British and American longhairs, Turkish Angora, Norwegian forest cat, Siberian, Turkish Van, Devon and Cornish Rexes, Japanese bobtail, Persian, Ragdoll and ragamuffin, Russian white, Khao Manee and LaPerm.

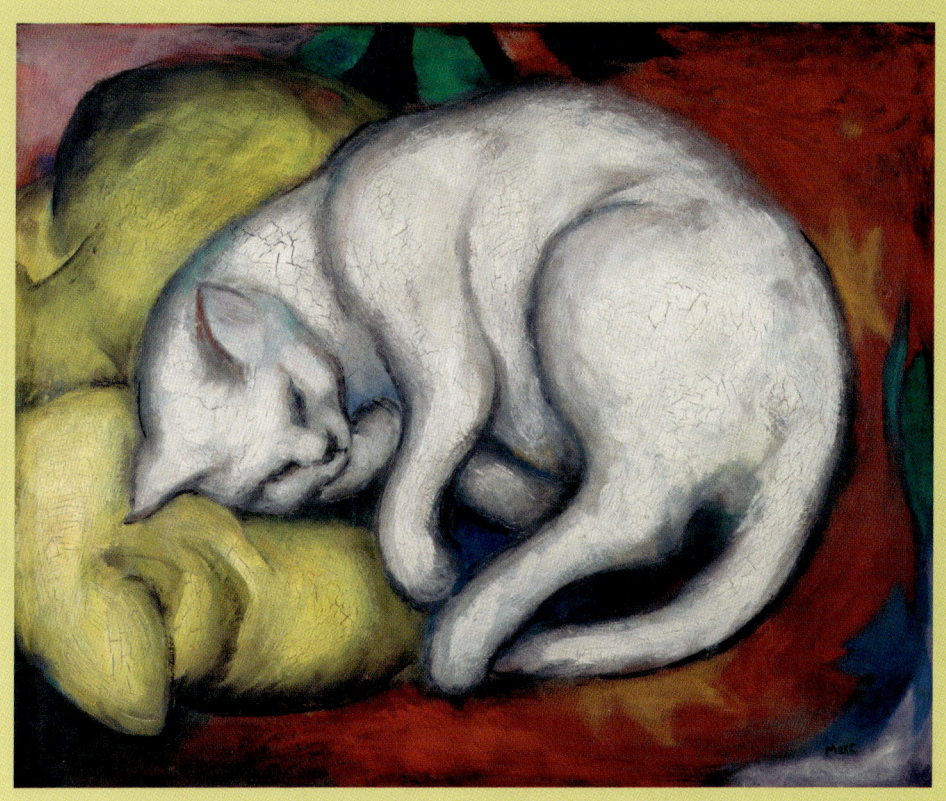

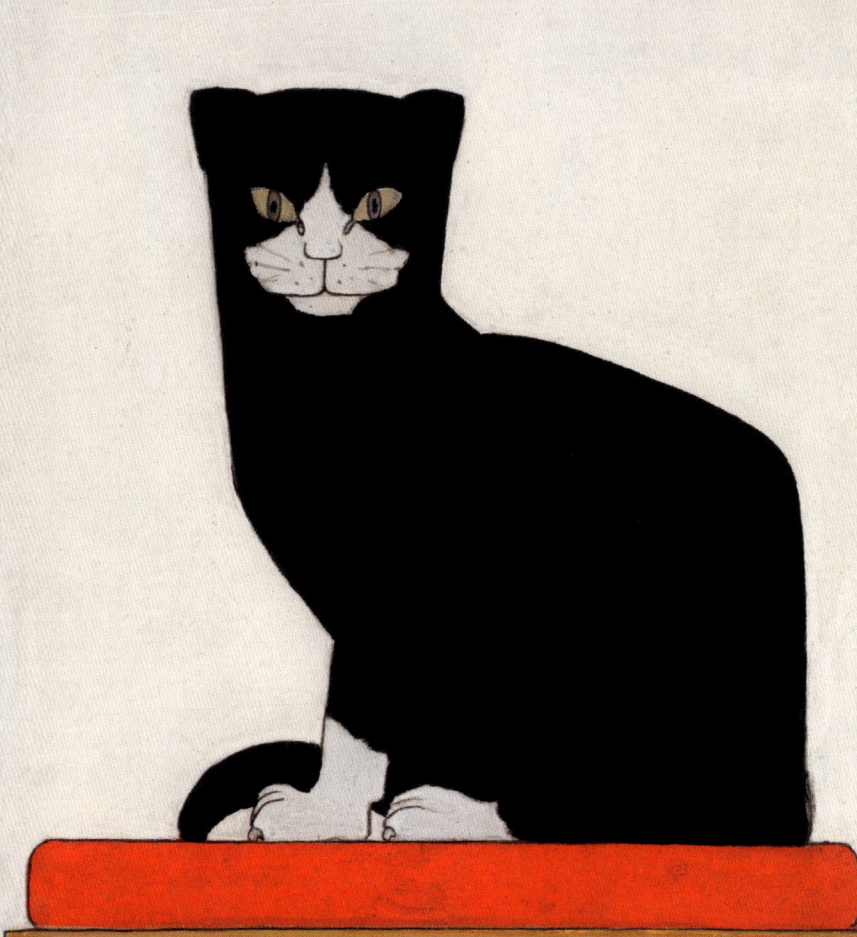

Reduced form

The Dutch painter, designer and ceramicist Bart van der Leck (1876–1958) was, with Theo van Doesburg and Piet Mondrian, a co-founder of the magazine *De Stijl*, which developed into an art movement of the same name. In 1916 Van der Leck began to rigorously abstract his paintings and reduce his colours to just red, yellow and blue, or sometimes, as here, to black, white, red and orange. These radical ideas evolved partly from theories discussed in the magazine, and partly from a visit to Paris, where he was impressed by the ancient Egyptian art he saw in the Louvre. In this painting, he depicts the cat both from the front and in profile, with no sense of depth or texture. The minimalist arrangement of shapes and colours emphasizes clarity and structure. The German art collector Helene Kröller-Müller, one of the first European women to put together a major art collection, bought more than 400 of Van der Leck's works between 1913 and 1939, including this painting. She wrote to the artist about the cat, saying: "I always call her 'my conscience', because her piercing eyes follow you everywhere."

44

BART VAN
DER LECK
The Cat
1914
Casein on cement
board (asbestos)
14½ × 11⅓ in
(37 × 29 cm)
Kröller-Müller
Museum, Otterlo,
The Netherlands

SCOTTISH FOLD

This distinctive breed of domestic cat is characterized by a natural dominant gene mutation associated with the rare genetic disorder osteochondrodysplasia, which affects cartilage throughout the body, causing the ears to fold forwards and down over the front of the head. Originally called "lop-eared" or "lops" after the lop-eared rabbit, the breed was named Scottish Fold in 1966. Because of their developmental abnormality, all Fold cats have malformed bones and can develop severe, painful degenerative joint diseases at an early age; consequently, breeding Fold cats is prohibited in several countries, and some major cat registries do not recognize the breed.

Transience and beauty

Born Marie-Clémentine Valadon at Haute-Vienne in southwest-central France, Suzanne Valadon (1865–1938) tried out many jobs, including being a circus performer, before becoming a model and close friend to some of the most famous artists of the time, including Degas, Steinlen (page 129), Renoir (page 99), Henri de Toulouse-Lautrec and Pierre Puvis de Chavannes. In the 1890s she gave up modelling to become an artist, and lived with her lover, her mother and her illegitimate son – as well as her dogs, cats and a goat – in a small apartment in rue Cortot, Montmartre. By 1894 she had become the first woman painter admitted to the Société Nationale des Beaux-Arts, and her bright, bold, flat-looking painting style became extremely popular in what was traditionally a man's world. Particularly fond of animals, Valadon, like Steinlen, fed the cats (and poor children) of Montmartre, and is also said to have given her own pet cats caviar once a week. Although she loved all animals, her "marmalade" cat Ravinou was one of her favourite subjects, and here she depicts him in her light-filled studio, curled up next to a vase of vibrantly coloured flowers. Along with a sense of domesticity, warmth, companionship, contemplation and independence, the image suggests themes of transience and beauty.

45
SUZANNE VALADON
Bouquet and a Cat
1919
Oil on canvas
26⅛ × 13¾ in
(66.5 × 35 cm)
Private collection

BRITISH SHORTHAIR

Researchers are not sure how cats first reached the British Isles, but British shorthair cats probably began as street cats before being refined and standardized by breeders. With short, dense coats and distinctive rounded head and face, these medium-sized or large cats were first known as the British blue, but were actually only blue-grey. Since the late nineteenth century, variations of colour and pattern have been developed, including solid, bicolour, tabby, tortoiseshell and calico, and the name has changed accordingly. A friendly and affectionate breed, the British shorthair was shown at England's first organized cat show in 1871.

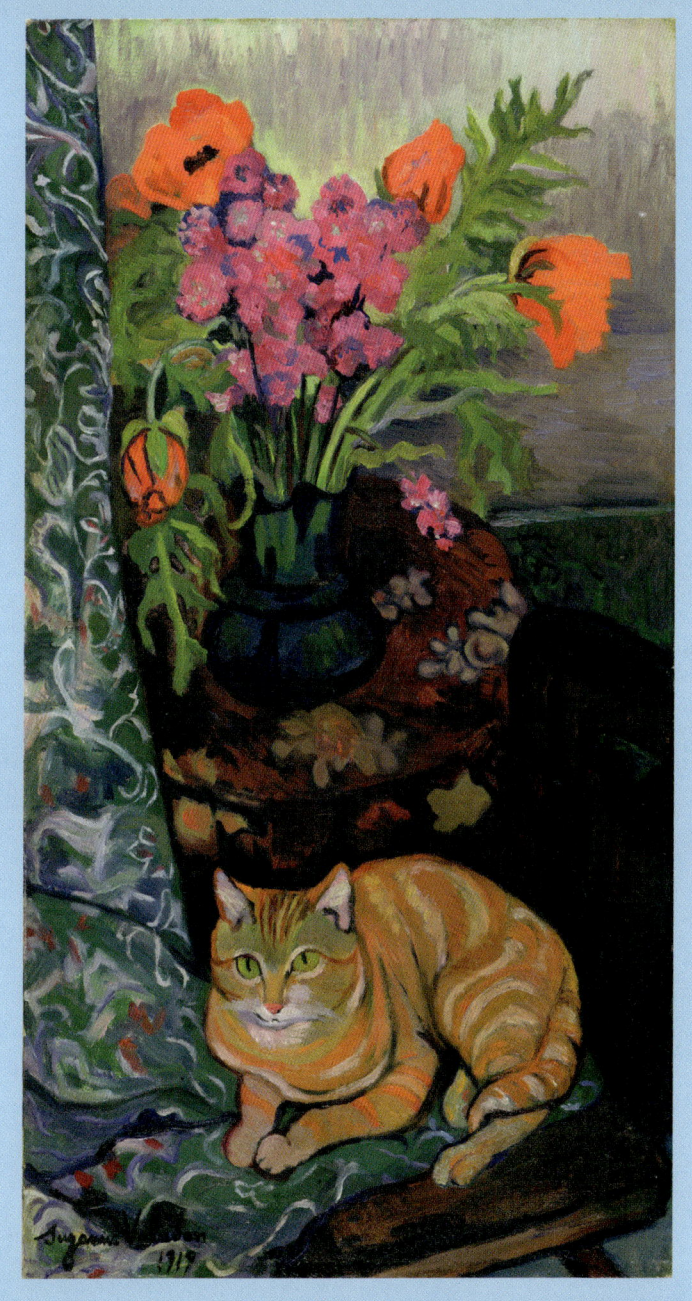

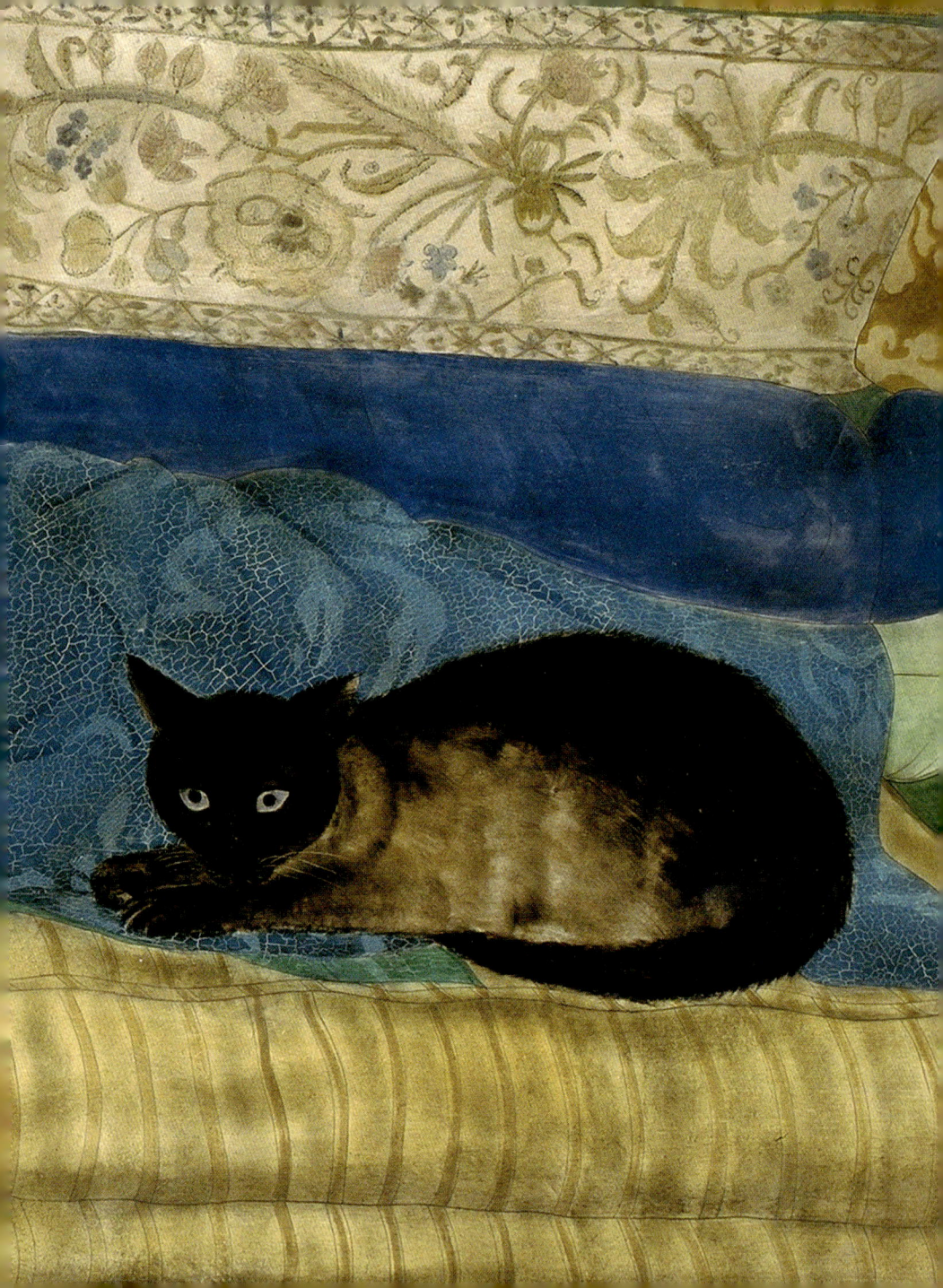

Blending traditions

From a young age, Léonard Tsuguharu Foujita (1886–1968) yearned to become famous as an artist in Europe. He studied Western-style painting at the Tokyo National University of Fine Arts, then moved to the bohemian area of Montparnasse in Paris. In the city, he befriended artists including Pablo Picasso, Amedeo Modigliani, Chaïm Soutine, Fernand Léger, Juan Gris and Henri Matisse, and he developed an eclectic style, blending Japanese and European artistic traditions, that proved to be immensely commercially successful. By 1925 he had received both the Belgian Order of Leopold and the Légion d'Honneur in France. A lover of cats, he included these animals in many of his paintings, with beautiful women or himself. He once said, "The reason I so much enjoy being friends with cats is that they have two different characters: a wild side and a domestic side." In 1930 his *Book of Cats*, with 20 etchings, was published. The portrait illustrated here is of the American heiress Emily Rockwell Crane Chadbourne, who was known both for her art collection and for her philanthropy. Looking serious, with a fashionable band in her hair, she reclines, her long gown draping over a sofa and her Burmese cat sleeping comfortably on both.

46

LÉONARD TSUGUHARU FOUJITA

Portrait of Emily Crane Chadbourne

1922

Tempera and silver leaf on canvas

35¼ × 57½ in (89.5 × 146.1 cm)

The Art Institute of Chicago, USA

Opposite: detail

BURMESE

The cat shown here resembles the present-day Burmese. The earliest records of these cats come from Thailand, where they had lived for centuries. It is likely that during the Burmese–Siamese war of 1785–6, some of Thailand's temple cats were taken back to Burma by Burmese soldiers. In the late nineteenth century they may have travelled again, since two Siamese cats that closely resembled today's Burmese cats appeared in a cat show at the Crystal Palace in London. The breed became known as Chocolate Siamese before being recognized as the Burmese breed in its own right in Europe and America in the early twentieth century.

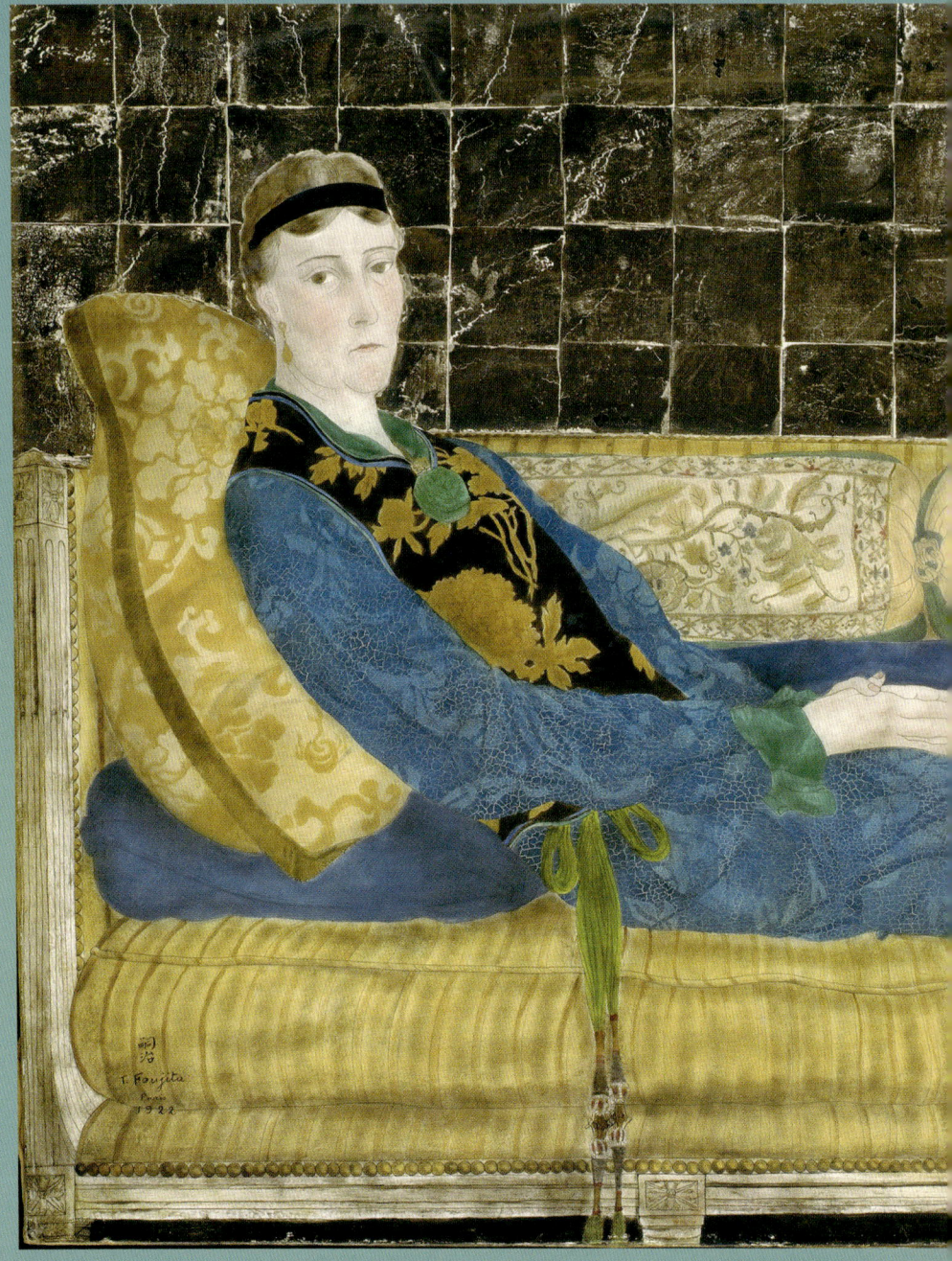

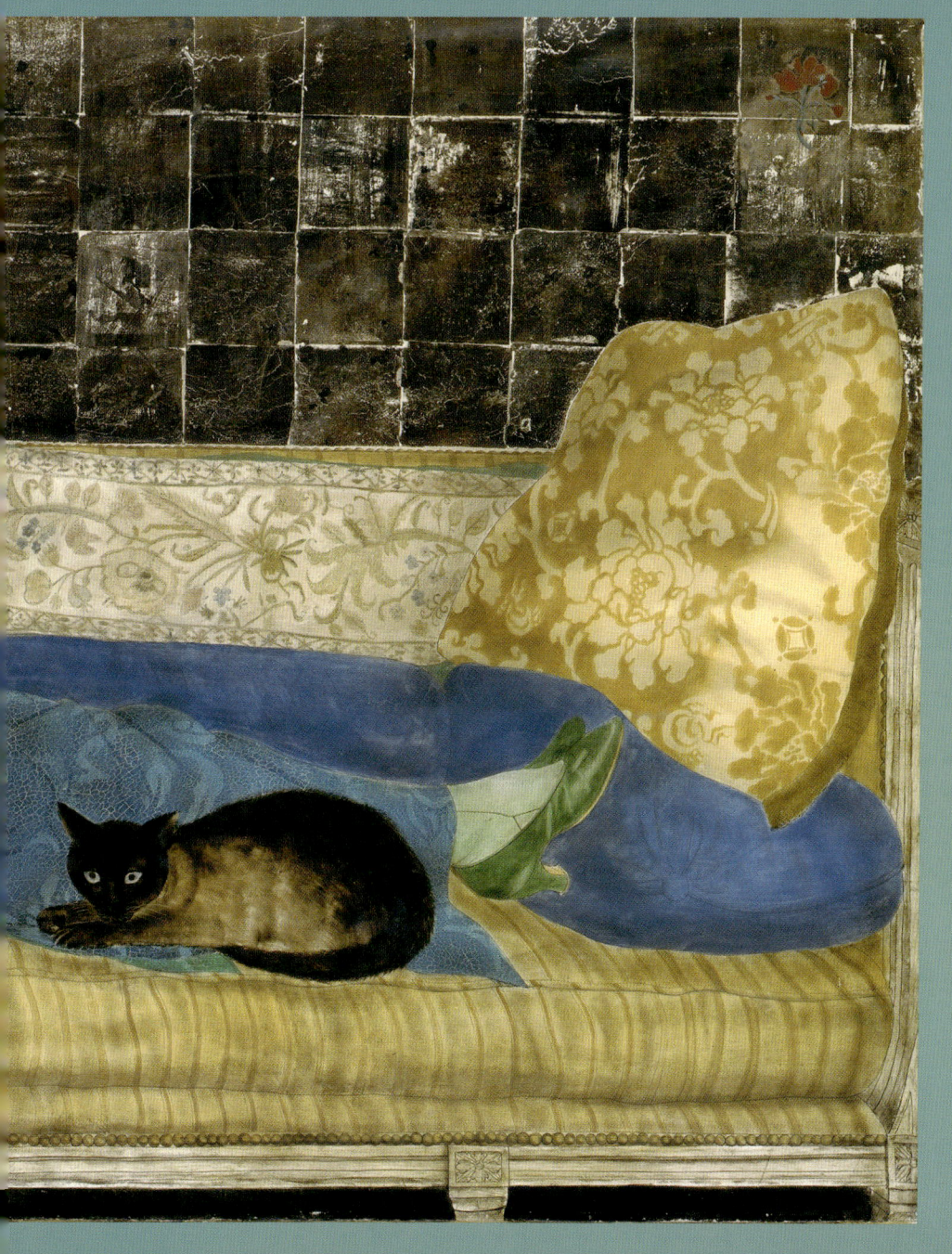

Matching blue eyes

Christopher "Kit" Wood (1901–30) was born in northern England. Although he considered becoming a doctor, at Liverpool University he met the artist Augustus John (1878–1961), who encouraged him to paint. Wood moved to Paris and studied at the Académie Julian. There he met Pablo Picasso, Jean Cocteau and Sergei Diaghilev, and established himself among the Parisian avant-garde, gaining commissions for many projects, including set design for Diaghilev's company, the Ballets Russes. He also travelled around Europe and North Africa. This is Wood's portrait of his friend Jean Bourgoint. Cocteau wrote about Bourgoint and his twin sister, Jeanne, in his book *Les Enfants Terribles* (1929). At the time of painting the portrait, Wood was involved in a brief relationship with Jeanne. The Siamese cat is meant to reflect aspects of Jean's personality, including his own capricious relationships and delicate appearance, his blue eyes reiterated by the blue eyes of the cat. On the narrow canvas, he leans slightly to the right; he appears relaxed, but the composition seems unfinished. Next to his head, some larger, faint features have been drawn. This may have been Wood's first plan for the composition, visual notes to help him complete the actual face when Bourgoint was not there, or a mistake that has not been erased.

47
CHRISTOPHER WOOD
Boy with Cat (Jean Bourgoint)
1926
Oil and graphite on canvas
58¼ × 23 in (148 × 58.5 cm)
Kettle's Yard, Cambridge, UK

SIAMESE

First described in the ancient *Tamra Maew* or *Cat Book Poems* in about 1350 CE, Siamese cats were originally bred in the kingdom of Siam (now Thailand). They were considered sacred, so only royalty and Buddhist monks were allowed to keep them. When European dignitaries began visiting Siam in the nineteenth century, they admired the cats and were given some as gifts by members of the Siamese royal family. However, with their distinctive colourpoint coats, blue almond-shaped eyes, triangular heads, large ears and slender bodies, today's Siamese cats bear little resemblance to the original foundation stock, which had a rounder head and body. The Siamese is one of the oldest pedigree cat breeds in existence.

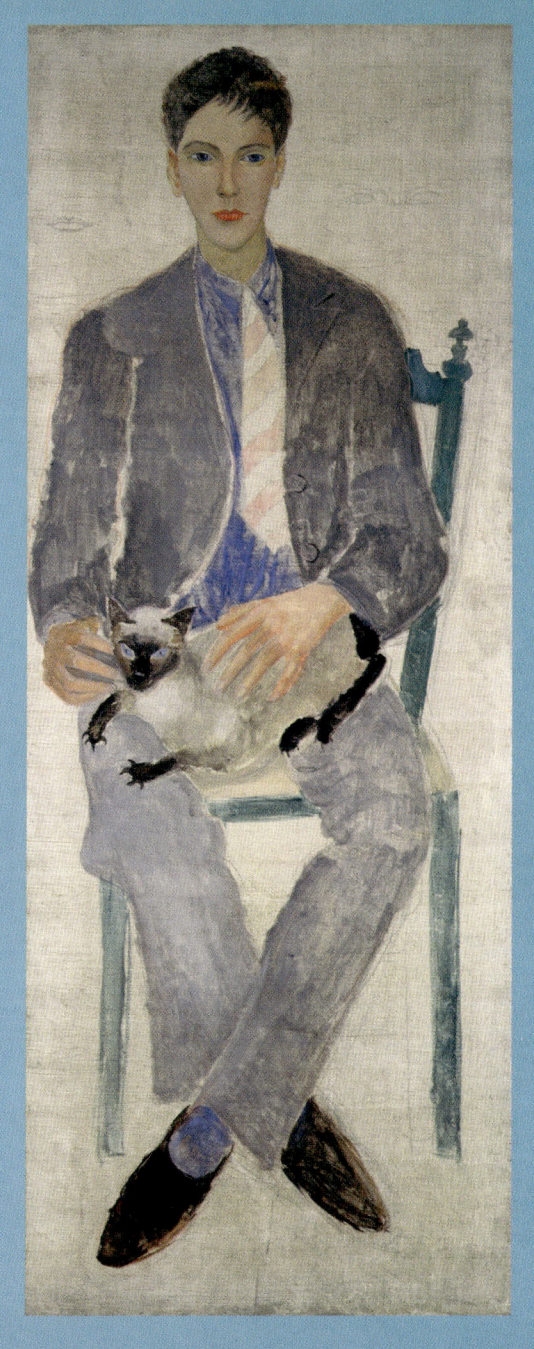

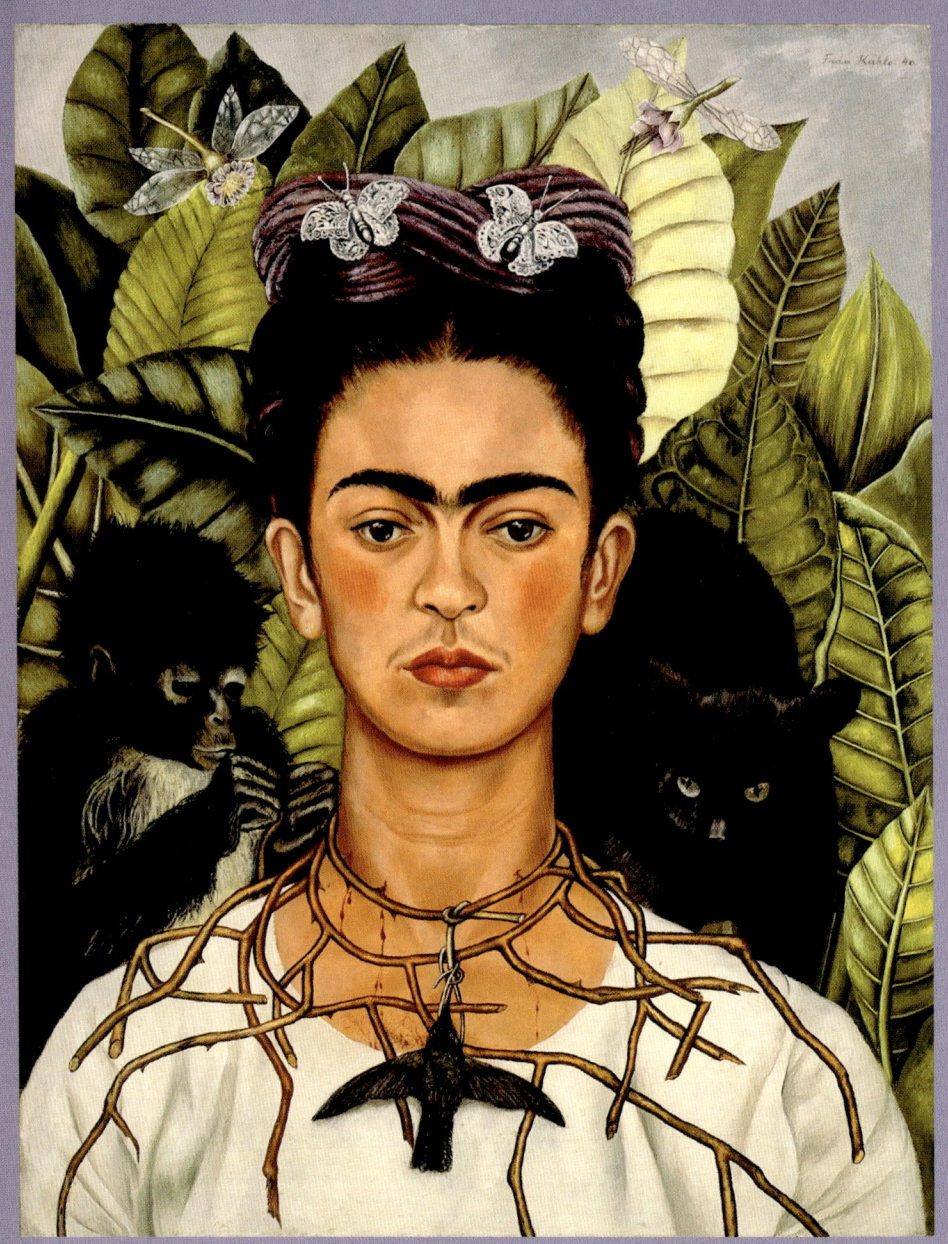

Art as therapy

Known for her autobiographical paintings, the Mexican artist Frida Kahlo (1907–54) used art to explore her tragic life. After suffering from polio as a child, she aimed to study medicine, but at the age of 18 she was injured horrifically in a bus accident that left her with lifelong pain and medical problems. She painted this self-portrait after temporarily divorcing her unfaithful husband, the celebrated muralist Diego Rivera. Surrounded by leaves, she faces the viewer, the corpse of a small black hummingbird hanging at her throat from a thorn necklace. A spider monkey sits behind her, tugging the necklace, making her bleed. Above her, two dragonflies float over butterfly clips in her hair, and a black cat looks over her shoulder. In Mexican culture, a dead hummingbird means good fortune, or it can symbolize Huitzilopochtli, the Aztec god of war. Although the cat was one of Kahlo's beloved pets, black cats can imply bad luck and death, and the monkey can symbolize evil. Rivera gave her the monkey as a gift, which suggests that it could represent him. Kahlo loved all animals, seeing them as the children she could not have. She had a special bond with Mitsu and Minou, her black domestic shorthair cats. The necklace could refer to Christ's crown of thorns, implying martyrdom, while the butterflies and dragonflies denote resurrection and hope.

48

FRIDA KAHLO

Self-Portrait with Thorn Necklace and Hummingbird

1940

Oil on canvas on Masonite

25 × 18½ in (61.2 × 47 cm)

Harry Ransom Center, Austin, Texas, USA

BLACK DOMESTIC SHORTHAIR

The result of cross-breeding between native wild cats and the domestic cats introduced to Britain by ancient Romans, domestic black cats have sturdy bodies and short, dense coats, and are usually curious, playful and affectionate. Their sleek, solid black fur is typically glossy and soft, with a thick texture that requires minimal grooming. Some of these cats may have "ghost markings", faint tabby patterns that can be seen in sunlight. In many countries, black cats are believed to be lucky. British sailors welcomed them aboard ship, believing they would ensure a safe return.

A sense of tension

An important member of the School of London – a group of artists who painted figuratively when it was not fashionable to do so – the British artist Lucian Freud (1922–2011) painted this portrait of his first wife, Kathleen "Kitty" Garman. Between 1947 and 1951 he painted eight portraits of her, usually including a rose, one of the bull terriers that had been a wedding present to the couple, or a kitten. This portrait is painted in Freud's early style, when he used a sable brush to enable him to apply paint smoothly and precisely. Subtle shading gives a sense of flatness. Garman, who was the daughter of the sculptor Jacob Epstein, is shown against a beige wall. She looks blankly to the side, her lips slightly parted, with an anguished expression that conveys a feeling of discomfort. Freud paid attention to the smallest details, such as eyelashes, wisps of hair and highlights in the eyes, but this serves to make the image seem less realistic, rather than more so. Garman's eyebrows and wavy hair echo aspects of the tabby kitten, which she grips tightly around its neck. The white knuckles create a worrying feeling of tension, but the kitten seems relaxed and looks directly at the viewer through wide-open, soft-green eyes illuminated by a pale light.

49
LUCIAN FREUD
Girl with a Kitten
1947
Oil on canvas
16 × 12 in
(41 × 30.7 cm)
Tate Britain,
London, UK

GREEN-EYED CATS

Cats of many breeds have green eyes, which can vary from yellow-green to grey-green, emerald to olive, and hazel to blue-green. Some green-eyed cats have flecks of gold or yellow in the iris. Green eyes are found in various cat breeds, including the Egyptian Mau, with its soft green eyes; the Havana, which has emerald-green eyes; the Russian blue, with vivid green eyes; the Abyssinian, with bright green eyes; the Chartreux, which has soft-green eyes; the Burmese, with gold-green eyes; and the Norwegian forest cat, with eyes in various shades of green. Generally, the more melanin there is in the iris, the darker the cat's eyes will be.

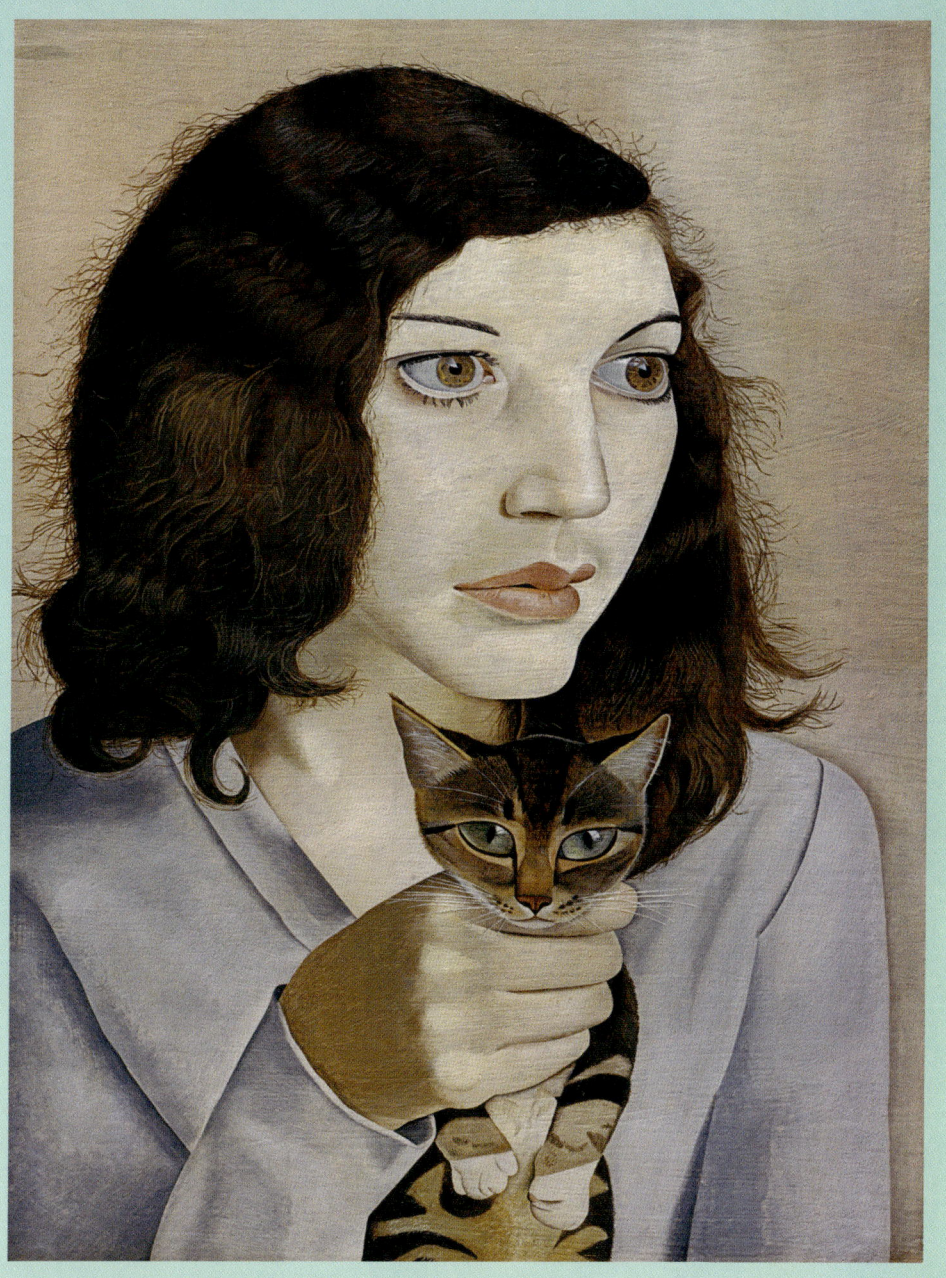

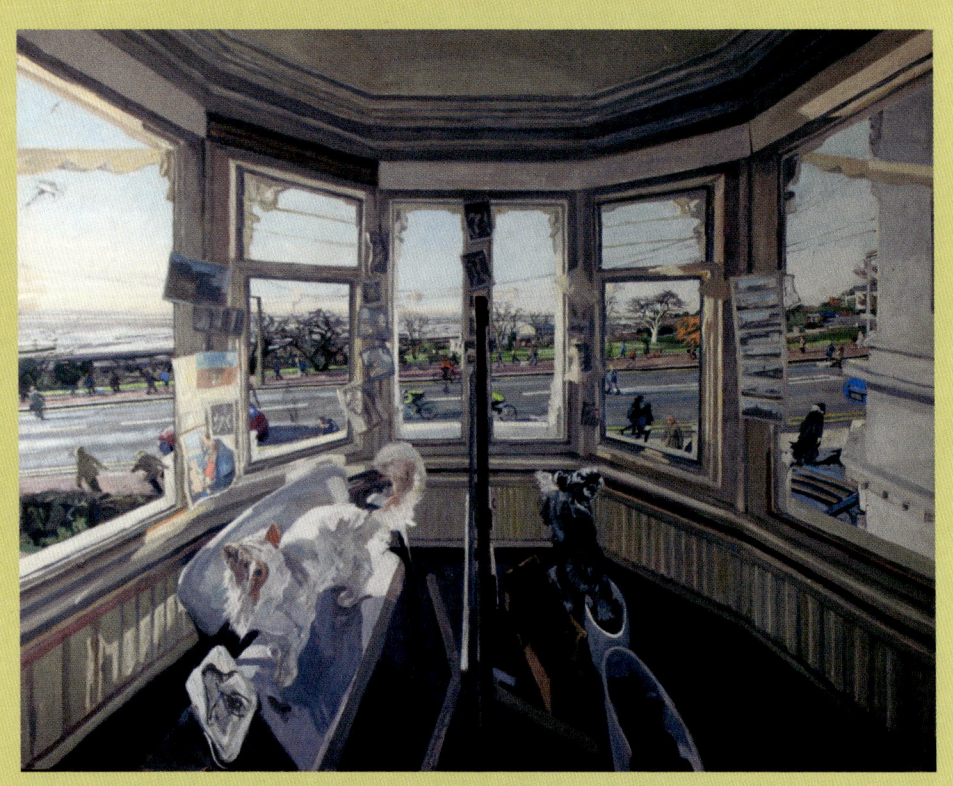

Beyond realism

Known for his atmospheric works, the British artist John Wonnacott (b.1940) studied art at the Slade School of Fine Art in London under the significant artists Frank Auerbach and Michael Andrews. He has become recognized for his distinctive figurative paintings, which show attention to detail, a skilful rendering of form and explorations of the effects of light. Often including architectural elements, with a restrained use of colour, Wonnacott creates compositions that subtly draw the viewer's eye. Since moving to Leigh-on-Sea, on the Thames Estuary in Essex, in 1959, he has frequently painted the people and places around him, and here he captures the view through his studio window. It is a blustery day. The seaside is in the distance, and several pedestrians and cyclists are on the street below, their hair and clothing moving in the wind. Inside the studio, Wonnacott's work can be seen, along with his playful dog jumping up at the window, and his white cat, which is trying to reach the seagulls outside. Beyond the surface realism, this painting seems to contain underlying messages. The bay window of the studio creates a frame within the frame, while the white cat – a recurring motif in Wonnacott's work – brings a touch of domesticity and tranquillity to the scene.

50

JOHN
WONNACOTT

*Estuary Bay
Window with
the White Cat
Watching Gulls*

2012–15

Oil on board

48 × 60 in
(122 × 152.5 cm)

Private collection

Overleaf: detail

SIBERIAN CAT

Wonnacott's cat is a white Siberian or, more formally, Siberian forest cat, an ancient Russian breed that is believed to have existed for centuries. These cats probably roamed the dense forests of Siberia, protected from the cold by their long, thick triple coat and developing their distinctive characteristics over generations. It has been speculated, although not proved, that the Siberian is the distant ancestor of all present-day long-haired breeds. However, Siberians are genetically closely related to Norwegian forest cats and some other northern European cats. Written history on them is scarce, but many ancient Russian fairy tales feature these friendly animals.

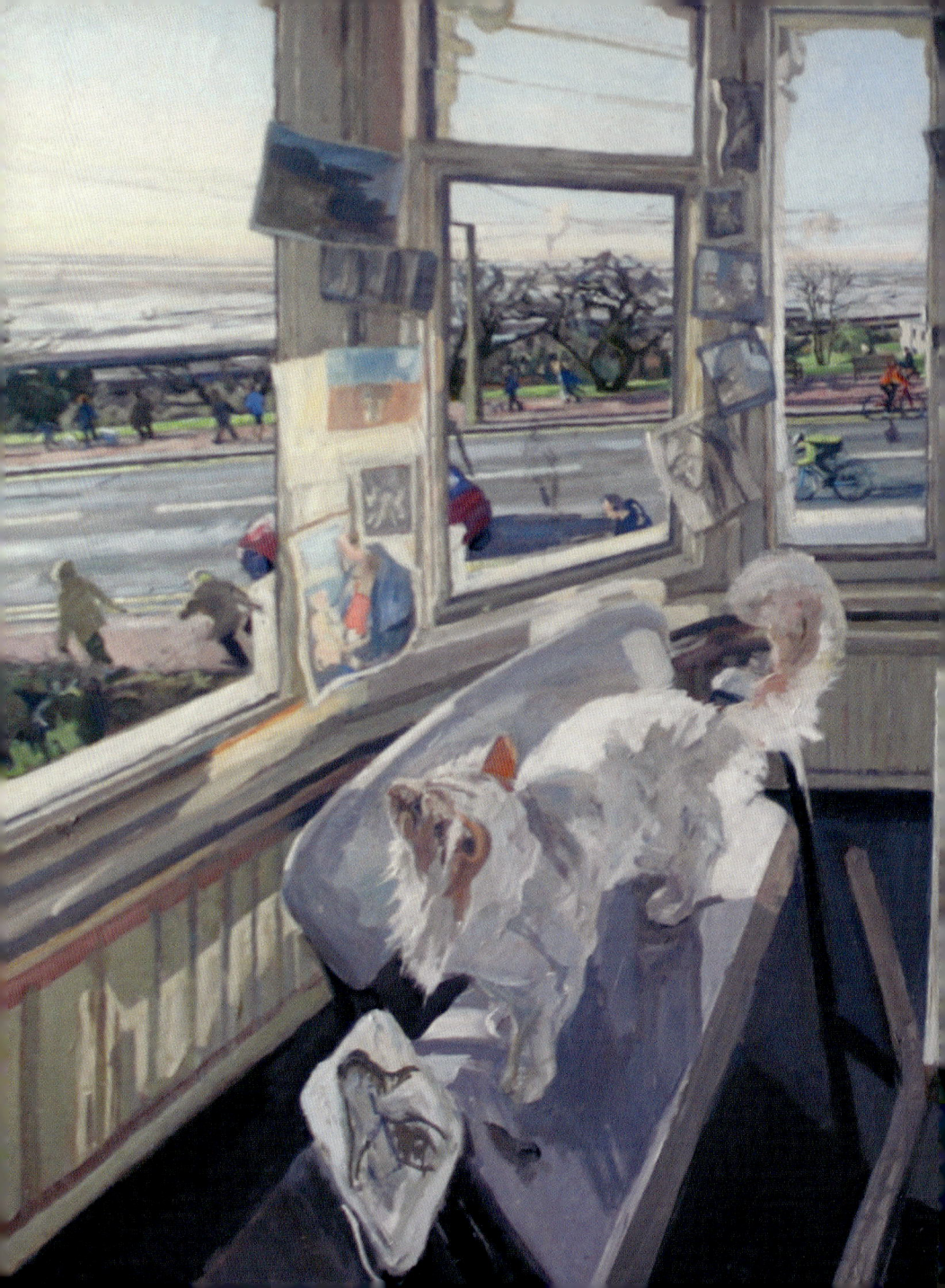